Counterpoint to a City

THE FIRST ONE HUNDRED YEARS OF THE
WOMEN'S MUSICAL CLUB OF TORONTO

COUNTERPOINT TO A CITY is a history of the Women's Musical Club of Toronto, which has been sponsoring chamber music and solo recitals for nearly one hundred years. The story of the club is told within the framework of the changing role of women in Canadian society and the evolution of the musical life of Toronto over the past century. In writing the book, the author made use of archival documents, interviews with club members, newspaper reports and reviews, and recent scholarship in the field of women's music studies. The book is perhaps the most in-depth work that has been written to date on the history of a single Canadian musical organization.

ROBIN ELLIOTT was born in Kingston, Ontario, in 1956. He was educated at Queen's University, where he studied violin with Dezsö Vághy and contemporary music with Istvan Anhalt. After receiving his B.Mus. in 1978, he studied violin at the Vienna Conservatory. Upon returning to Canada, he began graduate studies in musicology at the University of Toronto, where he obtained an M.A. in 1981 and a Ph.D. in 1990. His doctoral thesis, "The String Quartet in Canada," is a study of the history of the performance and composition of string quartets in Canada from the late-eighteenth century to 1990.

Elliott was an associate editor for the second edition of the *Encyclopedia of Music in Canada* (1992), contributed eighteen articles to that reference work, and has also edited two volumes of chamber music for the Canadian Musical Heritage series. He has taught at numerous Canadian universities and is currently a lecturer in music at University College Dublin.

COUNTERPOINT
to a CITY

*The First One Hundred
Years of the Women's
Musical Club of Toronto*

Robin Elliott

ECW PRESS

THE CANADA COUNCIL | LE CONSEIL DES ARTS
FOR THE ARTS | DU CANADA
SINCE 1957 | DEPUIS 1957

We acknowledge the support of the Canada
Council for the Arts in our publishing program.

This book has been published with the assistance
of grants from the Ontario Arts Council.

This book has been published with the help of a grant from the
Canadian Federation for the Humanities, using funds provided by
the Social Sciences and Humanities Research Council of Canada.

Copyright © ECW PRESS, 1997

CANADIAN CATALOGUING IN PUBLICATION DATA

Elliott, Robin, 1956–
Counterpoint to a city : the first one hundred years
of the Women's Musical Club of Toronto

Includes bibliographical references and index.

ISBN 1-55022-306-2

1. Women's Musical Club of Toronto. 2. Concerts –
Ontario – Toronto – History – 20th century. I. Title.

ML28.T6W644 1997   780'.6'0713541   C97-930116-5

Cover design by Ove Design. Cover painting Raoul Dufy, *La Console jaune
au violin / The Yellow Violin* (1949) © Raoul Dufy / KINÉMAGE, Montréal,
1996. From the collection of the Art Gallery of Ontario, Toronto.

Design and imaging by ECW Type & Art, Oakville, Ontario.
Printed by Imprimerie Gagné Ltée, Louiseville, Québec.

Distributed by General Distribution Services,
30 Lesmill Road, Don Mills, Ontario M3B 2T6.

Published by ECW PRESS,
2120 Queen Street East, Suite 200,
Toronto, Ontario M4E 1E2.
www.ecw.ca/press

A BRIEF HISTORY
of the
WOMEN'S MUSICAL
CLUB *of* TORONTO

ON 23 JANUARY 1899 a group of women musicians and music lovers met in a studio in the Yonge Street Arcade and founded the Women's Musical Club of Toronto. Thus was born an organization which, nearly a century later, continues to enhance the cultural life of Toronto by sponsoring an annual recital series and providing performance opportunities and scholarships for young Canadian musicians.

In its early years the club had two types of membership — active and associate — and most of the concerts in the initial seasons were performed by the local women musicians who made up the active membership of the club. There were two types of concerts — "closed," for members only; and "open," which the public was invited to attend. For many years now, all of the concerts have been open to anyone who loves fine music — men and women, young and old, from all walks of life.

In November 1899 the concerts began to be held in the Temple Building at the corner of Bay and Richmond Streets, and four years later the club moved to the Conservatory of Music concert hall. Many other concert venues have been used over the years, including Massey Hall, the Masonic Hall, and Hart House Theatre. For over thirty years, from 1946 to 1977, Eaton Auditorium was the regular venue for the Women's Musical Club recitals. Since 1985 the concerts have been given at Walter Hall in the Edward Johnson Building of the University of Toronto.

On 7 May 1902 the club sponsored its first concert by a visiting professional group, the Kneisel Quartet of Boston.

During the tenth season, two U.S. musicians were presented by the club in their local débuts — the baritone Francis Rogers and the pianist Olga Samaroff. In the ensuing ninety years the list of artists who have made their Toronto or Canadian débuts for the Women's Musical Club of Toronto reads like a who's who of the great musicians of this century: Myra Hess; Wanda Landowska; Mitsuko Uchida; the Flonzaley and Kolisch String Quartets; the Vienna Boys' Choir; Andrés Segovia; the violinsts Joseph Szigeti, Georges Enesco, and Arthur Grumiaux; the cellists Gregor Piatigorsky, Emanuel Feuermann, Paul Tortelier, and Lynn Harrell; and the singers Alexander Kipnis, Marian Anderson, Leontyne Price, Dietrich Fischer-Dieskau, Hermann Prey, Christa Ludwig, and Elly Ameling, to name but a few of the many. The list continues to grow, as each season features the exciting new talents of the future.

During the First World War, the Women's Musical Club of Toronto was active in charitable work for worthwhile causes; this activity continued during the Second World War, when the club raised thousands of dollars for the Red Cross. In more recent years the charitable impetus of the club has centred on the awarding of scholarships to talented young music students. Teresa Stratas and Robert Aitken in the 1950s, Russell Braun and James Ehnes in the 1990s — these and many other young Canadian musicians have received valuable help in the early stages of their careers via the club's scholarships. In this way the Women's Musical Club of Toronto is not only providing for the enjoyment and enrichment of its members and audiences but is also helping to ensure a brilliant musical future for Canada and the world.

CONTENTS

LIST OF ILLUSTRATIONS

PREFACE

This book was commissioned by the Women's Musical Club of Toronto (WMC) as part of the celebrations of the centennial of the founding of that organization on 23 January 1899. I am grateful to the WMC for entrusting me with the task of telling the club's story on this historic occasion.

The earliest history of the WMC is an anonymously authored article that appeared in 1922 in *Saturday Night*, a weekly review of business and the arts published in Toronto.[1] The article was written to celebrate the WMC's twenty-fifth anniversary, and it is based on interviews with Mary Wylie Meikle, who was the president of the WMC at the time, and Mary Henderson Flett Dickson, one of the founders of the club. It provides much useful information about the early years of the WMC, although unfortunately it also contains a number of factual errors which have been propagated over the years. No doubt influenced by Mary Dickson's social gospel philosophy, the writer of the article stressed the good deeds accomplished by the WMC, especially its patriotic and charitable activities during the First World War.

The fiftieth anniversary of the WMC passed by without any retrospective account, likely because the club was still recovering from four years of inactivity during the Second World War. Two WMC presidents, Kathleen Irwin Wells and Jessie Macpherson, wrote short articles about the club five years apart, in 1956 and 1961 respectively.[2] Neither account adds much historical information beyond what the *Saturday Night* article contained, although Macpherson's essay is a well-reasoned and perceptive apologia for the continued relevance of the WMC in particular and women's musical clubs in general. In between these two articles came a fairly lengthy and entertaining piece written by Brian Magner for the *Globe and Mail*.[3] Magner's article is based in part on an interview with Eustella Burke Langdon, who was the newly elected WMC president at the time.

The approach of the seventy-fifth anniversary season (1972–73) produced four short articles and a thirty-two-page pamphlet about the WMC: each of the three major daily local newspapers ran an article in the fall of 1971, the periodical *Performing Arts in Canada* added another in the spring of 1972, and the WMC commissioned a past president to write a short history of the club.

John Fraser in the *Telegram* described the club's attempt to update its image, an effort that was hampered, he felt, by reason of "the Victorian scent that hovers about the group's name."[4] The article was accompanied by a picture of WMC scholarship winner Teresa Stratas, smiling alluringly and wearing bell-bottom pants that were no doubt very up to date indeed in 1971. William Littler in his article for the *Star* concentrated on the history of the WMC and the many eminent artists it had brought to Toronto for the first time; his paper ran pictures of Uday Shankar and Madeleine Grey to illustrate his point.[5] Betty Lee in the *Globe and Mail* wrote that "the WMC consistently looks abroad for talent and should perhaps search more diligently for good Canadian musicians,"[6] resurrecting a complaint first raised by Lawrence Mason in the *Globe* thirty-two years earlier.[7] The opposite tack was taken by Carl Morey. He noted the many Canadian musicians who had performed in WMC concerts, and he listed some of the young Canadians who had won WMC scholarships and gone on to make their mark on the national or international music scene.[8] Each article had something interesting to say about the WMC, but the articles also said much about the individual interests of the respective authors as well.

The most substantial earlier history of the WMC is Helen Christilaw Goudge's *Look Back in Pride*.[9] As a past president of the WMC, Goudge was well familiar with the recent activities of the club, and she searched through the WMC archives and a few Canadian music periodicals for information about the early years of the organization. Goudge completed her work in seven months, and the booklet was published in time for the opening concert of the seventy-fifth season. There are large gaps in her account, but nevertheless Goudge's work provided a valuable basis for the present book.

The ninetieth anniversary celebrations brought forth one further article outlining the history of the WMC, this one by John B. Withrow.[10] Withrow based his article in part on Goudge's book, although he also had access to the WMC archives and added a fair amount of detail from early concert programs and annual reports.

In preparing *Counterpoint to a City*, a good deal of new research was undertaken in order to shed light on the founding and early years of the WMC, to fill in the gaps in Goudge's narrative, and to bring the story up to date by giving an account of the twenty-five years since *Look Back in Pride* appeared. The local history of Toronto and the story of the women's musical club movement in general have also been drawn upon to help place the WMC in a wider context, and theoretical issues and current scholarship pertaining to class and especially gender have also been examined for their relevance to the story of the club.

The main business of the WMC has been and continues to be the sponsoring of concerts, and consequently the writing of this book has necessarily entailed, among other things, a survey of one hundred years of music criticism in Toronto.

The early records of WMC activities that have been preserved in the club's archives are very incomplete, but it has proven possible to make a fairly detailed survey of the first decade or so of the club's activities from information in *Saturday Night*, in the "Social and Personal" column for the earliest years, and later in the music page. The society columns of the local newspapers also provided thorough coverage of WMC events in the early years. Indeed, a fairly detailed account of the activities of the WMC can be pieced together in the pages of the "On Dit" column of the *Mail and Empire*, from the club's first meeting in January 1899 to November 1936, when that newspaper amalgamated with the *Globe* to form the *Globe and Mail*. The *Globe*'s "Chit Chat" column also reported extensively on WMC events in the early years of the century.

With the transformation of the WMC from an amateur cooperative of women musicians and music lovers into an organization sponsoring concerts by visiting professional artists, the club's activities were increasingly brought to the notice of Toronto's music critics. The shift from mere reporting of concerts to actual music criticism of them occurs gradually in the first half of the century in Toronto newpapers and periodicals. The golden era of music criticism was perhaps the 1960s, when all three of the major newspapers had professionally trained music critics turning out extensive and insightful reviews of Toronto's daily concert life.

Music criticism, like conducting, seems to foster long careers. Edward W. Wodson worked for the *Telegram* for some twenty years, Augustus Bridle was on staff at the *Star* for thirty years, William Littler has already served that same paper for as long, and John Kraglund was the critic at the *Globe and Mail* for thirty-five years. Hector Charlesworth's career as a music critic for various Toronto publications still holds the record, spanning almost fifty years; he died in 1945 while writing a review of a Toronto Symphony Orchestra concert. I am indebted to these five critics and the many others who have provided regular commentary on WMC concerts over the years.

The main source of information about the later years of the WMC is the club's archives which, from the 1920s on, provide a fairly complete account of the organization's activities. Annual reports exist for only eight of the first thirty-five seasons, but are available for every year after that, and the minutes of executive committee meetings are preserved, with some gaps, from 1925 on. The major portion of the wmc archives was recently transferred to the Metropolitan Toronto Reference Library.

A note on names. Where possible, women are referred to at first mention in this book by their given name, maiden name, and married name (if applicable), in that order. If four names are cited, then the second is either a commonly used given name or else the maiden name of the person in question's mother. Until recently it was most common for women to use their husband's name as their official, "public" name; in appendix 1 this form of the name is given for all the wmc presidents, and on occasion it is used in the text if the given and maiden names were not found.

Despite the great advances made in recent years in women's studies, and more particularly in the field of women and music, it is still difficult to find information on many women who have been involved in music, even if they had important careers. If these women married someone famous, the most detailed account is often to be found in a biography of their husbands. The same principle applies to the women who have been involved with the wmc. The only substantial account of the life of Anna Farini (the president of the wmc during the 1907–08 season) is in Shane Peacock's vivid biography of her husband, *The Great Farini: The High-Wire Life of William Hunt*. Information about other wmc members was only available in a biographical sketch of their husband or father in *Canadian Who's Who* or other similar biographical compendiums, in which a rich life in music or a significant contribution to arts patronage is reduced to a sentence or less. If this book has managed to shed some light on even a few of these talented and generous women, as well as on the organization that they created and nurtured, then I feel that its purpose has been served.

NOTES

1 "An Important Event in Toronto's Musical History: The Silver Anniversary of the Women's Musical Club," *Saturday Night* 4 Nov. 1922: 26, 34.

2 Kathleen Irwin Wells, "The Women's Musical Club of Toronto," *BSS Bulletin* Apr. 1956: n.p.; Jessie Macpherson, "Women's Musical Clubs," *Canadian Music Journal* 5.4 (1961): 45–47.

3 Brian Magner, "Impresarios with a Mission," *Globe and Mail* 17 Oct. 1959, Globe Magazine: 14, 25.

4 John Fraser, "Name's Victorian Scent Keeps This Myth Lingering On," *Telegram* [Toronto] 23 Sept. 1971: 56.

5 William Littler, "The Musical Teacup Brigade of Toronto," *Toronto Daily Star* 30 Oct. 1971: 69.

6 Betty Lee, "Getting the Musical Best for a Bargain," *Globe and Mail* 7 Sept. 1971: 10.

7 Lawrence Mason, "Case Histories of Canadian Artists," *Globe and Mail* 14 Jan. 1939: 21; 21 Jan. 1939: 7; 28 Jan. 1939: 23; 11 Feb. 1939: 17. See chapter 7 for a discussion of these articles.

8 Carl Morey, "Toronto Women's Musical Club," *Performing Arts in Canada* 9.1 (1972): 19.

9 Helen Goudge, *Look Back in Pride: A History of the Women's Musical Club of Toronto 1897–98 to 1972–73* (Toronto: Women's Musical Club of Toronto, 1972).

10 John B. Withrow, "Celebrating 90 Years: The Women's Musical Club of Toronto Celebrates 90 Years of Achievement," *Bravo* Sept.–Oct. 1987: 70, 73, 74.

ACKNOWLEDGEMENTS

The WMC centennial history project received funding from the Eaton Foundation. This support was particularly welcome and apt, given the historic ties between the WMC and the Eaton organization.

This book has been published with the help of a grant from the Humanities and Social Sciences Federation of Canada, using funds provided by the Social Sciences and Humanities Research Council of Canada.

It is a pleasure to record here the assistance which I have received from many other quarters in the course of working on this project. Isabel Laidler Jackson and Esther Spence McNeil, the original co-conveners of the WMC centennial history book committee, were generous with their time, and Isabel Jackson in particular was helpful far beyond the call of duty. Much information on the workings of the WMC was gained in the course of personal interviews with Mary Dennys, Hanna Gätgens Feuerriegel, Betty Taylor Gray, Isabel Jackson, Esther McNeil, Božena Naughton, Muriel Jones Roberts, Muriel Gidley Stafford, and Françoise Dreyfus Sutton, to all of whom I am very grateful. In addition I would like to thank Hanna Feuerriegel for providing me with a copy of the indexed fifty-page list of WMC concerts from 1899 to 1995 which she prepared with her husband. The list was at my side during the entire time I worked on the book and was an indispensable aid. I also thank Hanna Feuerriegel, Isabel Jackson, and Pamela MacKenzie of the WMC, and the two anonymous readers for the Aid to Scholarly Publications Program of the Humanities and Social Sciences Federation of Canada, for their insightful comments on the typescript of the book.

For library assistance I thank especially Nicholas Barakett and the rest of the helpful staff at the Metropolitan Toronto Reference Library, and also the staff of the University of Toronto Faculty of Music Library, the Thomas Fisher Rare Book Room and the University of Toronto Archives, the Robarts Library, the Music Division of the National Library of Canada, the Greater Victoria Public Library, and the McPherson Library at the University of Victoria. Thanks also to Peggy Reuber for putting the WMC Archives in order before I began working on them, and to Grace Heggie, the current WMC archivist.

For computer assistance I am indebted to Shari and Gord Langdon and to Darcy Brewer. I thank Robert Lecker of ECW PRESS for his interest in this book and agreeing to undertake to publish it, and also Holly Potter of ECW PRESS for her kind help. I would like to record here my debt of gratitude to Patricia Wardrop for reading the entire typescript and making many useful corrections and suggestions based on her encyclopaedic knowledge of music in Canada.

And finally, I would like to thank Korina Wynd, who not only provided research assistance and computer help for the book, but also a supportive and loving environment during the time I worked on it.

SOURCE OF ILLUSTRATIONS

1. Metropolitan Toronto Reference Library photo collection, no. T12415
2. *Saturday Night* 4 Nov. 1922: 26
3. *Saturday Night* 4 Nov. 1922: 26
4. *Globe and Mail* 26 Feb. 1945: 12
5. *Greater Toronto and the Men Who Made It* (Toronto: Inter-Provincial Publishing Co., 1911): 150
6. WMC Archives, Metropolitan Toronto Reference Library, Special Collections, Baldwin Room
7. WMC Archives, Metropolitan Toronto Reference Library, Special Collections, Baldwin Room
8. Farini Papers F 1073, S17238, Archives of Ontario
9. Metropolitan Toronto Reference Library photo collection, no. S-1997
10. Austin Seton Thompson, *Spadina: A Story of Old Toronto* (Toronto: Pagurian, 1975) 182
11. Metropolitan Toronto Reference Library photo collection
12. *Saturday Night* 15 Mar. 1941: 30
13. Publicity flyer, WMC Archives, Metropolitan Toronto Reference Library, Special Collections, Baldwin Room
14. *Globe and Mail* 16 Nov. 1951: 15
15. *Globe and Mail* 19 Oct. 1955: 13
16. *Toronto Daily Star* 8 Nov. 1957: 8
17. *Globe and Mail* 21 Mar. 1958: 9
18. *Toronto Sun* 27 Oct. 1972

I

Setting the Scene

When the Women's Musical Club of Toronto was founded in January 1899, Toronto was on the brink of a major expansion as a metropolitan district and a musical centre. At the same time, the role of women in Canadian society and within the music profession was undergoing important changes. To trace the history of the Women's Musical Club (hereafter WMC) over the course of its one hundred years of activity is to reflect on the growth and development of Toronto as a musical centre, and also on the changing status of women, especially within the world of music. Before turning to the history of the WMC itself, it is worth examining what conditions were like in Toronto, and more particularly for women musicians in Toronto, at the time of the founding of the club.

The population of Toronto was just under 200,000 in 1899, but it doubled in the course of the next fifteen years. Although Canadian-born citizens were in the majority beginning in 1871, there continued to be a steady flow of immigrants from Britain and Ireland who, as they integrated into the city, nourished strong ties with the British Isles. In addition, the early years of the twentieth century witnessed the first large influx of ethnic immigrants, who formed the basis for the city's later cosmopolitan mosaic. Citizens of British origin made up nearly ninety-two percent of the total in 1901, but that proportion had fallen to about eighty-five percent by 1921.[1]

The British majority itself, though, was subdivided along religious and cultural grounds, and in addition there were fairly marked class distinctions. It has been pointed out that the dominant ethnic group included "both well-to-do British families and military types from abroad as well as destitute Scots and Irish refugees from the great potato famine."[2] Furthermore, Robert Harney has noted that "ethnic differences among immigrants from Great Britain created patterns of separateness which foreshadowed the post–First and Second World War ethnocultures and ethnic enclaves in the city."[3] Church life and strict morality continued to be the overall guiding principles of the day, as evidenced by the ongoing strength of the local chapter of the Lord's Day Alliance of Canada, and by the popular label for the city — "Toronto the Good." But C.S. Clark exposed in lurid detail the seamy side of the city that hid behind that popular label,[4] and it was a small but perhaps significant blow against the Lord's Day Alliance when it was on the losing end of a plebiscite in 1897 on the issue of allowing city streetcars to run on Sundays.

The year-long celebration of the Diamond Jubilee of the reign of Queen Victoria garnered the most attention in 1897, however. The festivities culminated in the spectacular Victorian Era Ball held at the Toronto Armouries on 28 December 1897. Sponsored by Lord Aberdeen (the governor general of Canada from 1893 to 1898) and Lady Aberdeen, the ball was called "the largest and most brilliant function in the history of Canada"[5] and was attended by nearly 3,000 celebrants. The original idea was that the fancy dress ball would illustrate themes from Canadian history, but in the end, not surprisingly, it turned into a celebration of the accomplishments of the British Empire under Queen Victoria. The event was the talk of the town for months and even years to come.

During the 1890s, Toronto's growing size and importance and its burgeoning aspirations led to the construction of many fine new buildings. Among these were the Ontario Parliament Buildings in Queen's Park, which opened on 17 September 1892, and the new City Hall at Queen and Bay, which opened on 18 September 1899. The integral role that music played in the life of Victorian Toronto is illustrated by the fact that the opening festivities for the Parliament Buildings included a marching band and a chorus of five hundred schoolchildren singing "The Maple Leaf for Ever,"[6] while the City Hall opening featured an outdoor band concert and vocal recitals in two of the chief courtrooms.[7]

Manufacturing was quickly becoming the largest employer in Toronto. The growing industrial strength of the city was typified by the farm machinery manufacturer Massey-Harris, which was the largest company of its kind in the British Empire. Here too there was an important connection with music. Hart Massey (1823–1896), the son of the founder of the company, had given Toronto the splendid Massey Music Hall, which opened on 14 June 1894 with a performance of Handel's *Messiah* that featured a 750-voice choir.[8] (A number of important WMC concerts have taken place in Massey Hall over the years.) But tractors and ploughs were not all that Toronto was turning out: it was also an important centre for the large piano industry of the day. The Toronto city directory for 1899 lists no less than sixteen piano manufacturers, including major firms such as Mason & Risch, Heintzman, and Nordheimer.[9] As a sign of things to come, in 1899 Nordheimer's store was also offering gramophones for sale at fifteen and twenty-seven dollars, and recordings for sixty cents each.

Robert Simpson opened his six-storey department store at the corner of Yonge and Queen Streets in 1894; it was destroyed by fire shortly after occupancy, but was rebuilt as the first fireproof store in Canada by January 1896.[10] Nearby, at 190 Yonge Street, Timothy Eaton continued to preside over the flagship store of his retail empire. He celebrated the arrival of 1899 by hosting a mammoth New Year's Eve dinner for 2,475 of his employees.[11] In 1930, nearly a quarter of a century after Timothy Eaton's death, his company added new premises at the corner of Yonge and College streets. The new store housed an auditorium that, among other great musical events, would serve as the venue for WMC concerts for over forty-five years. Timothy Eaton's widow, Margaret Wilson Beattie Eaton, and his daughter-in-law, Flora McCrea Eaton (Lady Eaton), both enjoyed a close association with the WMC over the years.

The musical life of Toronto at the turn of the century was dominated by three recently founded educational institutions. The oldest of the three (by one year) was the Toronto Conservatory of Music, which opened for business in 1887. The conservatory moved into its new home on the southwest corner of College Street and Queen's Avenue (now University Avenue) in the fall of 1897, and expanded these premises over the next few years to keep pace with the vigorous growth of its activities. For many years most of the concerts of the WMC were held in the fine concert hall of the Conservatory of Music. The Toronto College of Music, founded in 1888, was located on Pembroke Street, around the corner from Massey Hall. The Metropolitan School of Music, which staked out the western suburbs of the city as its domain, began offering instruction in 1894 on Queen Street West, at the corner of Macdonell Avenue, in Parkdale. Many of the early members of the WMC were drawn from the teaching staff of these three institutions. In 1900 there were sixty-six women teachers thus employed: twenty-three at the Conservatory of Music, twenty-five at the College of Music, and eighteen at the Metropolitan School of Music.[12]

Toronto's main claim to fame as a musical centre during this era was in the field of choral performance. There were many fine church choirs, the more illustrious ones employing professional singers as soloists. Of the larger choirs, the most important eventually proved to be the Toronto Mendelssohn Choir (founded in 1894), which resumed its activities in 1900 after a three-year hiatus. By 1909 there were nine major choral societies in operation with a combined total of over 2,500 choristers. One writer claimed improbably but enthusiastically that Toronto thus boasted the largest number of choral forces of any city in the world.[13] Others were certain that at the very least it was the choral capital of North America. The WMC was not immune to this choral fever; a Women's Choral Club flourished within its ranks under a succession of conductors during the club's early years.

Operatic performances in the 1890s were in decline compared to the previous few decades, but were still offered with some regularity by visiting companies, notably the Metropolitan Opera in 1899 and 1901. For orchestral fare, apart from sporadic local efforts, Toronto audiences again had to rely on visiting U.S. groups, at least until the Toronto Symphony Orchestra began its first full season in December 1907.[14] Professional chamber music concerts by visiting groups were sponsored by the Toronto Chamber Music Association, founded in 1896, and local musicians also performed such concerts on occasion. Private music making at home flourished; the proof of this is in the society columns of the day, which are full of references to piano, song, and instrumental recitals during afternoon teas, at homes, and a variety of other private social entertainments that were a part of day-to-day life in Victorian Toronto. In all other areas of musical activity, including band performance, music publishing and journalism, and even composition, business was booming.

In all public arenas, the face of musical Toronto was dominantly male. This was quite literally true in the case of the Toronto Symphony Orchestra, which under its founding conductor Frank Welsman instituted a policy whereby the women string players were seated at the inside desks to hide them from the view of the audience.[15] The other Toronto musical institutions may have been more subtle in their policies, but they were equally effective at keeping women in their place. Men ran all the leading institutions: F.H. Torrington was the principal of the Toronto College of Music, Edward Fisher was the director of the Toronto Conservatory of Music, and W.O. Forsyth was the principal of the Metropolitan School of Music.

But in the much larger, and in many ways more important, world of private music making in Toronto, the field was dominated by women. Marcia J. Citron has noted that in Western musical life from the nineteenth century on, "the public arena has been privileged, and its activities have been chronicled, preserved, and praised," but that "removed from written scrutiny, the private has been given much less attention."[16] Citron develops the idea that the private world of music making has been largely associated with women musicians and has consequently been undervalued. As we shall see, it was this very factor that shrouded the early years of the WMC in darkness for many years.

As far as the actual day-to-day work of music instruction was concerned, women clearly outnumbered men. The Toronto city directory in 1900 listed 391 names in the classified section as "music teachers"; 262 of them were women.[17] Teaching music, especially piano or voice, had long been regarded as a suitable occupation for women. The United States Census Report for 1870 revealed that sixty percent of music teachers in the U.S.A. were women, and it is likely that they had dominated this field in Canada for some time as well. From its inception the WMC thus had a large base of musically trained women on which to draw for its membership.

Advanced professional training in music was increasingly available for Canadian women in the period under consideration. Judith Tick has shown how, in the United States during this era, the nineteenth-century stereotype of the "piano girl" — a young woman without any particular talent forced to plod away at piano lessons because it was the proper thing to do — was giving way to a new model of professionalism among women musicians.[18] Women everywhere were coming to view music as a serious professional activity rather than an "accomplishment." Many of the early members of the WMC were young women performers who had begun their training under excellent teachers locally and then had completed their education abroad. The singers studied in New York, London, or Paris, while the school of choice for many of the instrumentalists was the Leipzig Conservatory. Meanwhile, Canadian academia had opened its doors to women musicians: in 1885 the University of Trinity College (later federated with the University of Toronto) began offering music degrees to women, and the first two female graduates received their degrees in 1886.

There were many role models for aspiring young Canadian women musicians. The most famous was the soprano Emma Lajeunesse Gye (1847?–1930) of Quebec, who adopted the stage name Emma Albani and appeared throughout Europe and North America in opera, oratorio, and concert performances, and was made a Dame Commander of the British Empire in 1925. In her youth, Albani also tried her hand at composition, and in this she was followed by Roberta Geddes-Harvey (1849–1930),

Eva Rose Fitch York (1858–ca. 1935), Susie Frances Riley Harrison (1859–1935), Laura Lemon (1866–1924), and others. In the next generation, the Canadian-born composer Gena Branscombe Tenney (1881–1977) achieved great success during a long career in the United States. Another notable expatriate Canadian woman musician was the violinist Nora Clench Streeton (1867–1938) who, like her friend Albani, settled in London and enjoyed a very successful career. Although no Canadian women pianists enjoyed an international career on the level of Albani or Clench, many appeared within Canada and abroad as soloists.

Canadian women musicians were indeed making great strides in professional accomplishment. But because the world of public music making was slow to open its doors to them, many thrived in the private world of women's music clubs, where they could play for each other or enjoy performances by their friends. The Toronto music critic Emma Stanton Dymond, in her article "Status of Canadian Women in Music," explained the situation as it stood in 1900:

> The dawn of a new century finds the position of Canadian women in Music firmly established, elevated and hopeful. Bearing in mind the youth of our country, the rapid growth of interest in music, the number of those engaged in music — both as an Art and as a Profession — are all alike amazing. . . . [W]e find an army of enthusiastic young women, born, trained and taught in Canada, winning places in the front ranks of teachers, pianists, vocalists and the music profession generally. . . . Music has, indeed, been a plant of rapid growth in our midst. . . . The educational value also of women's music clubs for study of different composers' lives and works cannot be too highly estimated. These have sprung up almost everywhere within the past ten years.[19]

Women's musical clubs were indeed ubiquitous throughout North America by 1900. The women's musical club phenomenon was part of the much larger women's study club movement, which began in the United States in the 1860s. The focus and activities of these study clubs ranged far and wide. In recent years these clubs have been analysed variously as service organizations, educational institutions, and latent feminist groups.[20] The General Federation of Women's Clubs was formed in the United States in 1890, and by 1906 it embraced some five thousand local organizations, thought to be only a fraction of the women's clubs then in existence. Meanwhile the first women's musical clubs had been formed in the United States in the 1870s.[21] An all-women

National Federation of Music Clubs was founded in Springfield, Illinois, in 1898. By 1899 this organization represented hundreds of U.S. women's musical clubs with a combined membership of over twenty thousand women, and by 1930 it had four hundred thousand members.

Canadian women in the late-nineteenth century were also banding together in ever greater numbers to form a variety of local and national clubs and special interest groups. The women's club movement continued to gather steam in Canada during the early years of the twentieth century. Marjory MacMurchy in 1916 estimated that 250,000 women belonged to one or more national associations; as she concluded, "Canadian women have a genius for organisation."[22] She went on to describe the average club woman:

> The typical member . . . is married, not single. She is middle-aged. She is a woman with household occupations and yet with some leisure. Her children are wholly or half-way grown up and she is able to undertake some work outside. . . . She also has sufficient initiative and energy to make other occupation necessary. She must have social intercourse. Few things are more unhealthy mentally than for a woman whose work is keeping house to remain indoors alone, all day, every day. The need of this middle-aged, married woman for work and social co-operation, her impulse to help others and accomplish something worth doing in the world outside, are the forces which have created women's organisations.[23]

Add to this that she was likely of the middle class, and we have a good portrait of the average women's club member.

Improvements in domestic technology, together with a gradually declining birth rate and the introduction of compulsory education in 1871, all contributed to a greater amount of leisure time for middle-class women in the late-nineteenth century. For many of these women, this increased leisure time led to an increased need for companionship, and this in turn found a natural and structured outlet through participation in women's clubs. The attraction of these clubs has been explained as follows:

> To those stepping outside the home for the first time they provided the security that went with being associated with like-minded women. . . . Through these clubs many Canadian women learned the skills of organization, public speaking, and social investigation, and this may have been of more importance than the aims for which the women had allegedly come together.

Perhaps most significant, these were *women's* organizations, founded, organized, and run by and for women. Men were excluded. In these clubs women could create and enjoy their own social values, free from those of the normally male-dominated society in which they lived.[24]

The groups which these women were joining in Canada ranged in focus from reform-minded bodies like the Woman's Christian Temperance Union, whose first Canadian local was founded in 1874, to cultural activity clubs such as the Women's Art Association of Canada, which was founded in Toronto in 1890 and opened branches in other cities across the country before the turn of the century. An important umbrella organization for many of these clubs and societies was founded in 1893. This was the National Council of Women of Canada, whose first president was Lady Aberdeen.[25]

There was no national organization for women's musical clubs in Canada, and so the extent of the movement in this country is difficult to estimate. The earliest such organization in Canada seems to have been the Duet Club of Hamilton, founded in 1889.[26] There were certainly dozens of such groups in existence by 1900. In Ontario, women's musical clubs flourished not only in larger urban centres such as Toronto, Ottawa, and Hamilton, but also in smaller towns such as Listowel and Napanee. Montreal in 1900 was home to three such clubs, including one called the Arion Club that was exclusively for unmarried women. In Toronto there were some eight women's musical clubs of various types in existence by 1900, including one, founded in January 1899, that was destined to achieve great things.

NOTES

[1] Robert F. Harney, ed., *Gathering Place: Peoples and Neighbourhoods of Toronto, 1834–1945* (Toronto: Multicultural History Society of Ontario, 1985) examines various ethnic groups that arrived in Toronto during this period.

[2] Raymond Breton et al., *Ethnic Identity and Equality: Varieties of Experience in a Canadian City* (Toronto: U of Toronto P, 1990) 14.

[3] Harney 2–3.

[4] C[hristopher] S[t. George] Clark, *Of Toronto the Good* (1898; Toronto: Coles, 1970). About a quarter of the book, for example, deals with prostitution in the city.

[5] *Leslie's Weekly* [New York] 27 Jan. 1898, qtd. in Rieger and Williamson, *Toronto Dancing Then and Now* (Toronto: Metropolitan Toronto Reference Library, 1995) 7.

6 Roger Hall, *A Century to Celebrate, 1893–1993: The Ontario Legislative Building* (Toronto: Dundurn, 1993) 36–38.

7 May Hamilton, "Music in Canada," *Musical Courier* 4 Oct. 1899: 11.

8 William Kilbourn, *Intimate Grandeur: One Hundred Years at Massey Hall* (Toronto: Stoddart, 1993) 11–13.

9 "Piano Manufacturers," *Might's Toronto City Directory* (1899): 1006.

10 Toronto Historical Board plaque, 1979.

11 "A Mammoth Dinner Party," *Globe* 4 Jan. 1899: 9.

12 National Council of Women of Canada, *Women of Canada: Their Life and Work* (1900; Ottawa: National Council of Women of Canada, 1975): 231.

13 *Conservatory Bi-monthly* Nov. 1909: 186.

14 See Carl Morey, "Orchestras and Orchestral Repertoire in Toronto before 1914," *Musical Canada: Words and Music Honouring Helmut Kallmann*, ed. John Beckwith and Frederick A. Hall (Toronto: U of Toronto P, 1988) 100–14, for details.

15 Morey 112. It should be noted, though, that the Toronto Symphony Orchestra under Welsman had more women players than it did when it was reorganized in 1923.

16 Marcia J. Citron, *Gender and the Musical Canon* (Cambridge: Cambridge UP, 1993) 102.

17 "Music Teachers," *Might's Toronto City Directory* (1900): 988–90.

18 Judith Tick, "Passed Away Is the Piano Girl: Changes in American Musical Life, 1870–1900," *Women Making Music: The Western Art Tradition, 1150–1950*, ed. Jane Bowers and Judith Tick (Urbana: U of Illinois P, 1986) 325–48.

19 In National Council of Women of Canada 228–29.

20 Theodora Penny Martin, *The Sound of Our Own Voices: Women's Study Clubs 1860–1910* (Boston: Beacon, 1987), provides an excellent survey of this movement. See also Karen J. Blair, *The Clubwoman as Feminist: True Womanhood Redefined, 1868–1914* (New York: Holmes & Meier, 1980).

21 Clara A. Korn, "Women's Musical Clubs," *Etude* 17.5 (1899): 150, cites the Rossini Club of Portland, Maine, founded in 1871, as the oldest in existence. Linda Whitesitt, "'The Most Potent Force' in American Music: The Role of Women's Music Clubs in American Concert Life," *The American Woman: An International Perspective*, ed. Judith Lang Zaimont (Westport, CT: Greenwood, 1991) 3: 664, states that the Rossini Club was founded in 1869 but existed informally for several years prior to its official organization.

22 Marjory MacMurchy, *The Woman — Bless Her* (Toronto: Gundy, 1916) 14.

23 MacMurchy 16–17.

24 Ramsay Cook and Wendy Mitchinson, eds. *The Proper Sphere: Women's Place in Canadian Society* (Toronto: Oxford UP, 1976), 199.

25 See N.E.S. Griffiths, *The Splendid Vision: Centennial History of the National Council of Women, 1893–1993* (Ottawa: Carleton UP, 1993).

26 "Women's Musical Clubs," *Encyclopedia of Music in Canada*, 2nd ed., 1992.

2

Origins

Toronto at the turn of the century was home to a variety of musical clubs, some for men, others for women, and a few that were open to both. The Toronto Male Chorus Club, founded in 1893, was a men's choir which gave an annual concert in Massey Hall. The Toronto Clef Club was formed in 1895; its object was "the fostering of a fraternal feeling amongst professional musicians, the welcoming of musicians of standing and personal integrity who may settle in the city, the entertaining of visiting artists of eminence and the encouragement of any means calculated to elevate the status of music and musicians in Canada."[1] Omitted from this lofty statement of principles was the fact that the club was only open to men; women were entertained in the clubroom only on special "ladies' nights" beginning in 1896. The Toronto Vocal Science Club, formed in 1897 and open to both men and women, gathered regularly to hear papers on issues related to vocal physiology, especially in its practical relations to voice production. The Toronto Singers' Club was also open to men and women; it was a mixed choir formed by the conductor Edward W. Schuch in 1899.

To narrow the field down to women's musical clubs, there were at least eight such groups operating in Toronto by the end of the nineteenth century. The oldest was the Toronto Ladies' Choral Club, a choir founded by Norah Hillary in 1889. The Toronto Chamber Music Association, sometimes called the Women's Chamber Music Association, was founded in 1896. The University of Toronto was home to a Ladies' Glee Club and a Ladies' Guitar and Mandolin Club, both founded circa 1897.

The Home Music Club, founded in 1897 and still active today, started out as a women's musical club but began to admit men to its ranks early in the twentieth century. The Toronto Musical Improvement Club was also founded in 1897, and it was primarily a women's musical club, although some men and children also participated in its concerts and events. A group called the Wednesday Club was holding musicales early in 1899, at about the same time that the WMC was founded. The Thursday Musical Club was founded at the Toronto Conservatory of Music in October 1899 by the director's wife, Florence Lowell Fisher. Before turning to the story of the WMC's founding, let us describe some of the other clubs in more detail here, as one or two of them have been confused with, and others may well have amalgamated with, the WMC.

The Toronto (Women's) Chamber Music Association was founded on the initiative of Mrs. F.H. Torrington in the fall of 1896 to sponsor chamber music concerts by visiting professional string quartets. Mrs. Torrington was the second wife of the principal of the Toronto College of Music, and she was a leading organizer of women's groups; she was president of the National Council of Women from 1911 to 1918.[2] Mrs. Torrington served as the secretary-treasurer of the Toronto Chamber Music Association. The founding president was Elizabeth Campbell Mason, Lady Gzowski was the honorary president, and among the twenty or so other founding members were three women who were later involved in the WMC: Mary Henderson Flett Dickson and Mary Irene Gurney, two of the founders of the WMC, and Mary Richmond Kerr Austin, an early president of the WMC.

At the time of the founding of the Toronto Chamber Music Association, chamber music was conspicuous by its absence from Toronto's concert life, as the *Saturday Night* music critic complained in October 1896:

> Chamber music, which is perhaps the most elevated form of musical expression, has of late years been woefully neglected in this city. Not only have capable local organizations been discouraged owing to lack of support, but visiting quartettes have fared so poorly that the much vaunted musical culture of the city has seemed the wildest kind of a romance.[3]

Visiting U.S. groups such as the Mendelssohn Quintette Club and the Beethoven Quintette Club, both of Boston, had been appearing in Toronto since the 1870s, and an earlier Chamber Music Association had been founded by Samuel Nordheimer in 1886, yet chamber music still occupied a precarious position in Toronto's concert life.

It was the goal of the Toronto Chamber Music Association to redress this problem. In the program for the second concert sponsored by the organization, the following announcement was printed:

> It is the aim of this Association to so encourage and promote Chamber Music in Toronto that it will become an established feature of art in our city. . . . The members of this Association hope to have the assistance of all lovers of music in the city, and of all who realize what an educational factor concerts of this kind must be.[4]

The association sponsored two concerts per season during the four seasons of its existence, from 1896 to 1900. The visiting groups were the Yunck String Quartet of Detroit (1896, 1897), the Spiering Quartet of Chicago (1898, 1899), the Dannreuther Quartet of New York (1898), and the Kneisel Quartet of Boston (1897, 1899, and 1900); all but the Yunck Quartet were making their Toronto debuts, according to contemporary reviewers.

A feature of these concerts is that one or more singers would perform arias or songs with piano accompaniment between the string quartet numbers. Music critics of the day, curiously, usually reserved the phrase "classical music" for the chamber repertoire, and the educational value of this music was stressed, as was its refined and elevated quality. But evidently the audiences of the day liked to have this uplifting fare in smaller doses, separated by the perhaps more visceral attractions of a good singer. The women who organized and ran the Toronto Chamber Music Association obviously had a tough time in educating Toronto audiences as to the merits of chamber music. Their concerts consistently lost money, so they had to bring the sensational boy soprano Earl Gulick of Brooklyn to appear with the Kneisel Quartet on 30 April 1900 in order to attract a large audience and recoup their losses. Having thus eliminated its accumulated deficit, the association promptly retired from the field forever.

But the Toronto Chamber Music Association must have whetted Toronto audiences' appetite for professional chamber music concerts, and its departure created a void in the local concert schedule that, as we shall see, the WMC would fill by sponsoring annual visits by the Kneisel Quartet starting in 1902. The experience gained in working for this association was put to good use by those of its members who later helped to run the WMC.

Just as the Toronto Chamber Music Association prefigured the WMC's activities as a presenter of professional chamber music concerts, so the

Home Music Club of Toronto foreshadowed the WMC's early emphasis on private musicales by and for club members. This club was founded at 383 Markham Street, the home of the soprano Mrs. Charles Crowley, in 1897; only women were admitted at first.[5] The club held weekly afternoon meetings, and each member was expected to contribute by performing on the programs from time to time.

In 1900 the Home Music Club began to admit men and hold its twice-monthly meetings in the evenings rather than the afternoons. The club has continued to function in much the same way ever since. Its constitution states that "The Club exists to provide a forum wherein its members may perform, and hear performed, vocal and instrumental music at the highest attainable standard," and it sets our four classes of membership — active, associate, life, and inactive; it also provides guidelines for membership fees, the election of the executive committee, annual general meetings, and all the other necessities of a well-run club.[6] The club is limited to seventy-five members, and new members must be proposed and seconded by existing members. In these respects this group bears a striking similarity to the earliest incarnation of the WMC. For many years the Home Music Club has flourished in its own quiet way, out of the scrutiny of the public eye, and it may legitimately claim to be the second oldest existing musical organization in Toronto, after the Mendelssohn Choir.

One other club which was similar in many respects to the WMC has on occasion been confused with it. The Thursday Musical Club was founded in the same year as the WMC. Both clubs held their meetings on Thursdays: the WMC in the morning and the Thursday Musical Club in the evening. The latter was founded in October 1899, as reported in the *Musical Courier*:

> At the Toronto Conservatory of Music a club has been formed, the object of which is to increase the love of art for art's sake and to enrich the musical life of the students. That cultured and beautiful woman, Mrs. Edward Fisher, wife of the musical director, has been elected president. The vice-president is Miss Maud Masson.[7]

During its first season of activities the Thursday Musical Club had a membership of two hundred. It was intended mainly for staff and students of the Conservatory of Music, and its stated aim was "mutual improvement, encouragement and inspiration in the study of vocal and instrumental music."[8] In practice this meant that the members played music for each other, or on occasion read an essay on some aspect of music appreciation. The membership was predominantly female, although not exclusively so. Florence Fisher was not a musician herself, but she was described by Hector Charlesworth as "a woman of the highest musical taste and general culture"; he also noted that "her kindness and hospitality toward pupils and graduates was proverbial."[9] In all these respects, Florence Fisher was remarkably similar to Mary Dickson, the founding president of the WMC. How long the Thursday Musical Club lasted is not known, but there seems to be little record of its activities after the first few seasons. Possibly the club amalgamated with the WMC in 1903, for in the fall of that year the WMC began meeting in the concert hall of the Conservatory of Music, which previously had been the venue for the Thursday Musical Club concerts. Florence Fisher had joined the WMC by 1905 at the latest, and she later served on its executive committee.

This brings us to the story of the founding of the Women's Musical Club of Toronto, a story that has been told several times over the years, but unfortunately in various conflicting versions. The founding date has been set at various years between 1889 and 1902, with 1897 and 1898 being the favoured choices in the past (neither is correct, as it turns out). Two slightly different tales of who was involved in the founding of the WMC have circulated, and in many other respects the early years have been a source of some confusion. There are several reasons why this should be so. The archives of the WMC shed no light on the founding of the club, and apart from printed programs little has been preserved from the period before 1907.[10] The club was largely a private organization in its early years, and so its activities were not often reported by the press of the day. Membership in the club was only open to women, and nearly all of the music critics in Toronto at the time were men. A further source of confusion, as we have seen, is the fact that there were many women's musical clubs operating in Toronto at the turn of the century, and thus it is not always clear which club is being referred to in newspaper and magazine reports of the day.

Nevertheless, the story of the founding of the WMC was indeed recorded in at least five different contemporary sources. Only one of these sources is a music column. The Canadian correspondent for the *Musical Courier*, a weekly music periodical published in New York City, was a young Toronto music journalist named May Hamilton, who contributed a regular column titled "Music in Canada." At the end of one of her columns, dated 27 January 1899, she noted in passing "A Woman's Musical Club has recently been established in this city."[11] In December 1899 she reported "The Woman's Musical Club, of Toronto, is meeting every week and giving creditable programs. The president is Mrs. George Dickson, of St. Margaret's College."[12] May Hamilton was the only woman music critic in Toronto at the time, and she was a member of the WMC during its first few seasons. A second source which confirms the January 1899 date is the book *Women of Canada: Their Life and Work*, compiled by the National Council of Women of Canada for distribution at the Paris International Exhibition, which opened on 15 April 1900. The book included a section titled "Musical Clubs Organized and Conducted by Women," which gives the following information:

> Woman's Morning Music Club, Toronto. Organized in January, 1899. Object, "mutual improvement in vocal and instrumental music." Membership, active and associate, 40 of the former, 125 of the latter. Meets for one hour weekly. President — Mrs. George Dickson.[13]

Incidentally, the confusion over the name of the WMC is not unique to these two sources. Over the years the club has been referred to in print as the Woman's Musical Club, Woman's Morning Music Club, Woman's Thursday Musical Club (hence the confusion with the Conservatory's Thursday Musical Club), and a number of other variations, notwithstanding the fact that every program of the organization, from 1899 on, has consistently used the same name — Women's Musical Club of Toronto.

A search through Toronto newspaper and periodical music columns for January 1899 failed to reveal a single mention of the founding of the WMC. In the social columns however, three substantial reports were located: those of the *Globe*'s "Chit Chat,"[14] the *Mail and Empire*'s "On Dit,"[15] and *Saturday Night*'s "Social and Personal."[16] Piecing together the information found in these three sources, the following account of the founding of the WMC emerges. On Monday morning, 23 January 1899, an organizational meeting was held in Mary Hewitt Smart's studio in the Arcade on Yonge Street.[17] Mrs. J.D. Tyrrell chaired the meeting, and a resolution to found a "morning musicale" club was passed. It was decided that the club should meet every two weeks on Monday mornings at 10:30 a.m. in Miss Smart's studio. The fee for active and associate members was set at one dollar; professionals could join without charge. Members were then enrolled, and it was decided that the number of active and associate members would be limited. The business part of the meeting concluded with the election of the following officers: Mary Dickson, president; Mary Irene Gurney, vice-president; Grace Boulton, secretary; and Ethel Street, treasurer. A vote of thanks was passed to Mary Smart for the use of her studio and to Henry Mason for the loan of a grand piano to the club. The meeting concluded with a recital by the pianists Ethel Street, Mary Irene Gurney, and Florence Taylor; the singers Margaret Huston and Mrs. Le Grand Reed; and the violinist Hilda Boulton. Florence Taylor was from Detroit, but the rest of the recitalists were local musicians. (For more information on this recital, see the beginning of chapter 3.) Other women present at this founding meeting included Mrs. Torrington, Elizabeth Campbell Mason, Evelyn de Latre Street, and at least a dozen others. The meeting concluded at noon.

Obviously a fair amount of behind-the-scenes organizational work had preceeded the 23 January 1899 meeting. One column mentioned that Mary Irene Gurney was "one of the chief movers in the scheme."[18] A substantial account of the founding of the WMC was written for *Saturday Night* in 1922 on the occasion of the twenty-fifth anniversary of the club. The unsigned article reports as follows:

> Miss Irene Gurney, now Mrs. Sanford Evans of Winnipeg, associated with a few others, originated the idea, and Mrs. Dickson was asked by Miss Gurney, Mrs. Stewart Houston, Mrs. H.H. Langton, and Miss Grace Boulton to accept the Presidency, a post which she filled for the first five years.[19]

If this account is true, the election on 23 January 1899 would seem to have been a formality. With the exception of Mrs. Houston, the women mentioned above were the very ones who formed the first WMC executive.

It seems likely that most of the credit for starting up the WMC should go to Mary Irene Gurney. Irene Gurney was well placed in Toronto social circles of the day, as she was the daughter of Edward Gurney, a prominent local manufacturer and president of Gurney Foundry and Stove Works. But she won respect from local music critics on the strength of her piano playing rather than her social position. She was one of F.H. Torrington's star pupils, and also studied at the New England Conservatory of Music in Boston, from which she graduated in 1890. Upon returning to Toronto, she gave her recital debut in Association Hall[20] on 14 October 1890, eliciting high praise from the music critic of *Saturday Night*:

> Miss Gurney needed none of the good feeling which surrounds the acceptance of a social invitation to popularize her work on that evening. . . . [S]he is possessed of a thoroughly artistic temperament,

FIGURE I

The interior of the Yonge Street Arcade;
the WMC was founded here on 23 January 1899.

FIGURE 2

Mary Irene Gurney Evans,
the founder of the WMC.

excellent technical ability, and a proper conception of the spirit of the pieces she played. . . . She has a rich, warm touch, and she plays with a freedom and ease which is delightfully refreshing. . . . Her rapid work is clear and distinct, with nice gradations of tonal and rhythmic effects.[21]

For the next ten years Gurney had an active local career, making her mark as a piano accompanist and on occasion giving a solo recital. She also had a song published by the Anglo-Canadian Music Company in 1896. In January 1900, one year after she was involved in the founding of the WMC, she married William Sanford Evans, a local journalist and financier. Among her wedding gifts was a music cabinet from the WMC.[22] She continued to perform in and arrange WMC concerts until 1901, when she moved with her husband to Winnipeg. Sanford Evans turned to politics and served as the mayor of Winnipeg and later as Winnipeg's MLA in the Manitoba Legislature. Mary Irene Gurney Evans returned to Toronto for a WMC concert in her honour on 7 February 1903, and she was an honorary member thereafter. She also became active in, and from 1903 to 1906 served as the president of, the Women's Musical Club of Winnipeg, and from 1908 to 1910 she served as the first president of the Women's Canadian Club.[23] During the First World War, while living temporarily in Ottawa, she returned to Toronto for a WMC concert on 30 March 1917, which seems to have been her last appearance at a WMC event. She was still living in Winnipeg at the time of her husband's death in June 1949.

Mary Irene Gurney Evans deserves credit for founding the WMC, but it was Mary Henderson Flett Dickson who nurtured it for many years. Mary Dickson, who was a generation older than Mary Irene Gurney, was the president of the WMC for twelve of its first twenty seasons. She was born in Hamilton, Ontario, in the mid-nineteenth century. In 1882 she married the educator George Dickson, who was the headmaster of Hamilton Collegiate Institute at the time. The Dicksons moved to Toronto in 1885, when George Dickson became the principal of Upper Canada College. After a difficult ten years with UCC, George Dickson left in unhappy circumstances in 1895.[24]

In 1897 the Dicksons founded St. Margaret's College, a Presbyterian ladies' school which offered instruction up to the level of university matriculation. St. Margaret's was formally opened by Lord and Lady Aberdeen, who were in town for the Victorian Era Ball, on 12 November 1897; Lady Aberdeen and Mary Dickson were acquainted through their work for the National Council of Women.[25] The college was located at

FIGURE 3

Mary Henderson Flett Dickson, the
first and longest-serving WMC president.

403 Bloor Street West, at the corner of Spadina Avenue, and had 80 pupils registered for its first year of operation. In 1907 it moved to 144 Bloor Street East. Many of the pupils were from the United States, and for a time there was a branch of St. Margaret's in New York City.[26] When the college opened, George Dickson was the president and Mary Dickson was the principal; both were on the teaching staff. Upon George Dickson's death in 1910, Mary Dickson became the president and Miss J.E. Macdonald became the principal. Mary Dickson served as the president until 1920, and continued to live on the college grounds until St. Margaret's closed in 1923. She then moved to 58 Elm Avenue, where she lived until her death.

St. Margaret's offered excellent instruction in a wide variety of academic subjects (Lucius R. O'Brien, for example, was the first art instructor), but was particularly noted for the strength of its music department. After the move to new quarters in 1907, the college boasted twenty soundproof practice rooms and a large concert hall, which was the site of a number of WMC events over the years. The music staff of about a dozen instructors consistently included the leading Toronto musicians of the day.[27] After St. Margaret's College closed, the building was renamed Rosary Hall. It was operated as a boarding house until circa 1931 and was demolished sometime thereafter. By sheer coincidence, the first WMC office was established in 1992 at 160 Bloor Street East, adjacent to the former St. Margaret's College property.

While St. Margaret's College took up a lot of Mary Dickson's time and energy, she had plenty of both left over for other projects in addition to the WMC. One of the most dedicated volunteers of the day, Mary Dickson served as president of the Toronto Council of Women and the Women's Canadian Club, and was also on the executive committees of the Toronto Symphony Women's Committee, the Women's Association of St. Andrew's Church, and the Women's League of the Presbyterian Church of Canada.[28]

Mary Dickson died on 18 October 1940. The funeral took place on the afternoon of 21 October, at the very same time, ironically, as a WMC concert in Hart House Theatre. Mary Dickson had not been associated with the WMC for fifteen years at the time of her death, but her passing was noted in the annual report for the 1940–41 season. It was hardly an adequate recognition for the woman to whom, as we shall see, the WMC probably owes more than just about any other. The obituary in *Saturday Night* best captures what made Mary Henderson Flett Dickson a remarkable woman, and is worth quoting at length by way of tribute to her importance in the history of the WMC:

It seems likely that the nearest thing to a "Salon" to be found in Canada . . . was the gatherings which Mrs. George Dickson used to assemble in her home in Rosedale, and in which, while music usually predominated, all forms of intellectual activity were invariably represented. But intellectual activity is not enough to make a salon; social grace is also essential, and of that Mrs. Dickson was one of the country's finest practitioners and most scrupulous guardians. With the dignity and wit of a Marquise of the *ancien régime* she combined a ready and generous appreciation of every kind of artistic talent which made her social relations "catholic" in the fullest sense of the word.

An ardent and discriminating patron of music, she was one of the most energetic founders of the Women's Musical Club, and a well-known figure at every musical event of quality in Toronto. But her greatest achievement was unquestionably the contribution which she made to the refinement of social behavior. . . . There is an art of living, which is more important because more inclusive than all the other arts of the human race. It is too often neglected in new and aggressive communities, but Mrs. Dickson understood and practised it, and her own long life, which closed last week, was in consequence one of the most perfectly rounded and satisfactory that any human being could desire.[29]

We shall have occasion to return many times to the contributions of Mary Dickson to the WMC over the years.

Mary Hewitt Smart provided the studio where the WMC was founded and in which its meetings were held during the first season. She was born in Brockville, Ontario, in 1857. After studying singing in Boston, Philadelphia, and with Edward Hayes in New York, she moved to Toronto in 1889 to teach music at Moulton Ladies' College at 34 Bloor Street East. She resigned her position there in June 1897 to set up her private music studio in the Yonge Street Arcade. In October 1897 she began hosting private musicales at this studio; among those participating was Mary Irene Gurney.[30] It may well be that these private musicales planted the seed for the WMC, and possibly as a result of confusion with the initiation of these musicales, 1897 has sometimes been cited as the founding year of the WMC.

Also in the fall of 1897, Mary Smart joined the music staff of the newly opened St. Margaret's College, where she would have made the acquaintance of Mary Dickson. In the fall of 1907 she closed her private studio and began teaching at the Toronto Conservatory of Music.[31] In 1909 she

FIGURE 4

Mary Hewitt Smart Shenstone. The founding
meeting of the WMC was held in her music studio
in the Arcade Building at 131-9 Yonge Street.
Portrait by WMC member Dorothy Stevens, 1934.

resumed teaching duties at Moulton College and remained on staff there until her retirement in 1927. In 1925, after sixty-eight years of unmarried life, she became the second wife of the manufacturer Joseph N. Shenstone.

Perhaps Mary Smart's most important contribution to the cultural life of Toronto was the founding of the Heliconian Club early in 1909. She was the honorary president of this club until her death in 1945, and a striking portrait of her, painted in 1934 by the Toronto artist Dorothy Stevens, hangs in the Heliconian Club's permanent home at 35 Hazelton Avenue. Like other early members of the WMC, Mary Smart was active in several women's groups. She was a member at one time or another of the Toronto Symphony Women's Committee, the Women's Art Association, and the Toronto Ladies' Club.

The other women who assisted in the founding of the WMC may be dealt with more briefly. Augusta Louisa Robinson Houston was the daughter of John Beverley Robinson, who was the mayor of Toronto in 1856 and served as the lieutenant governor of Ontario from 1880 to 1887. Her mother, Mary Jane Hagerman Robinson, was an accomplished singer. Augusta Louisa Robinson studied singing in Toronto, New York, Paris, and London. Following her return to Canada in 1895, she sang with Emma Albani's concert party for two years, and then in 1899 she gave a series of benefit concerts for the Dominion Patriotic Fund of the South African War, raising $10,000. Also in 1899 she gave a vocal recital as part of the opening ceremonies for Toronto City Hall. In 1898 she married the barrister Stewart Field Houston, who was the manager of Massey Hall from 1900 until his death in 1910. In 1900 she retired from the public stage, but she continued to perform for the WMC, of which she remained a member into the 1920s. She died in Toronto on 9 September 1935.

Ethel Beatrice Street, the founding treasurer of the WMC, was the daughter of William Purvis Rochfort Street. Her younger sister, Evelyn de Latre Street, was an accomplished violinist and a graduate of the Leipzig Conservatory who often played in WMC concerts. Ethel Street was born in London, Ontario, circa 1870 and moved to Toronto with her family in 1887 when her father was appointed an Ontario High Court judge. On 2 May 1899, towards the end of the first season of the WMC, she married Hugh Hornby Langton, a noted Canadian historian and the librarian of the University of Toronto for thirty years. The Langtons were both passionately fond of music and played the piano, though not in public. They also owned what was at the time perhaps the only copy in Canada of the original Bach complete works edition.[32] Ethel Street

Langton arranged many of the earliest WMC concerts, and she was one of the first honorary members of the club. She died in 1946.

Grace Boulton was one of five sisters, three of whom were early WMC members; the others were Hilda Boulton, a violinist, and Edith Boulton, an associate member. Their cousin Constance Boulton also appeared in an early WMC concert as an elocutionist. These women were all members of the famous Boulton family of The Grange.[33] Grace Boulton was a pianist and for a dozen years or so was the secretary (from 1907 the secretary-treasurer) of the WMC. This was the club's only paid position; her job was to order music for the concerts and to look after the general business affairs of the club. Grace Boulton, Ethel and Evelyn Street, H.H. Langton, and Mary Irene Gurney had all been members of yet another earlier musical club for men and women that flourished in Toronto circa 1895–96.[34]

These then, were the remarkable and accomplished individuals who founded the Women's Musical Club of Toronto. We turn now to their activities during the first decade of the club's life.

NOTES

[1] "Music," *Saturday Night* 17 July 1897: 10.

[2] Griffiths 86, 113.

[3] "Music," *Saturday Night* 10 Oct. 1896: 10.

[4] Toronto Chamber Music Association program, 5 Apr. 1897, in the collection of the Metropolitan Toronto Reference Library.

[5] "Our Musical Clubs," *Musical Canada* Dec. 1910: 229.

[6] *The Constitution and Rules of the Home Music Club*, as amended March 1987.

[7] May Hamilton, "Music in Canada," *Musical Courier* 1 Nov. 1899: 12.

[8] National Council of Women of Canada 229.

[9] Hector Charlesworth, "Death of Mrs. Edward Fisher," *Conservatory Quarterly Review* 7.1 (1924): 12.

[10] WMC *Tenth Annual Report*, covering the 1907–08 concert season, has been preserved in the Music Division of the National Library of Canada.

[11] May Hamilton, "Music in Canada," *Musical Courier* 1 Feb. 1899: 6.

[12] May Hamilton, "Music in Canada," *Musical Courier* 6 Dec. 1899: 35.

[13] National Council of Women of Canada 229.

[14] "Chit Chat," *Globe* 24 Jan. 1899: 8.

[15] "On Dit," *Mail and Empire* 24 Jan. 1899: 2.

[16] "Social and Personal," *Saturday Night* 28 Jan. 1899: 3.

[17] The Arcade building, known as the Toronto Arcade or the Yonge Street Arcade, was built in the 1880s. It was located at 131–9 Yonge Street, between

Adelaide and Richmond, and ran east to Victoria Street. On the south side of the third floor, in unit 71, were studio rooms, and Mary Hewitt Smart operated a private music studio in Room U. The Arcade building was demolished in 1955.

18 "On Dit," *Mail and Empire* 24 Jan. 1899: 2.

19 "An Important Event in Toronto's Musical History: The Silver Anniversary of the Women's Musical Club," *Saturday Night* 4 Nov. 1922: 26, 34.

20 Association Hall was located in the YMCA building at the corner of Yonge and McGill Streets. It was the venue for many of the early open concerts of the WMC.

21 "Music," *Saturday Night* 25 Oct. 1890: 6.

22 "Social and Personal," *Saturday Night* 27 Jan. 1900: 2.

23 C.W. Parker, ed., *Who's Who in Western Canada* (Vancouver: Canadian Press, 1911): 171.

24 Richard B. Howard, *Upper Canada College 1829–1979: Colborne's Legacy* (Toronto: Macmillan, 1979): 109–27, describes George Dickson's term as principal of UCC.

25 "Good Wishes for the New College," *Mail and Empire* 13 Nov. 1897: 6.

26 Seranus [Susie Frances Harrison], "Canada," *The Imperial History and Encyclopedia of Music*, ed. W.L. Hubbard (Toronto: Ford, n.d. [ca. 1910]): 249.

27 "St. Margaret's College, Toronto," *Musical Canada* Nov. 1908: 265.

28 "Canadian Women in the Public Eye: Mrs. George Dickson," *Saturday Night* 8 Jan. 1921: 25.

29 "Late Mrs. George Dickson," *Saturday Night* 26 Oct. 1940: 3.

30 "Music," *Saturday Night* 6 Nov. 1897: 10.

31 "Miss Mary Hewitt Smart," *Conservatory Bi-monthly* July 1909: 115.

32 Isabel Erichsen Brown, "Bach Gesellschaft in Toronto," *Conservatory Review* Mar. 1934: 5–7. This copy of the Bach edition formerly belonged to the German composer Carl Reinecke and is now in the University of Toronto Music Library.

33 A genealogical table, printed circa 1913 and titled "Boulton of Moulton," traces the family's roots back to the seventeenth century in England. A copy is preserved in the University of Toronto Archives.

34 H.H. Langton, private diary, vol. 1 (1895–1904), Thomas Fisher Rare Book Room, University of Toronto.

3

The First Decade

The wmc began holding morning recitals immediately upon its founding. The organizational meeting on 23 January 1899 concluded with a mixed recital that featured six different performers. The *Mail and Empire* gave the details for part of the program of this first wmc concert.[1] Margaret Huston sang Jules Massenet's "Départ," the popular Scottish song "The Land o' the Leal," and Benjamin Godard's "Angels Guard Thee" (the "Berceuse" from his opera *Jocelyn*); Mrs. Le Grand Reed sang Clayton Johns's "Where Blooms the Rose" and Cécile Chaminade's "Summer"; and Hilda Boulton played two violin solos — an arrangement of Handel's famous "Largo" from his opera *Serse*, and a Spanish serenade by Boehm.[2] In addition there were unspecified piano solos by Ethel Street, Mary Irene Gurney, and Florence Taylor.[3]

The first season of the wmc lasted from 23 January to 23 May 1899, with recitals on every other Monday morning in Mary Hewitt Smart's studio in the Yonge Street Arcade. From time to time, reports on these recitals appeared in the local society columns of the day. After the recital on 6 March 1899, dedicated to works by Schumann, one paper reported that "The growth of the young club is almost phenomenal, and its life and success is easily assured."[4] The club had reached the limit established for associate members by that date and was planning a move to larger quarters for the coming season. By the final regular meeting for the season the wmc had outgrown Mary Smart's studio; this recital was held on 15 May 1899 in St. George's Hall on Elm Street,[5] and a printed constitution was distributed at this time.

The first season closed with a special musicale on Tuesday evening, 23 May 1899, in St. George's Hall. This was the first open concert of the WMC; nonmembers were invited to purchase tickets. The hall was decorated with flowers and Persian rugs for the occasion, evening dress was requested, and, after an hour-long musical program, refreshments were served. The performers on this occasion were the singers Mrs. Le Grand Reed, Julie Wyman, Margaret Huston, and Adele Strauss Youngheart, the violinists Kate Archer and Evelyn Street, and the pianists Katherine Birnie and Mary Irene Gurney, all local musicians and likely active members of the WMC. Mary Richmond Kerr Austin acted as the accompanist. At the conclusion of the evening, as one paper reported, there were "many congratulations on all sides on the great success of the club's first venture, and prophecies of great things for the future of the Women's Musical Club."[6]

The second season of the WMC saw a number of changes. The meeting time was switched to Thursday mornings at 10:00 a.m., and the venue was moved to the Temple Building at the corner of Bay and Richmond streets.[7] The season opened on 2 November 1899 and ended on 11 May 1900, with a special program held in the Normal School at the corner of Church and Gould streets.[8] The program for the latter event has been preserved in the WMC Archives and is of interest because the club's logo — the intertwined letters WMCT — is printed on it in embossed gold lettering. This is the earliest preserved use of the logo.

There were 165 members in the second season, divided into two categories. The 40 active members performed in the weekly concerts and in return were entitled to a reduced membership rate of two dollars. The 125 associate members, who formed the bulk of the audience, paid an annual membership fee of three dollars. There was no longer any mention of professional members being admitted without charge. Visitors to Toronto who were guests of WMC members could be admitted to a recital for twenty-five cents.

The average fee for associate members in U.S. women's music clubs at this time was five dollars a year. This would have been expensive for working women, representing about a week's wages for a teacher. Linda Whitesett has made an interesting observation about this fact:

[I]t was difficult at first to convince women to pay such a high fee for the privilege of hearing talent that they had heard previously in the homes of friends and neighbors for no charge. However, the increase in associate membership in most clubs at the turn of the century indicates that the benefits of belonging to a music club soon

FIGURE 5

The Temple Building, where WMC
concerts were held from 1899 until 1903.

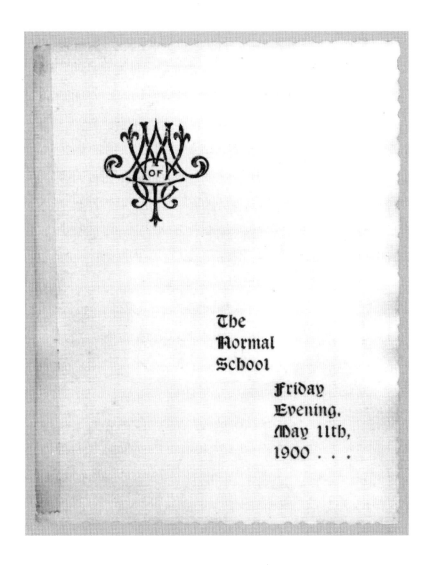

The
Normal
School

Friday
Evening,
May 11th,
1900 . . .

FIGURE 6

Program from a special concert at the end of the second
season, with the earliest preserved use of the WMC logo.

outweighed the disadvantages of the expensive fee. As membership fees remained unchanged for many decades, membership gradually became available to women of lesser means.[9]

Whitesett's comments apply with equal validity to the WMC. The fee for joining the club remained unchanged until 1914, by which time the number of associate members had more than tripled.

The early WMC seasons consisted of weekly recitals each Thursday morning from November to April, with two weeks off at Christmas — some two dozen events in all. A plan of work published in the early annual reports itemized the date and theme of each recital for the coming season and the member of the program committee who was responsible for arranging it. The annual reports also contained a page titled "Rules for Active Members." These state that not more than two nonmembers could perform in any recital without the permission of the executive committee, that a paper read at any regular meeting could not exceed fifteen minutes in length, that the program for the recital had to be submitted one week in advance, and that the music to be performed had to be purchased through the secretary.

Most of the recitals were private events, held exclusively for WMC members and their guests, but each season a few open recitals were given to which the general public was invited for twenty-five cents. For each weekly recital there was a small printed program. Fifty or so programs from the WMC's first decade have been preserved. Nine of these programs date from the second season, and they are typical of the WMC concerts for the first two decades. Piano and vocal solos predominate, with a violin solo or chamber music ensemble from time to time. The recitals lasted about an hour, with between five and ten items on each program. The music was mostly Romantic-era repertoire, from Beethoven to Brahms, although earlier works were occasionally featured and living composers were represented with some frequency.

Four men participated in the recitals during the second season for which programs have been preserved: the cellist Paul Hahn; Dr. Crawford Scadding, a physician and amateur singer (no relation to the Toronto historian Henry Scadding); and two singers identified only as Mr. Spratt and Mr. Drummond. The rest of the performers were women, most if not all of them active members of the WMC.

The earliest preserved WMC program is dated 16 November 1899; it was the third concert of the second season. The performers were Florence Marshall, Evelyn de Latre Street, Ada Hart, and Margaret Huston. These women will be described in some detail here to give an idea of the level of musicianship typical of the active members of the club during its first decade.

Florence Marshall had just returned to Toronto in the fall of 1899 from piano studies at the Leipzig Conservatory with Harry Field, the Canadian musician who served there from 1896 to 1900 as the teaching assistant of the Liszt pupil Martin Krause. She taught piano at a private studio at 328 Wellesley Street. Miss Marshall played three etudes by Chopin in the WMC recital.

Evelyn Street was born in London, Ontario, in 1874. She was a pupil of Joseph Baumann of Hamilton (who was also Nora Clench's teacher) and then studied for five years with Hans Sitt at the Leipzig Conservatory, from which she graduated in 1892. Her first public appearance upon her return to Canada was with the New York Symphony Orchestra under Walter Damrosch as part of a concert in Toronto on 27 April 1893; she played the Bruch Violin Concerto in G Minor.[10] On the 16 November 1899 WMC concert she played the Violin Concerto No. 1 in A minor, Op. 20, by Saint-Saëns. Evelyn Street later became the second violinist of the American String Quartet of Boston, an all-women ensemble that was organized by the violinist and composer Charles Martin Loeffler. After moving to the United States she married W.M. Boykin and settled with him in Vineland, New Jersey.

Ada Hart, like Gena Branscombe, was born in Picton (near Kingston), Ontario. She had been a piano pupil of J.W.F. Harrison in Ottawa and also studied in Leipzig with Krause and in Vienna with Theodor Leschetizky, Paderewski's teacher. She played for Paderewski on the occasion of his visit to Toronto in April 1896. On the 16 November 1899 WMC program she performed works by Paderewski and Chaminade. In 1900 she married Alex D. Cartwright (son of the politician Sir Richard Cartwright, of the powerful and wealthy Cartwright family of Kingston), but she continued to be an active member of the WMC, arranging or performing in many recitals for the club.

Margaret Huston, the older sister of the actor Walter Huston, was a young mezzo-soprano just starting out on her career. She had sung in the first WMC meeting on 23 January 1899. Later that year she was the featured guest artist at the Kneisel Quartet concert of the Toronto Chamber Music Association on 4 October 1899. The *Saturday Night* critic on that occasion noted that she "acquitted herself, despite an accidental break-down, very creditably,"[11] which is as close as a critic of that day would come to saying that her performance was an utter disaster. She went on to study in Europe, however, and had a noted career as a recitalist, specializing in the music of Wolf and Debussy, until she

Women's Musical Club

OF TORONTO.

△ △

Programme.

November 16th, 1899.

1. VIOLIN CONCERTO—Op. 20................... *Saint Saëns*

   MISS EVELYN STREET.

2. PIANO SOLO—Theme and Variations........ *Paderewski*

   MISS ADA HART.

3. SONGS—(*a*) Le depart........................ *Massenet*
   (*b*) It was in a Land................. *Chaminade*
   (*c*) Separation.................... *Hillmacher*

   MISS MARGARET HUSTON.

4. PIANO SOLO—Three Etudes .... *Chopin*
   (C-sharp minor, F major, G-flat major.)

   MISS FLORENCE MARSHALL.

5. SONG—Berceuse............................... *Godard*
   (With Violin Obligato.)

   MISS MARGARET HUSTON.

6. PIANO SOLO—(*a*) Elevation }............. *Chaminade*
   (*b*) The Flatterer }

   MISS ADA HART.

FIGURE 7

The earliest preserved WMC program.

married and retired in 1915.[12] On 16 November 1899, she again sang Massenet's "Départ" and Godard's "Berceuse" (this time with violin obligato by Evelyn Street) along with other songs by Chaminade and Hillemacher.[13]

These four women were typical of the active members of the WMC in its first decade. Many were born or married into the upper levels of Toronto social circles, but at the same time they were highly trained and skilled performers. This posed something of a dilemma, as many people still thought that it was not suitable for women of a certain class to appear in public as performers, or even to earn wages of any kind. It was common for these women to abandon their public careers after marrying, whether at the instigation of their husbands or as a result of societal pressures. Nancy B. Reich has explained the situation as follows:

> The upwardly-mobile middle-class male may well have feared that accepting money for work performed by the women of his family would weaken his control of the household and reflect on his ability to provide. Worse than this possible disgrace, however, was the shadow of unrespectability . . . that still clung to the world of theater and, by extension, to music. The appearance of a woman on the concert stage could undermine the hard-won social status of her bourgeois family; consequently, even the most gifted were expected to confine their musical activities to the home.[14]

One of the many benefits of the WMC concerts was the opportunity that they provided for these women to continue to perform before an audience under socially approved conditions.

In later seasons most concerts had a special theme, but of the nine programs preserved from the second season only two such recitals were given. These were a Bach program on 30 November 1899 and a Chopin program on 22 March 1900; the other recitals were labelled "miscellaneous." Bach was still a rarity in concerts at the time, and it was unusual to have an entire recital devoted to his music. The WMC program included the Air from the Orchestral Suite No. 3, played by a string quartet; the Bach-Gounod "Ave Maria" with violin obligato; a Prelude and Fugue in C-sharp major for piano (likely from Book One of the *Well-Tempered Clavier*); the Concerto for Two Violins (with piano accompaniment); the song "My Heart Ever Faithful" ("Mein gläubiges Herz," a popular soprano aria from the Cantata No. 68); and the *Chromatic Fantasia*.

The regular meetings of the second season ended on 5 April 1900 with "Request Day," which began with a sketch titled "Personal Reminiscences of Liszt" by Madame Anna Farini. Anna Mueller Farini was

FIGURE 8

Anna Mueller Farini, WMC president 1907–08.

one of the great personalities of the early years of the WMC. A native of Germany, she was the daughter of Count von Mueller, who, according to her account, had been an aide-de-camp to Kaiser Wilhelm I. Anna Mueller had studied piano at the Leipzig Conservatory under Carl Reinecke and Karl Klindworth, and she claimed to have been the first student to have lectured on music history there.[15] She also called herself a pupil of Liszt, although another report stated rather more cautiously that she "was at Weimar from time to time during Liszt's residence there, and has many recollections and souvenirs of the great virtuoso, particularly many fine photographs."[16] Her "souvenirs" included a court jacket Liszt had reportedly worn, an autographed portrait of the pianist-composer, a letter Liszt wrote to her shortly before he died, and a jewellery box which contained the butt of a cigar that Liszt had smoked.[17] Among her other possessions was a Bechstein grand piano presented to her by the kaiser.

Anna Farini was clearly an impressive woman, and from the time of her arrival in Toronto early in 1898 she was held in high regard by the people who mattered in Toronto's musical circles. Critics wrote admiringly of her elegance, sophistication, refinement, and culture. In addition to her talents as an essayist and pianist, she was also a composer and, as we shall see, she assumed the presidency of the WMC for a year. Contrary to the custom of the day, she never went by her husband's Christian name, but was only ever known as Madame Anna Farini. This was perhaps a reflection of the fact that her reputation was quite independent from that of her husband, Guillermo Farini. Unlike the other early WMC executive members, who were married to financiers, businessmen, and the like, Anna Farini was married to a tightrope walker and circus performer.

Guillermo Antonio Farini (1838–1929), whose real name was William Leonard Hunt, grew up in the vicinity of Port Hope, Ontario, and made a name for himself in 1860 by crossing Niagara Falls on a high wire. He went on to perform in England and on the Continent, and was also associated for a while with P.T. Barnum in the United States. He met Anna Mueller in Berlin in 1884, and they were married in 1886. By 1898, at age sixty, Farini was tiring of the circus and show business life, and so he moved to Toronto with his German wife to begin a new life. A restless spirit, he turned his talents to various occupations while in Toronto. He is listed in successive city directories as a mining engineer, the manager of a whip company, an author, and an artist. The Farinis left Toronto in December 1910, for Guillermo wanted to study art in Europe. In 1921 they returned to Canada, settling in Port Hope, where Guillermo died on 17 January 1929 at age ninety-one and Anna died on 7 June 1931 at age seventy-seven.[18]

The third season of the WMC opened on 1 November 1900 and closed with another "Request Day" on 4 April 1901; ten programs have been preserved from this season. Once again only four men participated in the concerts; Dr. Scadding and Mr. Drummond returned from the second season, and two other male singers were featured, Edwin B. Jackson and Oscar Wenborne. The content of the recitals was similar to the second season — mainly piano and vocal solos, with the odd instrumental work. Seven of the ten events were theme programs.

"Mozart and Modern Composers" was the title of a program on 6 December 1900; the term "modern" was used in the sense of contemporaneous, rather than in the sense of new and adventurous. The "moderns" were minor figures and fairly tame, even by turn-of-the-century standards. They included Paolo Tosti (1846–1916), Eduard Schuett (1856–1933), Ovide Musin (1854–1929), Homer Newton Bartlett (1845–1920), and two U.S. women composers — Helen Hood (1863–1949) and Myra Chisholm (dates unknown). Mozart was represented by the first movement of a piano sonata and "Vedrai, carino" from *Don Giovanni*. The season also saw concerts devoted to Chopin and Nevin, Schumann, Schubert and Liszt, Chopin and Schubert, Wagner and Liszt (arranged by Madame Farini), and Grieg (who was still alive at the time). "Request Day" began with annual reports by the secretary and the treasurer, followed by the election of officers and a short recital.

A rival women's musical club was founded during this season, called St. Cecilia Musicale; it met on Thursday afternoons.[19] Thus for a time there were three women's musical clubs meeting in Toronto on Thursdays: the WMC in the morning, St. Cecilia Musicale in the afternoon, and the Thursday Musical Club in the evening! The St. Cecilia Musicale seems to have been short-lived; it may well have amalgamated with the WMC after a few seasons.

Five programs from the fourth season exist. The Choral Club, a women's choir made up of WMC members, sang works by W.H. Neidlinger and Alexis Hollaender under the direction of J.D.A. Tripp in a concert on 20 March 1902. The WMC choir was founded by Mary Smart (likely in the third season) before it was taken over by Tripp. Tripp was born near Toronto in 1867, and in 1889 he became the first person to graduate from the Toronto Conservatory of Music. He also studied piano in Europe with Moszkowski and Leschetizky. He founded the Toronto Male Chorus Club in 1893 and conducted it until 1908. In 1910 he moved to Vancouver, where he had a prominent career as a piano teacher until his death in 1945.

An important innovation for the WMC this season was the decision to sponsor concerts by the Kneisel Quartet. The first such concert took place on 7 May 1902, just after the end of the WMC's fourth season. Perhaps a surplus at the end of the regular season encouraged the WMC executive to risk engaging a professional ensemble in order to fill the gap created by the demise of the Toronto Chamber Music Association. The Kneisel Quartet was a logical choice for at least two reasons: it had given the last concert of the earlier organization on 30 April 1900, and it regularly performed for women's musical clubs across North America. The ensemble, which had been formed in Boston in 1885, was well known for its efforts to build audiences for chamber music. The sponsorship of this concert brought the WMC to the attention of the music critic of *Saturday Night*:

> The Women's Musical Club, which by the way is not a money-making society, but an association of enthusiastic amateurs to promote the cause of good music, has engaged the Kneisel Quartette of Boston for a recital in Association Hall on the evening of May 7. Lovers of classical chamber music will no doubt consider it a duty to encourage the ladies in their good and disinterested mission by giving the concert their patronage.[20]

The Kneisel Quartet played Beethoven's "Harp" Quartet, three movements of Dvořák's "American" Quartet, and the slow movement of Schubert's "Death and the Maiden" Quartet; Franz Kneisel and the cellist, Alwin Schroeder, each played solos. The concert was a success from all points of view. It was reviewed in the local papers and periodicals, serving to bring the WMC to the attention of the wider community. Although there was no assisting vocal artist, a good-sized audience nevertheless turned out, and the WMC was encouraged to continue sponsoring an annual appearance by the Kneisel Quartet from 1902 to 1908.

By the fifth season, the regular WMC concerts were being reported on in the press with more frequency, and thus we have some knowledge of this season even though no programs have been preserved. We learn from reviews that the concerts were still being held in the Temple Building. A review of the closing recital on 25 April 1903 noted that there was a guest vocalist, a Mrs. Palmer of San Francisco, and that "The Choral Club, under the direction of Mr. Tripp, sang five glees with a distinction that one expected from a chorus trained by Mr. Tripp."[21]

A special event during the fifth season was a concert on 31 January 1903, for which Mary Irene Gurney Evans returned to Toronto from Winnipeg. There was a review in *Saturday Night*:

The Women's Musical Club, an organization under the presidency of Mrs. Dickson, gave a most successful musicale on Saturday afternoon in the Temple Building, in honor of Mrs. Sanford Evans, the founder of the club. A choice programme consisting of compositions by Arensky, Dvořák, Liszt, Handel, Chopin, Bach, Sapellnikoff and Rubinstein was supplied by Mrs. A.D. Cartwright, Miss MacBrien, Miss Florence Marshall, Miss Katharine Birnie, Miss Kate Archer, Mr. David Ross and Mrs. Sanford Evans. With such a representation of brilliant Canadian talent, the music was rendered in a manner that gave the large gathering of about six hundred ladies and gentlemen a most delightful treat. Refreshments were served after the music, and Mrs. Dickson officiated as hostess with her usual tact and kindliness.[22]

The large attendance, the fact that the concert was held on a Saturday afternoon, and the presence of men in the audience all indicate that this was an open concert of the WMC, to which nonmembers were invited for twenty-five cents.

The Kneisel Quartet returned at the end of the fifth season for their second WMC concert in Association Hall on 6 May 1903. The patronage of Gilbert John Murray-Kynnymond Elliot, Lord Melgund and fourth earl of Minto, the governor general of Canada, had been secured for this event, but was of dubious benefit. The governor general and his party arrived forty minutes late, necessitating a change in and abbreviation of the program. The *Saturday Night* music critic pointedly noted that "The change caused annoyance and disappointment to a large number of the patrons of the concert" and added, "It would have been a gracious thing had his Excellency 'intimated' that the concert was not to be delayed by his tardy arrival."[23] Despite this wrinkle, the Kneisel Quartet was well received by a "large and fashionable audience," and the WMC season closed on a positive note. It was a good year for the Kneisel Quartet also; the members resigned their positions in the Boston Symphony Orchestra in order to devote themselves entirely to chamber music.

The WMC began meeting in the concert hall of the Toronto Conservatory of Music in the fall of 1903 when the sixth season began. Just one program has survived from this season, an all-Brahms recital on 25 February 1904 organized by Ethel Street Langton. The Kneisel Quartet returned on 13 January 1904 to play Tchaikovsky's String Quartet No. 2

and the second Razumovsky Quartet by Beethoven, which had been scheduled the previous year but dropped because of the late arrival of the governor general. The *Saturday Night* critic reported that it was the best ensemble playing that had ever been heard in Toronto.[24] This time there was an assisting vocal artist, the contralto Jean Rankin of Montreal, making her Toronto debut. Alwin Schroeder also played a solo, the Suite No. 3 for solo cello by Bach.

An extraordinary WMC debut took place during the sixth season on 7 January 1904, when a precocious ten-year-old boy performed two organ solos, as reported in the *Mail and Empire*: "Master Ernest MacMillan, son of Rev. Alex. MacMillan, held all spellbound with one of his own compositions on the organ. As an encore he played 'The Hallelujah Chorus,' the whole audience rising to their feet."[25] This marked the start of a long and mutually rewarding association between the WMC and MacMillan, who was to become the leading figure in Canadian music of his day. The ties continued into the next generation of the MacMillan family, for Ernest's son Keith MacMillan, who was the general manager of the Canadian Music Centre, assisted the WMC by allowing it to use the centre's boardroom for meetings, and Keith's wife, Patricia Dustin Mac-Millan, joined the WMC executive in December 1965 and was the club's recording secretary for many years.

The sixth season ended with a Saturday afternoon open concert on 9 April 1904. About 350 guests turned out to the hall of St. Margaret's College on this occasion for a mixed recital by a dozen of the active members of the WMC.

The seventh season saw the first change in leadership of the WMC. Mary Dickson stepped down after six seasons as president and was succeeded by the English-born musician and activist Constance Bodington Hamilton. Ethel Langton was the first vice-president for this season.[26] In 1888 Constance Bodington had become the second wife of the Canadian civil engineer Lauchlan Alexander Hamilton (1852–1941), who was the chief land commissioner for the Canadian Pacific Railway. L.A. Hamilton was in charge of the CPR's development of western Canada and laid out the townsites of Vancouver, Calgary, Regina, Saskatoon, and other cities. Constance Hamilton had been one of the founders and had served as the president of the Women's Musical Club of Winnipeg, and she joined the WMC soon after she moved to Toronto with her husband when he went into semi-retirement circa 1900. She sang the two Brahms alto songs with viola obligato, Op. 91, in the 25 February 1904 concert, and in later seasons she was also active as a pianist in WMC recitals. She was still alive at the time of her husband's death in 1941.

FIGURE 9

Toronto Conservatory of Music concert hall, the venue of club concerts from 1903 to circa 1914 and again from 1925 to 1929.

The art critic and writer Graham McInnes lived with the Hamiltons during the 1930s, and he has left a vivid description of Constance Bodington Hamilton, who was known to her friends as "Lady Mary":

> She was big and gawky and terrifyingly persistent: a wonderful wearer-down of pompous clerics; an unrelenting extractor of funds from cowed businessmen; an inexorable caller on civic politicians; and a passionate lover of the music of Bach.
>
> . . . And though tough and endlessly resilient in the pursuit of social justice or of favours for others, Lady Mary was unutterably careless of herself. She dressed like a scarecrow in rusty black and smeared old greys. She ate when and as she could, although she ran the ramshackle old house on time for her husband. . . .
>
> But Lady Mary was also frugal by nature except in the things of the spirit, and here she was brimful with the special brand of competent capable generosity that overwhelms with its kindness. Both my father and I were in turn the beneficiaries of this engulfing kindliness. She never spared herself in any cause that she deemed worthy and during the period that I lived [with the Hamiltons] at 30 St. Joseph Street . . . the tumbledown house was rarely empty.[27]

In addition to her activities with the WMC, Constance Hamilton was the first alderwoman to be elected in Toronto in 1920, she was a cofounder and treasurer of the Bach Society of Toronto, and she served as the chair of the Yorkville Library Association. Her efforts on behalf of indigent artists and musicians in Toronto, especially during the Depression years, were legendary.

The seventh season of the WMC opened on 3 November 1904 with a concert by the Klingenfeld String Quartet of Toronto. Only one program has been preserved from this season, a miscellaneous recital on 24 November 1904. However, some of the concerts were reported in the press; the critic May Hamilton felt that one of the most interesting events was a lecture-recital on Wagner by the pianist Evelyn Choate from Buffalo.[28] Once again the recitals took place in the concert hall of the Toronto Conservatory of Music, and the closing concert was held there on 15 April 1905.

The Kneisel Quartet made its annual appearance on 16 January 1905. The *Saturday Night* music critic felt that the program was a "trifle severe." It included the third Razumovsky Quartet by Beethoven, the Toronto premiere of the Debussy String Quartet, Wolf's *Italian Serenade*, an excerpt from the String Quartet in A minor, Op. 51, No. 2 by

Brahms, and the Bach *Chaconne*. One might have expected the Debussy work to be greeted with a certain caution; it was probably one of the more adventurous works heard that season in Toronto. But the critic complained about the length of the Beethoven quartet ("too extended for the average music lover, taking more than half an hour in performance") and longed, ironically, for the good old days when a vocal soloist assisted and only excerpts from chamber music works were given:

> I see no artistic necessity for playing the whole of a long quartette, sonata or symphony, even if a great composer's name is attached to it. . . . One would suggest, therefore, that it would be found an advantage to select only the most graceful movements from the large chamber music works, unless one is assured of audiences who have exceptional powers of absorption. It would make quartette concerts more popular and enjoyable, if a vocalist were engaged to sing between the string numbers, a practice resorted to for years at the London Monday Popular Concerts.

Clearly the WMC still had some work to do in educating Toronto audiences — and critics — as to the merits of the chamber music repertoire. The critic went on to complain about Bach's *Chaconne* for solo violin: it was "another very long composition. There is a good deal of dry scholastic material in it, and it is not well suited to the genius of the violin."[29]

There was another change in the WMC executive at the end of the seventh season, when Sarah Trumbull Van Lennep Warren became the new president, with Anna Farini as first vice-president. Sarah Warren, like Mary Dickson, was a cultivated music lover rather than a trained musician. She was born in New Jersey, and after marrying Harry Dorman Warren moved with him to England and then in 1887 to Canada. Her husband died before the First World War, and her eldest son was killed at Ypres. She then became chair of the board of directors of the family business, a large rubber company, proving to be a more than capable businesswoman.[30] She was also a noted philanthropist; among her many gifts was an important collection of lace donated to the Royal Ontario Museum.[31] Sarah Warren became an honorary member of the WMC after stepping down from the presidency.

The weekly concerts in the Toronto Conservatory of Music concert hall continued during the eighth season, which opened on 2 November 1905 with a performance of Arthur Somervell's highly regarded Tennyson song cycle *Maud* (1898), sung by Mr. R.S. Pigott with Frank Welsman at the piano. This same work would be given fifteen years later, on 15 February 1920, as part of a WMC concert of "Modern British Music" arranged by Ernest MacMillan. (*Maud* may have been "modern" in 1905 but was hardly so in 1920!) Only one program has been preserved from the eighth season, a miscellaneous recital on 15 February 1906 in which both Pigott and Welsman performed once again; the recital was arranged by Welsman's wife. Evidently audience decorum had been found wanting in some of the earlier WMC events; at the bottom of the program appears the plea "SILENCE is requested during the numbers."

The Kneisel Quartet made its annual appearance on 13 March 1906, and yet again Frank Welsman participated, this time in a performance of the Dvořák Piano Quintet. The other works played were Mozart's String Quartet in E-flat major, K. 428, and Smetana's String Quartet in E minor "From My Life." The *Saturday Night* critic noted, "The programme contained but three numbers, but each was a work of some dimensions, and the concert consequently occupied one hour and three quarters,"[32] but this time the WMC and the Kneisel Quartet were spared a lecture about how to mount a chamber music concert. The closing event for the season was a Saturday afternoon open concert on 21 April 1906 in the Toronto Conservatory of Music concert hall.

Not a single program has been preserved from the ninth season. From the *Conservatory Monthly* we learn that the recitals began on 1 November 1906 and were held each week as usual at the Toronto Conservatory of Music concert hall. The events included an appearance by the Toronto Ladies Trio, an all-women piano trio which had made its debut the previous season on 8 April 1905 at the Toronto Conservatory of Music. The trio's pianist, Eugénie Quéhen, was born near Liverpool, England, and received a licentiate in piano from London's Royal Academy of Music in 1899. That same year she moved to Canada, and in 1901, as a pupil of A.S. Vogt, she won the Toronto Conservatory of Music gold medal upon graduating. She was appointed to the piano faculty of St. Margaret's College in 1902 and joined the Toronto Conservatory of Music teaching staff in 1904.[33] The violinist was Lina Adamson (1876–1960), daughter of the prominent local violinist Bertha Drechsler Adamson. Like Evelyn Street, Lina Adamson had studied under Sitt at the Leipzig Conservatory.[34] Lois Winlow, a former pupil of Rudolph Ruth at the Toronto Conservatory of Music, was the cellist.[35] All three women were active members of the WMC and frequently appeared in the club's recitals as a trio or on their own as soloists.

The Kneisel Quartet concert was on 29 January 1907, this time at the Toronto Conservatory of Music concert hall instead of in Association Hall. Works by Schumann, Glazunov, Glière, and Grieg were played "as near perfection as it is perhaps possible to conceive" according to the *Saturday Night* review.[36]

The tenth season is the best documented of any in the first decade, thanks to the preservation of the *Tenth Annual Report* in the collection of the Music Division of the National Library of Canada. The season started off with a crisis when Sarah Warren retired from the presidency on short notice because of a prolonged absence from Toronto; Anna Farini was the first vice-president and so, in accordance with the WMC Constitution, she assumed the presidency. In January Mrs. Tower Fergusson, the new first vice-president, also resigned, and Mrs. J.A. Street was elected in her place. The positions of secretary and treasurer were amalgamated, and Grace Boulton filled that job.

There were 282 members for the season: 9 honorary, 61 active, and 212 associate. In all, twenty-one recitals were given, held as usual in the Toronto Conservatory of Music concert hall on Thursday mornings at eleven o'clock. As a suitable date for the Kneisel Quartet concert could not be arranged, two U.S. musicians were engaged instead for concerts: the baritone Francis Rogers for the season's first event on 7 November 1907, and the pianist Olga Samaroff on 17 January 1908. Samaroff had given her New York debut at Carnegie Hall in 1905 and was at the beginning of an important career as a pianist, music critic, and teacher. Both Rogers and Samaroff were featured in their local debuts; they were the first in a long line of outstanding musicians introduced to Toronto by the WMC. The two concerts were critical successes, but poorly attended. The excess of expenses over income for these two events was $222.45, a matter of some concern because it reduced the club's bank balance to just $92.25 on an operating budget of $1,355.70. It was not yet time to panic, but at the annual general meeting the members were scolded by the president for their lack of interest in the open concerts.

The programs for all twenty-one recitals and the two sponsored concerts are printed in the *Tenth Annual Report*. One interesting event was a program of fourteen short works by Torontonians on 6 February 1908. The composers represented were Anna Farini, W.O. Forsyth, Albert Ham, Albert Nordheimer, R.S. Pigott, T.B. Richardson, A.S. Vogt, and Frank Welsman. The twenty-fifth anniversary of Wagner's death was commemorated on 13 February 1908 with a concert of works by Richard Strauss and Wagner; the recital began with a rather flowery essay about Wagner's death in Venice by Anna Farini.[37] The Toronto Ladies Trio returned on 9 January 1908, and the Toronto String Quartet, an all-male ensemble which had been founded just over a year earlier, performed a recital on 27 February 1908. The closing event of the tenth season was another Saturday afternoon open concert on 25 April 1908.

Much had been accomplished during this first decade of activities. Some two hundred concerts had been given, many of them winning favourable press reviews. Six concerts by the Kneisel Quartet had been sponsored to great acclaim, and two young and promising U.S. musicians had been heard in their local debuts. There had been some difficulties to be sure, especially for the executive committee, but these had been successfully overcome. The achievements of the first decade ensured a healthy future for the WMC, one to which its members could look with optimism.

NOTES

[1] "On Dit," *Mail and Empire* 24 Jan. 1899: 2.

[2] The U.S. composer Clayton Johns (1857–1932) wrote about one hundred songs. Marcia J. Citron has noted that Chaminade's pieces "were written mostly for private settings, the non-professional, and women" (Citron 103). The Boehm referred to was likely the German composer Carl Böhm (1844–1920), who wrote many attractive miniatures for violin and piano.

[3] Florence Taylor of Detroit had appeared in a concert in Toronto in October 1898 and returned to the city to play in a concert on 24 January 1899 in Association Hall in which Margaret Huston also participated.

[4] "On Dit," *Mail and Empire* 7 Mar. 1899: 6.

[5] St. George's Hall at 14 Elm Street was built in 1891 and renovated in 1920 to become the new home of the Arts and Letters Club of Toronto (founded in 1908) and was purchased by that club in 1985.

[6] "On Dit," *Mail and Empire* 24 May 1899: 2. This report lists 50 people who attended the event.

[7] The Temple Building was constructed from 1895 to 1897 for the Independent Order of Foresters. At nine storeys high (a tenth was added in 1901) it was the skyscraper of its day and for a time was the tallest building in the British Empire. It was demolished in 1970.

[8] The Normal School was demolished in 1963 except for a single wall which serves as an entrance to the campus of Ryerson Polytechnic University.

[9] Whitesitt 667.

[10] This was the second concert of the eighth season of the Toronto Vocal Society, a choir conducted by E.W. Schuch; the program is in the collection of the Metropolitan Toronto Reference Library.

[11] "Music," *Saturday Night* 14 Oct. 1899: 10.

[12] James B. McPherson, "Huston, Margaret," *Encyclopedia of Music in Canada*, 2nd ed., 1992.

[13] The French composers Lucien and Paul Hillemacher were two brothers who collaborated in their compositions, signing their works P.L. Hillemacher.

[14] Nancy B. Reich, "Women as Musicians: A Question of Class," *Musicology and Difference: Gender and Sexuality in Music Scholarship*, ed. Ruth A. Solie (Berkeley: U of California P, 1993) 132.

[15] "Music," *Saturday Night* 1 Oct. 1898: 10.

[16] *Conservatory Bi-monthly* Mar. 1908: 53.

[17] Shane Peacock, *The Great Farini: The High-Wire Life of William Hunt* (Harmondsworth, Middlesex: Penguin, 1995) 453. The Liszt souvenirs were dispersed at a public auction in 1945.

[18] Peacock's book gives a wonderfully entertaining and richly detailed account of the life of Guillermo Farini. In addition to Farini's exploits as a circus performer, he was also an explorer and wrote a book about his purported discovery of the Lost City of Kalahari.

[19] "Music," *Saturday Night* 18 May 1901: 10.

[20] "Music," *Saturday Night* 3 May 1902: 10.

[21] "Music," *Saturday Night* 2 May 1903: 10.

[22] "Music," *Saturday Night* 7 Feb. 1903: 10.

[23] "Music," *Saturday Night* 16 May 1903: 10.

[24] "Music," *Saturday Night* 23 Jan. 1904: 10.

[25] "On Dit," *Mail and Empire* 8 Jan. 1904: 5.

[26] *Conservatory Bi-monthly* Nov. 1904: 186–87.

[27] Graham McInnes, *Finding a Father* (London: Hamish Hamilton, 1967) 123, 124, 127. The author's father was the baritone Campbell McInnes, who befriended the Hamiltons soon after his arrival in Toronto from his native England in 1919.

[28] *Conservatory Bi-monthly* May 1905: 91.

[29] "Music," *Saturday Night* 21 Jan. 1905: 13.

[30] Michael Kluckner, *Toronto the Way It Was* (Toronto: Whitecap, 1988) 161. The family business was the Gutta-Percha and Rubber Company Ltd., a local manufacturer of automobile tires and rubber goods.

[31] Jean Graham, "Among Those Present, XLII: Mrs. H.D. Warren," *Saturday Night* 5 Nov. 1932: 10.

[32] "Music," *Saturday Night* 17 Mar. 1906: 13.

[33] "Miss Eugénie Quéhen," *Conservatory Monthly* May 1912: 135. For the 1907–08 season Mrs. Gerard Barton substituted as the trio's pianist.

[34] See "Drechsler Adamson, Bertha," *Encyclopedia of Music in Canada*, 2nd ed., 1992.

[35] *Encyclopedia of Music in Canada* 383 misspells Lois Winlow's surname Winslow.

[36] "Music," *Saturday Night* 2 Feb. 1907: 15.

[37] The essay is printed in WMC *Tenth Annual Report* 68–71.

4

"A Splendid Vehicle of Musical Progress"

About fifty programs from the second decade of the WMC have been preserved, but almost all of them are contained in two of the three annual reports in the collection of the Music Division of the National Library of Canada: the *Eleventh Annual Report*, for the 1908–09 season, and the *Fifteenth Annual Report*, for the 1912–13 season. Fortunately there are extensive reports about WMC concerts in the newspapers and periodicals of the day, especially *Musical Canada* and the *Canadian Journal of Music*, allowing us to reconstruct the events of the other eight seasons in this decade in some detail.

Mary Dickson dominated the second decade of the WMC just as she had the first: she served as president for six of the ten seasons between 1908 and 1918. She was chosen to succeed Anna Farini at the election of officers towards the end of the tenth season on 16 April 1908[1] and served as president for two years during this term of office.

The *Eleventh Annual Report* provides a complete picture of the activities of the WMC during the 1908–09 season. The first event was a Saturday afternoon reception and recital hosted by the president at St. Margaret's College on 31 October 1908. There was a detailed report in the *Conservatory Bi-monthly*:

An excellent programme was given by Miss Cornelia Heintzman, Miss Eugénie Quéhen, Mrs. Frank MacKelcan, Mr. Frank Blachford, Mr. Walter Robinson of New York, Mr. Arthur Blight, and Mr. Carl Hunter. The hall of St. Margaret's College is a room of most delightful size and appearance and admirably suited to the proper performance of chamber music or recitals, being equipped with a fine platform and galleries on either side. The large gathering included many professional musicians and other friends of the Club, and before the programme Dr. Fisher, in a pleasing speech, commended the work of the Club in highest terms, referring to the superior class of music given at the meetings and its educational value to the members.[2]

The season proper got under way on 5 November 1908 with a recital by the local baritone David Ross, accompanied at the piano by Constance Hamilton, a former president of the WMC. They performed the Tennyson song cycle *In Memoriam* by the English composer Liza Lehmann.[3] The weekly Thursday morning musicales in the Conservatory of Music concert hall continued until 1 April 1909, and the season closed two days later with a Saturday afternoon open concert.[4]

There were several events of special interest. The annual Christmas concert on 17 December 1908 opened and closed with organ selections by Ernest MacMillan, who was just fifteen years old at the time but was already the organist-choirmaster at Knox Presbyterian Church.[5] The Toronto String Quartet and the Toronto Ladies Trio returned for concerts on 7 January 1909 and 1 April 1909 respectively. There was a recital dedicated to "Present Day Composers" on 14 January 1909 in which music by seven living and two recently deceased European composers was given, with three of the works receiving their Toronto premieres. Other theme concerts included "American Composers" on 18 February 1909 and "Women Composers" on 18 March 1909.

A second concert of music by Torontonians was given on 25 February 1909, a year after the first such concert. Five of the composers heard on the previous occasion were featured again, along with six newcomers: Humfrey Anger, Edmund Hardy,[6] John Ernest Lawrence, Francis Paget Macklem, Lionel Read, A. Easter Smith, and Valborg M. Zollner.[7] Fifteen local composers in all were presented in these two concerts.

On 11 March 1909, the WMC was invited to give a special program at the Margaret Eaton School of Literature and Expression. Among the performers was the pianist Mona Bates (1889–1971), a longtime active member of the WMC; her copies of the early annual reports are the ones preserved in the National Library of Canada. The school was named after Timothy Eaton's wife, Margaret Wilson Beattie Eaton. As Kluckner has explained, "The girls who enrolled wore a sort of Girl Guides' uniform, and learned deportment while performing gymnastics, massed calisthenics, theatricals and what were called 'dramalogues.'"[8]

The institution was housed from 1908 in a Greek revival building on the west side of North Street (now Bay Street) just south of Bloor; its concert hall was to be the site of a number of WMC recitals. In 1925 the Margaret Eaton School moved to Yonge Street, and in 1941 it became part of the University of Toronto.

The Kneisel Quartet played a Friday evening concert on 27 November 1908, which turned out to be its final performance for the WMC. Included in the program were works by Haydn, Beethoven, and Grieg, along with the middle two movements of the Debussy String Quartet. Despite the fact that the Debussy work had been given in its entirety by the Kneisel Quartet in 1905, it was still quite a novelty for the *Saturday Night* critic: "The Kneisel played so beautifully, the seeming lack of tonality giving the hearing the same weird feeling that a familiar landscape seen by moonlight gives a lover of nature. Everything seems vague, almost unreal, and yet a part of one's self."[9]

This season the number of members was the highest to date at 320, including 9 honorary, 62 active, and 249 associate. Seven of the regular recitals were open events, a greater number than ever before, and a total of 535 nonmembers paid twenty-five cents to attend on these occasions. This helped to improve the financial situation somewhat, and the club ended the season with a bank balance of $138.32. The operating budget was over $1,500; two-thirds of the income came from members' fees and visitors' tickets, with the remaining one-third provided mostly by ticket sales for the Kneisel Quartet concert. Coming after the financial concerns of the tenth season, it was something of a turnaround, thanks no doubt at least in part to the capable leadership of Mary Dickson.

The Choral Club, which had been inactive for four or five years, was revived this season. It was conducted by Mrs. H.M. Blight, a native of St. Catharines and a former pupil of F.H. Torrington; she was a local organist, pianist, and composer. Mrs. J. Willson Lawrence, a local singer, took over as conductor in the twelfth season, but Mrs. Blight stayed on as accompanist. In later seasons the choir was conducted in turn by James W. Galloway, Edward Broome, and Peter C. Kennedy.

Another Toronto women's club was created early in 1909 by Mary Hewitt Smart, one of the founders of the WMC. This was the Heliconian Club, whose members were artists, writers, musicians, and other women professionally engaged in the arts. The club had eighty members by its second season and was meeting in the rooms of the Arts and Letters Club.[10] In 1923 the club purchased the former Olivet Congregational Church at 35 Hazelton Avenue, which has continued to serve as its permanent home. In its early years the Heliconian Club sponsored private musicales which featured many of the same musicians that appeared in WMC recitals. If there was any sense of rivalry in the early years, however, it faded with time: the Heliconian Club and the WMC have flourished side by side for nearly ninety years.

The twelfth season ran from 4 November 1909 to 2 April 1910, and included twenty-one events, six of them open concerts. The season began with a Thursday morning open concert at the Conservatory of Music concert hall which featured the local debut of the American String Quartet of Boston, an all-women ensemble. The second violinist was former WMC member Evelyn de Latre Street; the other members were Gertrude Marshall, Edith Jewell, and Susan Lord-Grandegee. Once again the Debussy String Quartet was heard, as well as Dvořák's "American" Quartet and a sonata for two violins and piano by Handel, with Mrs. Blight as the accompanist. There was a positive review in the *Globe*:

> The ensemble of the party was remarkable for its singleness of interpretation, its sympathy of rendering, its beauty of tone, and its truth of intonation. The leader, Miss Marshall, is a most accomplished violinist. Her tone is not perhaps big, but it is of beautiful quality. She has a command of nuances of tone color that gives charming variety to her playing. . . . The Debussy Quartette was finely rendered, both in technique and in the sympathetic spirit of the reading. . . . Lovers of chamber music present must have felt indebted to the Women's Musical Club for their enterprise and judgment in engaging this admirable quartette.[11]

Perhaps the most noteworthy event of the season was an evening open concert on 26 February 1910 in which the Flonzaley Quartet was presented in its local debut. The Flonzaley Quartet was established in 1902 by a Swiss banker and had appeared widely throughout North America and Europe. It seems to have taken over the women's musical club circuit from the Kneisel Quartet at about the time of its Toronto debut. E.R. Parkhurst, reviewing the concert in the *Globe*, was impressed by the playing of the group but found the program not particularly to his liking: it included Mozart's "Dissonance" Quartet, a Sammartini trio for two violins and cello, and Schumann's String Quartet in A minor, Op. 41, No. 1.[12] Nevertheless there was a large and enthusiastic audience, and the WMC was encouraged to invite the Flonzaley Quartet back in the future.

Yet another chamber music group was presented in an open concert on 6 January 1910: the Brahms Trio, a new ensemble whose members were on the staff of the Conservatory of Music. The violinist was Lina Adamson, formerly of the Toronto Ladies Trio, the cellist was George A. Bruce, and the pianist was Richard Tattersall, who had recently arrived from Scotland. (Tattersall became the organist at St. Thomas' Anglican Church on Huron Street, where his assistant organist was the young Gerald Moore.) The group played the first piano trios of Mendelssohn and Brahms. The other Thursday morning recitals were the usual fare of vocal and piano solos. Five events were grouped by national theme: "Russian Composers," "Scandinavian Composers," "German Composers," "French Composers," and "Irish Ballads." A newcomer to the WMC was Genevieve Clark Wilson, who gave a full-length vocal recital — nineteen numbers in all — on 2 December 1909. She was a professional singer from Chicago and had recently arrived in Toronto with her husband, who had moved there on business. She taught at the conservatory and was highly praised by the local critics, but her stay in Toronto was brief; she returned to Chicago in 1911.

The activities of musical clubs in Toronto were being reported with some frequency in the pages of *Musical Canada* this season, and a bewildering number of them were flourishing. The WMC enjoyed pride of place as the largest and most active of the lot, but there were also reports about the Twilight Musicale, the Strollers' Club, the Heliconian Club, the Wagnerian Club (new this season, for younger musicians and having little to do, it would seem, with Wagner), the Home Music Club, and the Speranza Musical Club. Most of them were meeting regularly and were exclusively or predominantly for women musicians. It was clearly the heyday of the women's musical club movement, at least in Toronto.

For the thirteenth season a new president was in charge of the WMC: Mary Richmond Kerr Austin. Mary Richmond Kerr was born in Perth, Ontario, in 1860 and died in Toronto in 1942. She had been a piano pupil of F.H. Torrington, and in 1877 became the accompanist for his Toronto Philharmonic Society. In 1882 she married Albert William Austin (who bore a striking resemblance to Torrington!) and moved to Winnipeg with him. Mary Austin's father-in-law, James Austin, commissioned a portrait of her by John Colin Forbes and also gave her a Steinway grand piano as wedding presents. The couple returned to Toronto in 1894; Albert Austin became a director and in 1925 the president of the Dominion Bank, which his father had founded. The Austins lived in Spadina, the imposing house on Davenport Hill built in 1866 by James Austin (Albert's father) on a site first developed by the Baldwin family in 1818.[13] Mary Austin also served on the executives of the Toronto Chamber

FIGURE 10

Mary Richmond Kerr Austin, WMC president 1910–13.
Portrait by Colin Forbes, R.C.A, 1882.

Music Association and the Toronto Symphony Orchestra. She had been involved with the WMC from the start, having performed in the club's very first open concert at the end of the first season on 23 May 1899.

During the first two seasons under Mary Austin's presidency (1910–12) it was business as usual for the WMC. Continuity in the leadership was provided by Grace Boulton, who had been a member of the first executive committee and continued to serve as the secretary-treasurer. The regular Thursday morning meetings were held in the Conservatory of Music concert hall from November to April both seasons, with WMC active members and selected guest artists performing each week. The Choral Club flourished under Mrs. Willson Lawrence in the thirteenth season, followed by James W. Galloway, a conservatory staff member, in the fourteenth season.

There were about 350 members during the thirteenth season. The first event was an open concert held on the evening of 3 November 1910. It introduced three newcomers: Jessie Binns, a former pupil of Edward Fisher who had just returned to Toronto after studying for six years with Leschetizky in Vienna; the baritone A. McLean Borthwick, recently arrived from Scotland; and the cellist and composer Leo Smith, who had moved to Toronto from England earlier in the year. Smith appeared in several recitals this season, including a chamber music concert on 9 March 1911 with the violinist Lena Hayes, who later became his wife.

The Toronto String Quartet was featured in two recitals, on 17 November 1910 and 5 January 1911, and in each one an active WMC member performed a piano quintet. In the first concert Frances Sarah Mickle performed the Beethoven Piano Quintet, Op. 16 (arranged for piano and strings), and in the second one Mary Caldwell performed the Dvořák Piano Quintet. Frances Mickle had studied piano at the Toronto Conservatory and in Berlin; she was active publicly as a performer until her marriage to the lawyer H.W. Mickle in 1909, after which her appearances were confined to the WMC. Mary Caldwell was related to Edward Fisher; she was born in Iowa and came to Toronto in 1908.

Another newcomer to the WMC this season was the English pianist and lecturer Grace Smith, who was born in London and had studied under Teresa Carreño and Ferruccio Busoni. In 1908 she had moved to Canada and in 1910 she settled in Toronto, where in addition to teaching piano she was for a time a member of the Hambourg Trio.[14] She appeared frequently in WMC events as a lecture-recitalist up to 1927. Her first such performance was at an open meeting on 9 February 1911, when she lectured on and performed French keyboard music of the seventeenth and eighteenth centuries.

The fourteenth season saw a return appearance of the Flonzaley String Quartet for a Saturday evening open concert in the Conservatory of Music concert hall on 2 December 1911. This time the novelty on the program was the Ravel String Quartet, which was completed in 1903 but had only just been revised and published in 1910. The critic E.R. Parkhurst evidently found the work puzzling, although the audience, it seems, did not:

> The Maurice Ravel quartet shares the general characteristics of the composer's music, which has been described as of "radical harmonic structure, ingenious detail and pervasive imagination." The design of the quartet seemed to be very vague and to lack connected musical thought. However, evidence was given of warm appreciation of its performance, and it was a most interesting and suggestive novelty.[15]

A longer review of the work appeared in the *Mail and Empire*:

> Like Debussy, there is much in Ravel that is illusive and difficult to grasp, and this was especially true of the final movements, though the Flonzaleys gave a really remarkable rendering of the slow movement, in some passages of which they introduced an eerie suggestion that made the music seem almost to come from the spirit world. The second movement was the most striking, and was brilliantly performed. Altogether the quartette was a most interesting one, and showed the more robust side of the work of the Flonzaleys.[16]

Sadly, on the same day as the Flonzaley concert, Violet Welsman (Frank Welsman's first wife) died suddenly of a heart attack at age thirty-six. As a member of the program committee of the WMC for several years, she had organized many events for the club, and her loss was deeply felt. One of the weekly Thursday morning recitals was cancelled for the first time since the WMC was founded, to honour her memory.

The fourteenth season closed with the annual Saturday afternoon open concert on 13 April 1912 in the Conservatory of Music concert hall. It featured vocal, piano, and cello solos and choral numbers by the Choral Club under James W. Galloway.

The fifteenth season was a year of crises and tragedy within the ranks of the executive committee of the WMC. In the latter part of the season Mary Austin was bereaved by the death of her son Albert Edison Austin (1888–1913) and was unable to fulfil her duties as president. She stepped down at the end of the season, but the WMC, in appreciation of her efforts on behalf of the club over the years, created the new position of honorary president for her. Florence Lowell Fisher, as first vice-president of the WMC, fulfilled the duties of the office of president in Mary Austin's absence. This was an extraordinary gesture on her part, as her husband was extremely ill at the time. Florence Fisher also stepped down from the executive committee at the end of the season, and she was made the honorary president of the Choral Club executive committee, which was in charge of the women's chorus. On 31 May 1913, a month after the close of the season, her husband, Edward Fisher, the founding director of the Toronto Conservatory of Music, died of angina; it was a great loss to Toronto's musical community. Finally May Livingstone, who had succeeded Grace Boulton as secretary-treasurer, became so ill in January 1913 that she had to give up her position. Agnes Fulton took over, but she too resigned at the end of the season, and the positions of secretary and treasurer were again separated.

It is a measure of the maturity the WMC had attained that the club enjoyed one of its best seasons, notwithstanding the ongoing crises in the leadership. The club was larger than ever, with a membership of 485. There were twenty-three events, including three evening concerts. The Choral Club was enlarged and put under the distinguished leadership of Edward Broome (1868–1932), an English-born choral conductor and organist. Broome had come to Toronto in 1906 as A.S. Vogt's successor at Jarvis Street Baptist Church, and in 1910 he had founded the Toronto Oratorio Society, a two hundred-voice choir.[17]

The first event was a Thursday evening open concert on 7 November 1912. The Toronto String Quartet played a Haydn quartet and Wolf-Ferrari's Piano Quintet, Op. 6, with Frank Welsman, and A.L. Madeleine Carter sang five items accompanied by Mary Campbell. A review article in the *Conservatory Monthly* is worth quoting at length for the light it sheds on how the WMC operated at this time:

> The Wolf-Ferrari quintette, new to Toronto, made a marked impression and the entire programme was of a most artistic and enjoyable nature. The Club is entering upon what will probably be one of the most successful years in its history and is justly regarded as one of the genuinely musical organizations in our midst, the officials and members being inspired by laudable desires to further the cause of the best music, either by introducing new artists to their audiences or by carefully selected programmes of novelties and masterpieces.
>
> Any person may become an associate member of the Club by having her name proposed by a member of the Club, and on being

elected by the Executive and the payment of the fee of three dollars shall be entitled to admission to all the meetings of the Club.

Active members are required to play or sing before the Examining Committee before being admitted to membership, the fee for active members being two dollars.

The Choral Club will be . . . enlarged to fifty this year, a membership of the Choral Club constituting one an active member of the Women's Musical Club, the fee being two dollars. Application for membership may be obtained from Dr. Edward Broome. . . .[18]

The terms and conditions of membership outlined above probably reflect the earliest Constitution of the WMC, which was written in 1899 and seems to have remained in effect until the club was reorganized in June 1914. In actual fact, the Choral Club membership, according to the *Fifteenth Annual Report*, increased during the course of the season from 60 to 107, a reflection of the popularity of Edward Broome.

As usual there were a number of especially interesting events. Schubert's "Trout" Quintet was performed by three WMC active members and two guest artists on 6 February 1913 in what was claimed to be its Toronto premiere. A "Women Composers" recital on 6 March 1913 included works by the French composer Cécile Chaminade, the U.S. composer Mary Turner Salter, and the Canadian composer Gena Branscombe. Grace Smith gave three lecture-recitals, on Mendelssohn, Chopin, and Beethoven, and Benita Le Mar gave a lecture-recital on modern French song writers, including Ravel, Roussel, and Debussy. There was a rather curious joint recital on 28 November 1912. Loraine Wyman, a pupil of the celebrated French *diseuse* Yvette Guilbert, sang three sets of folk songs in costume, a popular way of presenting such material at the time. These were interspersed with piano pieces by Bach, Chopin, and Schubert performed by Edouard Hesselberg, a Russian-trained pianist who had just arrived in Toronto to teach at the conservatory.

The Choral Club performed only one recital in the regular Thursday morning series, but it scored a much bigger success when it appeared in Massey Hall on 31 March 1913 with the New York Philharmonic. The occasion was a concert of the Toronto Oratorio Society. Broome had suffered a breakdown in January and vacationed in Bermuda to recover his strength. Upon his return there was not adequate time to prepare the full Oratorio Society choir, so the WMC chorus stepped in to save the concert. The orchestra was conducted by Joseph Stransky, Mahler's successor, in a rousing program that included Berlioz's *Benvenuto Cellini* Overture, Liszt's *Les Préludes*, Strauss's *Don Juan*, and Wagner's

Rienzi Overture. The wmc choir sang two works for chorus and orchestra by U.S. composers: *A Legend of Granada* by Henry Hadley (1871–1937), and *Song of Sunrise* by Charles Fonteyn Manney (1872–1951). This was tame fare by comparison with the orchestral numbers, but nevertheless there was a positive review in the *Mail and Empire*:

> The first portion of the vocal programme was rendered by the choral section of the Women's Musical Club. This choir consists of about a hundred and ten voices, including some of the best known local vocalists. The ladies sang with a fine quality of tone and a perfect balance of parts.[19]

The other attraction on the program was a children's choir of nearly four hundred voices (a clever way to attract a large audience) which sang "O Canada" and *Vogelweid*, a cantata by the English composer George Rathbone.

The closing Saturday afternoon open concert was the usual miscellaneous program; it took place on 12 April 1913. This was followed by the annual general meeting on 24 April 1913, at which a new slate of officers was elected. Helen Daly Pepler became the new president and Grace Boulton was elected as first vice-president. The club was in healthy financial condition, with $272.64 in the bank; the total budget for the season was still under $1,500.

Helen Daly Pepler had served as second vice-president for the eleventh season and first vice-president for the twelfth season. Her rise to the presidency had been delayed for three years by Mary Austin's term of office, but in the sixteenth season she at last acceded to the position. Like Mary Dickson and Sarah Warren, she was a music lover rather than a trained musician. She was married to Arthur Pepler, an assistant general manager of the Dominion Bank.

Not a single program from the sixteenth season has been preserved. One report gives the details for the closing concert on 18 April 1914, in which the main attraction was the Academy String Quartet. [20] This group, led by Luigi von Kunits, was in residence at the Canadian Academy of Music, a music school which had opened in 1911, absorbed the Metropolitan School of Music in 1912 and the College of Music in 1918, and then amalgamated with the Conservatory of Music in 1924.

Helen Daly Pepler served for just one season as president. At the annual general meeting in April 1914, Mary Dickson was elected to her final term as president, which lasted for four years. As it turned out, she was the ideal person to guide the wmc through the difficult years ahead.

Many artistic groups had to disband owing to the First World War, but the WMC went from strength to strength during this period under Mary Dickson's inspired leadership.

Her first move was to reorganize the WMC in June 1914. The Constitution, which had been formulated in May 1899, was revised. The name and object of the club remained the same, but the terms of membership were changed. Article III, section 2(a) of the new Constitution stated, "There shall be an adult membership of one class."[21] Section 2(b) added a new category of junior auxiliary membership, for those eighteen years of age or under. The annual membership fee for adults was raised to five dollars, on top of a one-time entrance fee of three dollars; junior members paid only an annual fee of two dollars. Club membership was limited to eight hundred, and candidates for membership still had to be nominated and seconded by existing members. But the former distinction between active and associate members was gone forever.

It would be interesting to know the motivation behind this change in the membership structure. The old system had provided the active members of the WMC with an audience for their recitals, but there was also an element of exploitation involved. The open concerts, which the general public paid admission to attend, raised a fair amount of money for the WMC. The WMC performers, whether amateur or professional musicians, received no compensation for their participation in these events, despite the fact that many of them performed at almost the same level as the invited guest artists who were paid substantial fees.[22]

This issue had been debated vigorously in the pages of the "Woman's Work in Music" column of the periodical *Etude* at the turn of the century. Clara A. Korn, a U.S. composer, argued that women's musical clubs should pay all professional musicians for their services. "Such professionals as are engaged [by women's musical clubs] rarely obtain remuneration for their services," she wrote, "and it is cryingly unjust that this should be permitted."[23] Nevertheless the WMC active members who performed in the open concerts presumably did so of their own free will, although there may have been subtle pressure exerted on them by the concert arranger; in any event, they would have been free to withdraw their services and become associate members or, more drastically, leave the club, if they felt that the system was unjust.

It is highly unlikely that it was only because of qualms about the economic exploitation of its active members that the WMC Constitution was rewritten. The fact is that the club gradually was changing its focus. The recitals by WMC members were becoming fewer in number each season, and the number of events by invited professional artists was increasing. In short, the WMC was transforming itself from a predominantly private club that sponsored a few open events, to a club whose main object was the presenting of professional solo and chamber music concerts.

No doubt many factors contributed to this metamorphosis. Women were entering the professional world in greater numbers, and while there were to be setbacks, in general it was no longer held to be improper for a woman to earn wages for her work. Thus there were likely fewer professionally trained women musicians who felt the need for a private club as an outlet for their performing talents. In addition, there were also fewer women with the leisure time to attend the morning concerts.

With the proliferation of recordings and the rise in the 1920s of radio, music performances of a professional standard were readily available to all, and audiences came to expect these same standards at public concerts. It may be that the WMC's active members did not live up to these expectations, and so were eased out of their role as performers. At the same time, the custom of spending an evening making music informally around the parlour piano was on the wane, and one consequence of this is that the value of music as a social asset was correspondingly diminished. Perhaps as a result of this, fewer women were pursuing musical training, and the WMC may have had difficulty recruiting a sufficient number of active members. Whatever the reason, the WMC's active members seem to have lost respect as artists during this period. The club itself, however, continued to gain respect for women through the high standards set at the concerts it sponsored, which reflected well upon the women's talent and perspicacity as impresarios.

Meanwhile the musical world at large was changing rapidly in important ways. Popular music, which made its first tentative inroads in Toronto in the 1890s in the form of music hall, the cakewalk, ragtime, and other such genres, was winning ever greater numbers of followers and was also gaining in social prestige. Even within the world of classical concert music, audiences were becoming increasingly fragmented as new concert-giving organizations proliferated. The "superior class of music" that the WMC had always promoted was now just one of a variety of musical entertainments on offer each season in the rapidly growing city, and it no longer automatically exercised the same sort of exclusive social prestige and unqualified admiration that it had formerly. It was a more competitive world, but in many ways a more exciting one. The secret of the longevity of the WMC is that it has always been capable of adapting to the changing ways of the world, and it was Mary Dickson who showed the way in 1914.

The most pressing challenge for the WMC between 1914 and 1918 was to prove the club's relevancy in time of war. The WMC approached this task in two ways, as an article about Mary Dickson written in 1921 explained:

> During the war, this society [the WMC] had but two objects in carrying on the work — to comfort and relieve by the music and to aid the great Cause of patriotic and philanthropic effort. The financial result was eight thousand dollars to the Red Cross Society and other patriotic organizations — and to the activity of the officers, headed by their enthusiastic president, was due much of the success of the various concerts held.[24]

At the start of the seventeenth season, a Philanthropic Committee was organized to bring music into the poorer neighbourhoods of Toronto and to raise money for the war effort. By the end of the season there were 125 volunteer musicians involved in the program, helping out in five different neighbourhoods and two missions. The WMC supplied accompanists and conductors for musical groups and offered free tuition to deserving pupils. At the end of the season the entire profit for the year ($250) was donated to the University Base Hospital. As the *Canadian Journal of Music* wrote, "Much good can reasonably be expected from this band of sincere women who realize that music is a spiritual language for the many, not alone the favoured few."[25]

There were twenty-one events in all during the seventeenth season, of which only nine were recitals of vocal and piano solos by WMC members. There were two lecture-recitals by WMC members (Hope Morgan and Grace Smith) and four lectures by guest speakers: A.S. Vogt, Frank Welsman, Albert Ham, and J.C. McLennan[26] (the last named spoke on "The Physical Basis of Music"). There were exchange visits with the Duet Club of Hamilton and the Chromatic Musical Club of Buffalo, a special students' day, and the annual closing concert. Rounding out the schedule were two concerts by the Choral Club, which numbered forty-eight members this year and was conducted by Peter C. Kennedy, who had become the WMC choir director in 1914. Kennedy was born in Pennsylvania, raised in Scotland, and educated in Toronto under Giuseppe Dinelli and Edward Fisher. He was an organist, pianist, and composer who taught for over forty years at the Metropolitan School of Music, the Canadian Academy of Music, of which he was the director, and the Conservatory of Music. He died in 1949.

The WMC events were no longer held exclusively at the Conservatory of Music concert hall. During the war years several different venues were used, including St. Margaret's College, Massey Hall, Margaret Eaton Hall, and Oddfellows' Hall.

Massey Hall was the venue for a grand concert in the eighteenth season, on 7 February 1916, in aid of the War Emergency Fund, a project to raise money for children orphaned by the war. The WMC Choral Club was the featured attraction, and a dozen other local musicians participated, including Ernest Seitz, the young pianist who in 1918 wrote "The World Is Waiting for the Sunrise," one of the most popular songs of its day. The *Canadian Journal of Music* gave the Choral Club a glowing report:

> The interest naturally centred in the ladies' choir. The rare purity of their voices, the unanimous spontaneity of the attack, the careful shading and the well-prepared climaxes spoke volumes for the unusual drilling capacity, the experienced routine and the highly refined taste of their temperamental conductor, Peter C. Kennedy.[27]

Unfortunately the review also stated that a "discouragingly small audience" turned out for this worthy cause.

The war eventually began to have an effect on the WMC. The nineteenth season had opened a month late, in December 1916, with a recital by the Buffalo soprano Rebecca Cutter Howe and longtime WMC member Eugénie Quéhen. The review in *Musical Canada* noted that the program featured "non-Teutonic" selections.[28] For the twentieth season the number of events was cut back to fifteen, including lectures by the local musicians Herbert A. Fricker (newly arrived in Toronto to become Vogt's successor as conductor of the Toronto Mendelssohn Choir), Leo Smith, and Grace Smith. Nevertheless the WMC soldiered on and continued to raise a significant amount of money for charity — over four thousand dollars in the nineteenth season alone. In January 1918 the Masonic Hall at the corner of Yonge Street and Davenport Road became the new regular concert venue for the WMC.

The WMC continued to exercise great skill in introducing important young artists to Toronto. In the nineteenth season a special benefit concert for the Toronto Red Cross Society was held in Massey Hall on 20 February 1917. The U.S. soprano Anna Case of the Metropolitan Opera and the brilliant eighteen-year-old Brazilian pianist Guiomar Novaes were presented in their Toronto debuts. This time Massey Hall was full, and the event raised over $2,500 for charity. On 1 March 1917 the U.S. singer Emma Roberts "scored a distinct triumph," in the words of the *Musical Canada* reviewer, in her Toronto debut for the WMC at Oddfellows' Hall.[29] In the twentieth season the Spanish coloratura soprano Maria Barrientos made her Toronto debut for the WMC in a recital at Massey Hall on 5 January 1918.

The patriotic services of the WMC did not go unnoticed. The wives of the governor general of Canada and the lieutenant governor of Ontario had for some time been honorary members of the WMC. But after a special concert in honour of the duke and duchess of Devonshire on 1 December 1916, the duchess consented to become the honorary president of the club. For the duration of the war the WMC programs carried the heading, "Under the Distinguished Patronage of Her Excellency the Duchess of Devonshire and Lady Hendrie." The vice-regal sponsorship continued into the 1920s.

After outlining the twentieth season of the WMC in *Saturday Night*, Hector Charlesworth had concluded, "The profits on these events will go to various patriotic objects. Assuredly the Women's Musical Club had become a splendid vehicle of musical progress."[30] Under often trying conditions the WMC had continued to flourish, having sponsored another two hundred or so concerts during its second decade. Although major organizational changes were underway, at the end of the war the WMC found itself in sound condition with a large membership and a renewed sense of purpose.

NOTES

[1] WMC *Tenth Annual Report* 3, 60.

[2] *Conservatory Bi-monthly* Nov. 1908: 183–84.

[3] Lehmann (1862–1918) visited Toronto for a performance of her song cycle *In a Persian Garden* at Massey Hall in January 1910.

[4] An outline of the events for this season is given in Helen Goudge, *Look Back in Pride: A History of the Women's Musical Club of Toronto 1897–98 to 1972–73* (Toronto: Women's Musical Club of Toronto, 1972) [5–6].

[5] A letter dated 1 December 1908 inviting Ernest MacMillan to play at this recital was donated to the WMC by Patricia MacMillan in 1970 but is no longer in the WMC Archives.

[6] Hardy was a local pianist, not to be confused with his contemporary, the Montreal musician Edmond Hardy.

[7] Zollner, a pupil of W.O. Forsyth, later married and as Mrs. Andrew Kinghorn served on the WMC executive committee. She was second vice-president at the time of her death in January 1927.

[8] Kluckner 229.

[9] "Music," *Saturday Night* 5 Dec. 1908: 15.

[10] A.V., "Women's Musical Club," *Musical Canada* Feb. 1910: 346. Anna Farini was a founding member of the Heliconian Club.

[11] E.R. Parkhurst, "Music and the Drama," *Globe* 5 Nov. 1909: 16.

[12] E.R. Parkhurst, "Music and the Drama," *Globe* 28 Feb. 1910: 16.

[13] Austin Seton Thompson, *Spadina: A Story of Old Toronto* (Toronto: Pagurian, 1975) 180, 182, 203–06. The house was occupied by Kathleen Austin Thompson, Albert and Mary Austin's daughter, until 1982; it is now Spadina Historic House Museum, next door to Casa Loma.

[14] Augustus Bridle, "Chamber Music in Toronto," *The Yearbook of Canadian Art 1913* (Toronto: Dent, n.d. [ca. 1914]) 147.

[15] E.R. Parkhurst, "Music and the Drama," *Globe* 4 Dec. 1911: 9.

[16] "Musical Merits Wins Recognition," *Mail and Empire* 4 Dec. 1911: 11.

[17] Florence Hayes, "Broome, Edward," *Encyclopedia of Music in Canada*, 2nd ed., 1992.

[18] "The Women's Morning Musical Club of Toronto," *Conservatory Monthly* Dec. 1912: 307. The article is unsigned but was likely written by Susie Frances Harrison, who was the editor of the *Conservatory Monthly* and also a WMC member.

[19] "Oratorio Society Opens Festival," *Mail and Empire* 1 Apr. 1913: 4.

[20] "Club Musicales," *Canadian Journal of Music* June 1914: 38.

[21] *Constitution and By-Laws of the Women's Musical Club of Toronto*, framed 1914 and revised 1923, WMC Archives.

[22] Olga Samaroff received about $250 for her concert in January 1908, and the Kneisel Quartet was paid $350 in November 1908.

[23] Clara A. Korn, "Women's Musical Clubs," *Etude* 17.5 (1899): 150–51.

[24] "Canadian Women in the Public Eye: Mrs. George Dickson,". *Saturday Night* 8 Jan. 1921: 25.

[25] "Women's Musical Club of Toronto," *Canadian Journal of Music* Dec. 1914–Jan. 1915: 125.

[26] John Cunningham McLennan (1867–1935) had become head of physics at the University of Toronto in 1907. A scientist of worldwide reputation, he later pioneered the use of radium to treat cancer. He moved to England in 1932 and was knighted in 1935.

[27] "War Emergency Fund Concert," *Canadian Journal of Music* Mar. 1916: 204.

[28] "Women's Musical Club," *Musical Canada* Jan. 1917: 45.

[29] "Women's Musical Club Recital," *Musical Canada* Apr. 1917: 199.

[30] Hector Charlesworth, "Music and Drama," *Saturday Night* 3 Nov. 1917: 6.

5

Transformations
and Troubles

The twenty-first season of the WMC was scheduled to begin with a recital at the Masonic Hall on Monday, 11 November 1918, at 3:00 p.m. The celebrations started in the early morning hours of that day, and by noon Toronto was a chaos of confusion and clamour, with bugles, trumpets, cornets, and drums blaring forth from every street corner. One paper reported that "Jazz bands were to be found everywhere, and emitted a din that made itself popular with discord, while the antics of the performers provided a world of amusement for the bystanders."[1] A huge bonfire attracted a throng of onlookers opposite Britnell's Book Store. Cars were stolen for joyrides, business was at a standstill, and the theatres were empty during the day as thousands took to the streets. It was not the beginning of the WMC season that they were celebrating, of course, but rather the end of the war. In the event, the WMC wisely decided to postpone its concert for two days.

The delayed opening of the twenty-first season took place on 13 November 1918 at the Masonic Hall. The Australian-born New York pianist Ernest Hutcheson was presented in his Toronto debut, playing works by Bach, Schubert, Chopin, Liszt, Alkan, Franck, and Debussy. It was a wide-ranging program, but one calculated to appeal more to pianists than the general public. The review in the *Mail and Empire* was rather cool:

> Mr. Hutcheson is a very earnest and intelligent artist. He did not make an instantaneous impression on the audience, but as he unfolded his programme, the variety and the artistic integrity of his

work first riveted the attention of his hearers and then roused them to enthusiasm.... There is no sensationalism in Mr. Hutcheson's art. He does not rely on that artistic magnetism that is generally called personality. He is a pianist with an excellent understanding, and with the power at his command of catching and conveying the intention of the composer.[2]

Mona Bates likely secured the services of Hutcheson for the WMC, as she was his pupil and teaching assistant at the time. Hutcheson returned to Toronto as a performer on many occasions in subsequent years. He became the president of the Juilliard School of Music in 1937, and that same year he prepared an important report on music education in Canada at the invitation of the University of Toronto and the Conservatory of Music.[3]

May Thompson Lash succeeded Mary Dickson as the president of the WMC for the 1918–19 season. She was born in Cayuga County, New York, and married the Toronto lawyer and financier Miller Lash in 1898. Miller Lash was the vice-president (and later the president) of Brazilian Traction, Light and Power Company Limited, the largest privately owned corporation in South America.[4] The Lashes did not maintain a residence in Brazil, however. Miller Lash worked out of the company's head office in Toronto, and the family lived at 60 Lowther Avenue, which later became the Society of Friends (Quaker) House. May Thompson Lash only served as president of the WMC for one season, but she remained a member thereafter and was actively involved in the club until her death in 1926.

In the immediate postwar years, the WMC concerts were held every two weeks, usually on Thursday afternoons, from November to March or April. The recitals were still of two types: "regular" meetings, which were for WMC members only, and "open" concerts, to which the general public could purchase tickets. For several seasons the WMC also sponsored an annual concert in Massey Hall by up-and-coming professional artists, mostly from the United States. The Massey Hall concert and some of the open concerts were reviewed by the music critics. Nearly all of the WMC events were covered in the society columns of the day, but, as we shall see, with a rather different emphasis than in the music columns. Some WMC members continued to perform in the recitals during these years, but at least half of the performers were local men who were professional musicians.

The regular venue of the WMC concerts from 1918 to 1921 was the Masonic Hall. Among the local artists who performed there in recital during the twenty-first season were the violinist Frank Blachford, the pianists Alberto Guerrero (newly arrived in Toronto), Arthur Oliver, and Harvey Robb, and the singer Kenneth Angus. Visiting musicians included the English violinist Vera Barstow on 9 January 1919 and the U.S. soprano Gail Gardner in her Toronto debut on 6 March 1919, the final event of the season. Gardner was accompanied by longtime WMC member Jessie Allen.

The main event of the twenty-first season was a special "patriotic concert" given at Massey Hall on the evening of 21 January 1919. The entire proceeds of this recital went to the Permanent Military Convalescent Hospitals in Canada and to Belgian and French Refugee Work. The artists initially hired for the event were the U.S. soprano Helen Stanley, who had previously been heard in Toronto, and the Belgian cellist Maurice Dambois, who was to make his local debut. Helen Stanley had to cancel owing to illness, and her place was taken on one day's notice by the contralto Julia Claussen of New York. This was the first of many last-minute cancellations — followed by a frantic search for a replacement artist — that the WMC concert convenors have had to contend with over the years. In this case all turned out well, as Claussen covered herself with glory in this, her Toronto debut, and Dambois also performed well. The WMC had quite a reputation by now for introducing new talent to Toronto, as a review of the "patriotic concert" made clear:

> To the credit of the Women's Musical Club of Toronto let it be said that they have consistently adhered to the policy of introducing new artists of standing at each of their annual recitals at Massey Hall. Of course, it would be much easier to bring singers whose drawing power had already been tested locally, and whose reputation was established among the regular supporters of concerts, but an organization like the Women's Musical Club can be of real value in introducing new people to the city. . . . The Symphony Orchestra used to introduce new artists to the city each year, but now we have only the Women's Musical Club to carry on the good work.[5]

The Toronto Symphony Orchestra had been a casualty of the war: it disbanded in 1918, and a new local orchestra was not formed until 1923. The WMC concert in Massey Hall was well supported, to judge by a report in the society column the next day, which speaks of a "large audience" and lists the names of over two hundred people who attended.[6]

As the WMC became more involved in sponsoring professional concerts, the Speranza Musical Club took over the role of presenting private musicales by local women musicians. The two clubs had many of the same members and seem to have enjoyed cordial relations; indeed, it was as if the WMC acted as big sister to the Speranza Club. The new WMC president for the twenty-second season was Carrie Reid Lambe, who graduated to the position after having served as the president of the Speranza Musical Club the previous season. Carrie Reid Lambe was president of the WMC for two seasons.

As mentioned above, nearly all of the WMC concerts were covered in the society columns of the day. These give detailed accounts of who distributed the programs and served tea, how the hall was decorated, what the women performers wore, and which important society people attended. The report in "On Dit," the society column of the *Mail and Empire*, about the opening of the twenty-second season on 6 November 1919 is typical. It reads in part as follows:

> The programme was unusually interesting. Miss Jocelyn Clarke, who looked charming in a white crepe frock, with corsage of violets and wearing a black velvet hat, delighted the audience with her very effective rendering of two songs. Miss Virginia Cayne, in black satin and a smart orange colored hat, gave several piano selections, which were much appreciated. Mrs. Dilworth closed the programme with some very delightful songs. Mrs. H.M. Blight was a very sympathetic accompanist. The pretty tea table was decorated with white chrysanthemums in wicker baskets.[7]

Aside from the performers, who were all local musicians, some eighty women are mentioned in this column by name. Those who assisted in the event in any way are listed (in this case sixteen people), as are any notable members of the audience, who are listed according to strict protocol: vice-royalty first, followed by other titled figures, continuing with past and present members of the WMC executive, and concluding with other members of Toronto society. There was no vice-royalty present at the opening WMC concert of the season, but Mrs. Lionel Clarke, the wife of the lieutenant governor of Ontario, attended the final recital, a lecture-recital by Hope Morgan on "Composers Who Contributed Most to the Advancement of Opera between 1633 and 1871," on 25 March 1920.

An interesting juxtaposition of items occurs in the "On Dit" column for 23 January 1920. There is a report of a WMC recital held on the previous afternoon, in which Ernest MacMillan performed with the Academy String Quartet — "Dr. Ernest MacMillan, who has numerous admirers, received a hearty welcome and played the piano delightfully." Later in the same column, it is stated that "Mrs. Ernest MacMillan (formerly Elsie Keith), received for the first time since her marriage yesterday afternoon."[8] Ezra Schabas, in his book on Ernest MacMillan, explains the sequence of events on that hectic day:

> [A]fter a ten-day honeymoon, a full-scale wedding reception was held at the Keith home in Toronto's Casa Loma district. It followed a Women's Musical Club of Toronto afternoon concert at which Ernest played the Franck *Quintet* with the Academy String Quartet. . . . Combining business with pleasure, he invited the audience *en masse* to the reception, to be joined, in the early evening, by relatives and friends.[9]

It was a busy season for MacMillan with the WMC. In addition to the above-mentioned recital, he was the piano accompanist for a mixed recital on 11 December 1919, just three weeks before his wedding, and on 12 February 1920 he arranged, lectured at, and played piano in a concert of "Modern British Music."

Other local musicians performing for the WMC in the 1919–20 season included the violinists Harry Adaskin, Helen Hunt, and Luigi von Kunits, the pianist Reginald Stewart, and the singers George Aldcroft and Campbell McInnes. The English-born baritone McInnes had just arrived from London and created something of a sensation both on and off the stage. His singing in the WMC recital "held his listeners spellbound to the last note" in the words of one review,[10] but meanwhile his attempted elopement with Dorothy MacMillan was foiled at the last minute by the intervention of Dorothy's brother Ernest, according to Ezra Schabas.[11]

McInnes returned for the opening concert of the twenty-third season, a gala event on 9 November 1920 in Masonic Hall in honour of Her Excellency the duchess of Devonshire. The WMC pulled out all the stops for this event, which was clearly one of the main society functions in Toronto for the fall season. The duchess of Devonshire and Mrs. Lionel Clarke both attended, accompanied by their daughters, and they were received by the top-ranking WMC executive members: Mesdames Lash, Lambe, Meikle, and Bongard. (As it turned out, these were the four consecutive presidents of the WMC between 1918 and 1929.) The report in "On Dit" the next day lists the names of well over one hundred women in attendance, and waxed eloquent with extended descriptions of what the vice-royalty and WMC executive wore and how the hall was decorated.[12] The duchess of Devonshire and Mrs. Clarke are listed as the patronesses of the WMC in the *Torontonian Society Blue Book and Club List 1921*,[13] a club registry which was published between 1920 and 1942 and provides a complete list of WMC executive committees and club members for that period. There were 600 members for the 1920–21 season: 569 adult and 31 student.

The English pianist Katharine Goodson appeared in recital on 30 November 1920, performing works by Chopin, Schumann, Liszt, Palmgren, and Grainger, as well as an etude by her husband, the English composer Arthur Hinton. Sharing the platform with her was the English-born baritone Frank Rowe of Montreal, who later became a distinguished teacher and numbered Maureen Forrester and Louis Quilico among his pupils. The Canadian soprano Greta Masson was presented in her Toronto debut on 11 January 1921 and won rave reviews, but she seems not to have lived up to her early promise and was little heard from again. A rather unusual recital was given on 25 January 1921 by the violinist Frank Blachford, who performed pieces by various composers, including himself, for violin and harp. He was accompanied by Joseph Quintile, who was the first harp teacher at the Toronto Conservatory of Music. The twenty-third season closed on 10 March 1921 with an illustrated lecture on "Greek Drama in Relation to Classical Opera" by James Crowdy.

The first event of the twenty-fourth season was a recital by the Russian singer Boris Saslansky, accompanied by his wife at the piano, on 3 November 1921. The concert was given in a new venue, Jenkins' Art Gallery on Grenville Street. The indomitable Mary Dickson prefaced the concert with a short address, after which she introduced the WMC's new acting president, Mary Wylie Meikle. "On Dit" reported that "Mrs. W.G.A. Lambe, the club's capable president [has been] obliged to with-draw from active work for some time."[14] Carrie Lambe had been absent from some of the previous season's events owing to illness, and as it turned out she did not return to the WMC executive ranks. After a year of filling in for Carrie Lambe, Mary Meikle stayed on for a further two seasons as president. She oversaw the silver anniversary celebrations of the WMC during the 1922–23 season.

The Jenkins' Art Gallery did not prove to be a suitable concert venue for the WMC, and by January 1922 the recitals were being held in the Assembly Hall of the King Edward Hotel at the corner of King and Toronto streets. The "King Eddie," built in 1902, made a special effort to cater to its female clientele. The entire tenth floor was reserved for women, with a private parlour for entertaining. After the WMC concerts in the Assembly Hall, the women could retire to the adjoining drawing room for an afternoon tea served by the hotel for fifty cents. The WMC concerts were held in the King Eddie until the fall of 1923.

An outstanding roster of Canadian and international musicians appeared during the 1922–23 silver anniversary season of the WMC. The number of events was reduced to seven per season, and the more informal mixed recitals by club members assisted by other local musicians were discontinued. The transformation of the WMC into an organization which only sponsored professional concerts was now complete, and the Constitution was revised to reflect the new structure of the club. In future only a few club members who were talented pianists, such as Valborg Zollner Kinghorn, Georgina Dennistoun Russel, or Gwendolyn Williams Koldofsky, would perform in WMC recitals as the accompanist for a visiting singer.

The featured musicians during this celebratory season were the baritone John Barclay, the Hungarian violinist Emil Telmányi, the U.S. soprano Berta Rebiere in joint recital with the Canadian violinist Leslie Taylor, the Russian tenor Dmitry Dobkin, the Canadian pianist Germaine Malépart in joint recital with the Canadian soprano Nellye Gill, the English pianist Myra Hess, and the English cellist Felix Salmond.

Telmányi, though notorious today for having recorded the Bach solo violin sonatas with the discredited "Bach bow," was a leading violinist of his day and appeared in Toronto for the WMC a year before he made his debut in England. Taylor, Malépart, and Gill were all young musicians who had just finished their training. Of the three, Malépart went on to have the most important career; she performed throughout North America as a soloist and from 1942 until her death in 1963 was one of the most sought after piano teachers in Montreal. Myra Hess was on her first tour of North America, and Salmond had just moved to the United States; both were presented by the WMC within a year of having made their U.S. debuts. All of these artists were under thirty-five years of age and were being heard in Toronto for the first time. The WMC was clearly enhancing its reputation for finding and introducing important young musicians.

The silver anniversary of the WMC also provided a chance to reflect on the club's past; this took the form of a long article in *Saturday Night*.[15] Although this article contains some factual errors (it states that the WMC was founded in 1897, not 1899, and that the Toronto Chamber Music Association was part of the WMC, whereas it was actually founded over two years before the WMC), it nevertheless offers valuable information about the activities of the club. We learn that the Choral Club had dwindled in size to the point of extinction by 1922 (it seems to have disbanded soon thereafter), and that a Junior Musical Club had recently been formed within the ranks of the WMC under the leadership of Kathleen Maclennan. The article also states that Mary Meikle was hoping to organize a National Federation of Musical Clubs in Canada, a project that unfortunately never came to fruition, although the WMC did have a Federation of Music Clubs committee for many years which kept up contacts with women's musical clubs in nearby Ontario cities. Much of the information in the *Saturday Night* article was based on an interview with Mary Dickson, whose Presbyterian sense of social service is reflected in her views on the duties entailed in being a member of the WMC: "Mrs. Dickson has a very lively sense of the responsibility of Club membership, and has a profound belief in the good the Club may yet accomplish if each member lives up to her responsibilities and does her individual share unselfishly and conscientiously."[16] There can be little doubt that it was Mary Dickson who had been the driving force behind the charitable social agenda of the WMC during the First World War. Her days of running the WMC were now over, however, and the stability that the club had enjoyed during her period of leadership was slowly being eroded. By the end of the decade the WMC would reach a crisis point that would nearly bring about its demise, but already the warning bells were sounding.

One alarming sign was the fact that the WMC soon experienced more difficulty in mounting seven events per season than it had previously encountered in giving three times that number. The budget was roughly twice what it had been in the early years, and this brought with it concomitant risks. Artists' fees had increased roughly fivefold now that professional musicians were being hired for every recital, instead of using the free services of WMC members. The financial exposure became much greater as the club relied more heavily on ticket sales to supplement income from membership fees. Poor attendance at the one or two open concerts per season could spell financial disaster. Matters were not helped by the fact that the WMC switched halls regularly, indeed sometimes twice a season. Between 1921 and 1925 the concert venue changed no less than five times, from the Masonic Hall to Jenkins' Art Gallery to the King Edward Hotel to the Uptown Theatre, then back to the Masonic Hall, before returning in the fall of 1925 to the Toronto Conservatory of Music concert hall. Some of these switches were necessitated by the fact that the club could no longer fill the larger concert halls.

There was one notable feature of the twenty-sixth season: the WMC once again began hiring professional chamber music groups. The club's early sponsorship of concerts by the Kneisel and Flonzaley quartets had long since lapsed, and only solo artists had been brought to Toronto for the past decade. In the interim a new organization had stepped in to fill the void: the Toronto Chamber Music Society sponsored highly success-ful concerts by the Letz and Flonzaley quartets during the 1921–22 season. The WMC's belated response to this was to hire the Elshuco Trio (a piano trio led by the young U.S. violinist William Kroll, a former Kneisel pupil) and the New York String Quartet for concerts during the 1923–24 season.

Géza de Kresz performed in a WMC recital on 14 December 1923, accompanied by Reginald Stewart. It was the cellist Boris Hambourg who had invited de Kresz, a Hungarian-born violinist, and his wife Norah Drewett, an English pianist, to move to Toronto in 1923 to teach at the Hambourg Conservatory of Music.[17] Beginning in 1924, Ham-bourg and de Kresz played together in the Hart House String Quartet, which had been formed under the patronage of Vincent and Alice Massey.[18] De Kresz returned for a WMC recital on 5 February 1925 with his wife, and again on 5 November 1925 with the Hart House String Quartet for the opening concert of the WMC's twenty-eighth season. At that time the quartet had only been together for a year and a half, but it was already well on the way to becoming one of the premier chamber ensembles of its day. Later that season the Hart House String Quartet went on an extended tour, playing for women's musical clubs across Canada.

The new president of the WMC beginning with the twenty-seventh season was Elsie Johnston Bongard. A native of Toronto, she was married to the wealthy stockbroker Robert Ross Bongard. Their rambling home at 571 Jarvis Street, on the corner of Isabella, was the scene of many musical and artistic events while they lived there; later it became the headquarters of the YMCA. The WMC executive committee meetings and some of the annual general meetings were held at the Bongard residence during Elsie Bongard's term of office, which lasted from 1924 to 1929. Evidently Elsie Bongard or someone in her executive committee gave a thought to posterity, for beginning with the 1925–26 season, an exten-sive record of concert programs, annual reports, minutes of executive committee meetings, and scrapbooks of newspaper clippings has been preserved in the club's archives.

Distinguished visiting artists during the twenty-seventh season included Hans Kindler (on 22 January 1925), who had been the principal cellist of the Philadelphia Orchestra under Leopold Stokowski, and Carlos Salzedo (on 19 February 1925), the innovative harpist whose many students included Judy Loman, a longtime member of the Toronto Symphony Orchestra. Kindler returned to Toronto in later years as the conductor of the National Symphony Orchestra of Washington, D.C. According to Sir Ernest MacMillan, Kindler "visited Toronto often enough to become a familiar friend and always won wide acclaim alike from musicians and audience."[19]

The twenty-eighth season was mainly devoted to Canadian artists: in addition to the Hart House String Quartet, the singers Esther Dale, Earle Spicer, Elizabeth Campbell, and Marjorie Candee were featured. Candee, a local soprano who was studying in New York, substituted at short notice on 7 January 1926 for the Canadian baritone Allan Burt, who was ill. She shared a recital with the pianist Paul de Marky, who with singular bad luck had programmed the Chopin Piano Sonata in B-flat minor, which a large portion of his audience had heard Paderewski play the night before in Massey Hall. It is to de Marky's credit that the comparisons which the music critics inevitably made were not entirely in Paderewski's favour. De Marky, like de Kresz, had recently emigrated from his native Hungary to Canada; he was living in London, Ontario, but later settled in Montreal, where he numbered Oscar Peterson among his pupils.[20] The two open concerts for the season were real coups for the WMC: the Canadian debuts of Wanda Landowska on 21 January 1926 and of Joseph Szigeti in the season's last concert on 26 February 1926.

The Landowska concert was the only one that season not held in the Conservatory of Music concert hall: it was given in the New Hall of the Margaret Eaton School, which was filled almost to capacity. This was not the first time in the modern era that a harpsichord had been heard in Toronto. Knox Presbyterian Church Choir had put on what was billed as an "Olde Tyme Syngynge Meetinge" in Association Hall in 1911; the women wore fashions of the early Victorian era and were accompanied by a harpsichord that was one hundred years old.[21] But that event was a novelty, whereas the WMC recital introduced to Canada the leading figure in the harpsichord revival of the early twentieth century. Landowska, who also wore period costume, played a Haydn and a Mozart sonata on the piano, and works by Handel, Bach, Scarlatti, Pasquini, Daquin, Rameau, and Couperin on the harpsichord. Local reviewers differed in opinion as to the merits of the harpsichord. Hector Charlesworth found the concert a delight and wrote that "When played by Landowska, it is clear that the harpsichord has a soul of its own, expressed in gentle, tender tones."[22] Fred Jacob, on the other hand, admitted that the harpsichord pieces were the most interesting part of the program, but added that "as composition followed composition, the feeling increased that there was

not sufficient variety, and that the piano interludes showed good judg-
ment on the part of the performer."[23]

Baroque music also featured prominently in Szigeti's recital, which
included Corelli's "La Folia" and the Bach Sonata in G minor for solo
violin, in addition to pieces by Mozart, Bloch, Kreisler, and Paganini.
Szigeti returned for a second WMC recital the next season on 14 January
1927 with a program that ranged from the Bach *Chaconne* to the
Debussy Violin Sonata. Critical opinion on the *Chaconne* had not
changed much since 1905, when the work had been panned by the
Saturday Night critic after Franz Kneisel had played it in a WMC recital.
Twenty-two years later Hector Charlesworth still had reservations about
the piece:

> In common with the late E.R. Parkhurst I wonder why violinists
> insist on giving this work without piano when it is a fact that
> Mendelssohn composed a very fine and reverential accompani-
> ment. . . . The plea of the purists against such a practice can hardly
> be maintained in the case of Bach because the greater part of his work
> that is heard nowadays is given in ways quite dissimilar to the
> methods of his time. Even with so fine a Bach interpreter as Mr.
> Szigeti the repetitions of the "Chaconne" grow rather wearisome on
> the single instrument.[24]

Szigeti also played an arrangement of two of Milhaud's *Saudades do
Brazil* (1921) in the same concert, which the audience wanted to have
encored. This prompted Fred Jacob to overturn a piece of conventional
wisdom by observing that "Torontonians are by no means unappre-
ciative of the unique ideas to be found in modern music."[25]

Canadian artists once again dominated the roster for the twenty-ninth
season, including two newcomers to the WMC: the pianist Gertrude
Huntly Green (11 November 1926) and the soprano Eva Gauthier (25
November 1926). Gauthier sang eighteen numbers ranging from Monteverdi to Ravel, seventeen of which she had given the premiere or the
modern-day premiere of two weeks earlier in New York. The season
ended on 3 March 1927 with the final lecture-recital for the WMC by
Grace Smith Harris, who wore period costume and spoke on Romantic
piano music while performing works ranging from Beethoven to
Chopin. One of the more interesting events of the season took place at
the annual meeting on 10 March 1927: an exhibition of the Welte-Mignon
piano, courtesy of Heintzman & Co. The local tenor Alfred Heather
sang two Schumann songs accompanied by the reproducing piano,

and then Reginald Stewart played Dvořák's *Humoresque*, which was repeated by the piano.

At that same annual meeting, Georgina Dennistoun Russel, the convenor of the WMC's concert committee, warned the members that the end was near unless things began to turn around for the club quickly:

> [T]he musical world is beginning to be alarmed at the lack of interest taken in concerts. The concert-going public is vanishing away. This may be partly on account of the radio or it may be that there are too many concerts given and the public cannot patronize them all. The Musical Club is suffering with the rest of the musical world, and as we are entirely dependent upon our fees and visitors for capital to finance our concerts, it is becoming a serious matter. If the Members of the Club would consider this and assist the Committee by bringing visitors to our open concerts and also by procuring new Members, it would enable the Club to not only bring big artists but also to start a scholarship, which we are most anxious to do.[26]

The WMC membership had fallen to 361 from a high point of 600 just six years earlier. It was becoming clear to everyone involved that the club could not continue to operate unless it had at least 400 members. The Junior Club offered no hopeful signs for expansion in the near future, as it had stagnated at about 60 members during the past three seasons. For two dollars a season the junior members were offered four lecture-recitals a year (by Grace Smith Harris, Norah Drewett, and Boris Hambourg's wife Maria Bauchope in the previous three seasons) in addition to attendance at all the regular WMC concerts, but this did not seem to be enough inducement to attract new blood to the club.

While part of the blame for the WMC's problems may well have rested with radio or a saturated concert season, most of the trouble lay closer to home. The WMC simply was not planning for the future. Executive committee minutes reveal that as late as 23 September 1925, with recitals due to begin in a little over a month, the WMC had not yet engaged a single artist for the coming season and had not even settled upon a concert venue.[27] Fortunately the Conservatory of Music came to the rescue and offered the use of its concert hall for a token twenty dollars per concert. It is a measure of the more casual pace of the times that artists of the stature of Landowska and Szigeti could still be engaged under such conditions. While the WMC may have touted the preponderance of Canadian performers during this period as a patriotic gesture, in reality this bias was largely determined by the fact that these musicians were available on short notice to fill in the gaps, and in addition their fee was on average half that of a comparable international artist. This allowed the WMC to limp along from season to season, but a more farsighted approach was necessary if better things were to be accomplished.

A step in the right direction was taken during the thirtieth season: the artists had all been engaged by 16 September 1927 and a prospectus was printed ahead of time outlining the season's events. There were eight recitals, half of them involving Canadian artists. The season opened on 10 November 1927 with a concert of works by Healey Willan, the outstanding church musician, composer, and teacher who had moved to Toronto from his native England in 1913. Willan's two violin sonatas were played by Harry Adaskin, the second violinist of the Hart House String Quartet, and the local soprano Jeanne Dusseau sang eleven of Willan's songs. The composer accompanied both of these local artists and prefaced the recital with a short lecture. This marked Dusseau's fourth appearance in five seasons for the WMC. No doubt her talent earned her the return engagements, but the WMC must also have appreciated her fee: Adaskin and Willan received $150 for the event, but Dusseau was paid only $50. The injustice of this arrangement was passed over in silence by the executive committee and presumably also by Dusseau. Pay equity was not yet heard of.

Other Canadians who performed that season were the Hambourg Trio (5 January 1928), the baritone Hyde Auld (19 January 1928), and the Montreal pianist Ellen Ballon in her local debut (1 March 1928); visiting artists included the Russian violinist Nathalie Boshko in her Canadian debut (1 December 1927), the Czech-U.S. two-piano team of Anca Seidlova and Martha Thompson (2 February 1928), and the U.S. mezzo-soprano Alma Peterson (16 February 1928). The Hambourg Trio performed the Ravel Piano Trio; it was still considered a "modern" work, but as one critic presciently pointed out, "Twenty-five years hence, every concert-goer will wonder why Ravel's trio was ever considered difficult or challenging."[28] A capacity audience at the Conservatory of Music concert hall witnessed the recital by Auld, a war veteran and pupil of Campbell McInnes who was living in Paris. Peterson included in her recital two songs by the talented expatriate Canadian composer Edward Betts Manning, who was living in New York at the time.

The WMC returned to Massey Hall for the first time since the charitable concerts of the war era to mount a special evening concert by the English Singers on 23 November 1927. This time the benefit concert was for a charity closer to home — the WMC itself. The English Singers were a six-member vocal group that specialized in motets and madrigals of the

Tudor era. The group had appeared in Toronto the previous season before a small audience, but in the meantime it had scored a big success in New York. A capacity audience turned out to Massey Hall, so that even after the WMC had paid the substantial expenses involved, it still managed to clear a profit of $1,000 on this event alone. As a result, even though the rest of the concerts lost money, the club was $500 in the black at the end of the season. The WMC hoped to begin a scholarship fund with this surplus, but there would soon be a more pressing need for the money. The third decade of the WMC had been a troubled one. About ninety concerts had been sponsored during that period, as against two hundred or so in each of the first two decades. By the end of the 1927–28 season the WMC membership numbers had declined once again, to 314 adult and 51 junior members. The executive committee put on a brave face, but there was no hiding the fact that things were rapidly reaching a crisis point.

NOTES

1 "City Celebrated in Orgy of Joy," *Mail and Empire* 12 Nov. 1918: 1.

2 "The Hutcheson Recital," *Mail and Empire* 14 Nov. 1918: 10.

3 A copy of the Hutcheson Report is in the University of Toronto Archives.

4 See Duncan McDowall, *The Light: Brazilian Traction, Light and Power Company Limited 1899–1945* (Toronto: U of Toronto P, 1988).

5 "Joint Recital by Gifted Artists," *Mail and Empire* 22 Jan. 1919: 7.

6 "On Dit," *Mail and Empire* 22 Jan. 1919: 10.

7 "On Dit," *Mail and Empire* 7 Nov. 1919: 10.

8 "On Dit," *Mail and Empire* 23 Jan. 1920: 10.

9 Ezra Schabas, *Sir Ernest MacMillan: The Importance of Being Canadian* (Toronto: U of Toronto P, 1994) 59. Schabas gives the date as 19 January 1920. The same story is also related in Goudge [9].

10 "On Dit," *Mail and Empire* 12 Mar. 1920: 10.

11 Schabas 60.

12 "On Dit," *Mail and Empire* 10 Nov. 1920: 10.

13 *Torontonian Society Blue Book and Club List 1921* (Toronto: Covington, 1920) 309.

14 "On Dit," *Mail and Empire* 4 Nov. 1921: 10.

15 "An Important Event in Toronto's Musical History: The Silver Anniversary of the Women's Musical Club," *Saturday Night* 4 Nov. 1922: 26, 34.

16 "Important Event" 26.

17 The Hambourg Conservatory of Music, founded in 1911, was located at 194 Wellesley Street East, at the corner of Sherbourne Street, from 1913 until it closed in 1951.

[18] Vincent Massey, the grandson of Hart Massey, had overseen the completion of Hart House, named in memory of his grandfather, at the University of Toronto. Hart House Theatre was the venue for the first concert by the Hart House String Quartet on 27 April 1924, and for WMC concerts from 1929 to 1941.

[19] Sister Mary Virginia Butkovich, "Hans Kindler, 1892–1949," diss., Catholic U of America, 1965, 180.

[20] Robert Van Wyck, "de Marky, Paul," *Encyclopedia of Music in Canada*, 2nd ed., 1992. This article states that de Marky's first performance in Canada was on 9 October 1926, but the reviews of the WMC concert mention that de Marky had already given a recital in Toronto earlier in the 1925–26 concert season.

[21] "Olde Tyme Concert," *Globe* 4 Dec. 1911: 9.

[22] Hector Charlesworth, "Wanda Landowska Delights All," *Saturday Night* 30 Jan. 1926: 6.

[23] Fred Jacob, "Wanda Landowska and Her Harpsichord," *Mail and Empire* 22 Jan. 1926: 11.

[24] Hector Charlesworth, "Szigeti a Violinist of High Gifts," *Saturday Night* 22 Jan. 1927: 6–7.

[25] Fred Jacob, "Szigeti the Violinist," *Mail and Empire* 15 Jan. 1927: 4.

[26] "Concerts Committee Report," WMC *Twenty-Ninth Annual Report 1926–27*, WMC Archives.

[27] WMC *Executive Committee Minutes*, 1925–26 season.

[28] "Fine Modern Music by Hambourg Trio," *Mail and Empire* 6 Jan. 1928: 5.

6

Back from the Brink

It must have seemed to Elsie Johnston Bongard during her final year in office as president of the WMC that the world was definitely not unfolding as it should. Despite an attractive roster of concerts on offer for the thirty-first season, the WMC membership declined once again, to 284 adult and 40 junior members — the lowest numbers in nearly twenty years. Pablo Casals, who had been hired for an open concert at Massey Hall on 22 January 1929 to help bolster the club's shaky finances, cancelled his appearance and never returned to North America as a solo cellist. In retaliation the WMC cancelled its contract for a concert on 23 February 1929 by Andrés Segovia, who was managed by the same artists' agency (Ibbs and Tillett of London) as Casals. Meanwhile the turnout at the first lecture for the Junior Club in November 1928 was so pitifully small that the number of events offered to the junior members was cut back to save expenses and, at the end of the season, the Junior Club was disbanded. By that time the WMC itself was in serious trouble, with just $8.95 in the bank at a time of growing financial panic in the world at large.

And yet the average WMC member may well have been more or less oblivious to these behind-the-scenes problems. Eight fine concerts were mounted during the 1928–29 season, including a highly successful return appearance by the English Singers for an open concert at Massey Hall on 8 November 1928 that drew rave reviews from the local music critics. The seven closed events, available to members for a fee of just six dollars, featured five vocal and two piano recitals. Two of the vocal programs offered out-of-the-ordinary fare: on 1 November 1928, Marie Thomson of Edinburgh gave a concert of Hebridean folk songs, and on 7 March 1929 the Armenian singer Marie Bashian gave a recital of Ancient Greek and medieval music as well as folk songs of France, Russia, and the Near East, all of which were sung in costumes of the appropriate time or place. Two local pianists were heard on 31 January 1929, though neither was Canadian: Norman Wilks gave a group of solos and, with Alberto Guerrero, two duets. Only one Canadian was a featured artist that season: the baritone Allan Burt, who repaid a debt by stepping in on short notice to replace Segovia on 21 February 1929. This marked an abrupt reversal of the policy of the previous few seasons, when nearly half of the performers had been Canadian. For the next decade there was only a single "Canadian-content" concert offered each season, a point which would eventually land the WMC in a minor controversy. The change in policy was likely due to the WMC's increased reliance on foreign artists' agents, notably Solomon Hurok and Mariedi Anders in the United States.

At the annual meeting on 21 March 1929, Georgina Dennistoun Russel was acclaimed as the thirteenth president of the WMC. She was an accomplished pianist who had often performed as an accompanist in WMC recitals during the previous six years. If the number thirteen did not give her a sense of foreboding, the shape that the WMC was in surely must have. It was immediately evident that drastic measures would have to be taken. Elsie Bongard was asked by the WMC executive to try to get ten women to guarantee one hundred dollars each to help shore up the club's shaky financial situation. By September she had succeeded in securing eight women who were willing to do this, but the crisis had already deepened by then. Georgina Russel called for a general meeting of the WMC to be held in the Conservatory of Music recital hall on 24 September 1929, "to inquire into the possibility of carrying on the Club."[1] At that meeting she resigned as president, no doubt with mixed feelings, because she was leaving Toronto.[2] Elsie Bongard also resigned her position as second vice-president. A motion was tabled "That the Women's Musical Club be disbanded," but it did not pass. A new president and second vice-president were nominated, and the meeting adjourned with the WMC hanging onto its life by a thread. Among those participating in this meeting was Mary Smart Shenstone, one of the founding members of the WMC. She must have been surprised and disappointed at the state of affairs in the club, which she had only recently rejoined after many years' absence.

A second general meeting was held on 1 October 1929, and it began with the resignation of Jean Clark, the first vice-president, who wished to leave the new president free to act "unhampered by any of the traditions of the former Executive Committee."[3] Judith Grant Howse Finch was acclaimed as the new president, with Mary Osler Boyd as first vice-president. It was left to the executive committee to fill the remaining vacant positions, which the WMC Constitution entitled it to do. Judith Finch's first act as president was to dispense with a paid secretary-treasurer as an economizing measure. Next a committee was formed to look into ways of enlarging the WMC membership, and the Constitution was amended to dispense with the three-dollar initiation fee as a means to that end. The meeting concluded with "a sincere vote of thanks to Mrs. Gordon Finch, for accepting the office of President, thereby enabling the Women's Musical Club to carry on."[4]

Judith Grant Howse was born in Hamilton and married Gordon Finch, an investment dealer from Scotland (south of Brantford), Ontario, in 1910. They lived in London until the outbreak of the First World War, then returned to Canada. Gordon Finch became the vice-president of the Toronto-based investment firm Wood Gundy in 1915, and he stayed with that company through the stock market collapse and the Depression. Judith Finch guided the WMC through a similarly rocky period of its history, serving as president from 1929 to 1931 and staying on as a member of the executive committee until 1955 and as a regular member into the 1960s. She was fortunate in having Mary Osler Boyd as second-in-command during her presidency. Mary Osler Boyd had become the concert convenor of the WMC in 1927, and she was actively involved in the running of the club for the next twenty-seven years, eight of them as president. More will be said about her later on; for the time being it is sufficient to note that, together with Judith Finch, she was instrumental in rescuing the WMC from imminent disaster.

The first meeting of the new executive committee was held on 17 October 1929. The vacancies in the executive were filled, and a membership committee was formed. The plan of holding the coming season's events in the splendid new Royal York Hotel was dropped in favour of moving to Hart House Theatre, which was available for less than half the cost of the hotel. And finally, to replace the now-defunct Junior Club, a new membership for music students was inaugurated at this meeting, with an annual fee of three dollars. This move soon lead to the formation of the Rehearsal Club, which flourished from 1930 until 1947. Whereas the focus of the Junior Club had been to offer younger members music appreciation lectures, the Rehearsal Club was closer in its goals to the original purpose of the WMC: it met twice a month to provide an opportunity for music students to play for each other to prepare for their own concert performances.

As if matters were not already complicated enough for the new WMC executive, it soon had to deal with what the minutes refer to as the "Women's Music Club controversy."[5] A rival local organization had begun using the name Women's Music Club, which understandably lead to confusion with the WMC. In response, the WMC executive sent a letter asking the rival club to change its name. The other group agreed to this request, and became the Toronto Ladies' Music Club. Just to be on the safe side, however, the WMC executive formed a committee to look into getting the club incorporated in order to gain the exclusive right to use the name Women's Musical Club of Toronto. This was successfully carried out, and on 28 March 1930 the WMC received letters patent officially incorporating it as a nonprofit organization.

Somehow, in the midst of all these difficulties, the WMC managed to carry on with the job of sponsoring fine concerts. Seven events were mounted during the 1929–30 season, only one fewer than the previous year. The lineup included the Anglo-American pianist Harold Bauer, the Aguilar Lute Quartet from Madrid, the Russian composer-pianist Nicholas Medtner, the Russian cellist Gregor Piatigorsky, a Canadian program arranged by Ernest MacMillan, the Polish-American soprano Claire Dux, and the dancer and pantomime artist Angna Enters. The Aguilar family (three brothers and a sister), Enters, Medtner, and Piatigorsky were all presented in their local debuts.

Although the reputation of Medtner has faded greatly since his death in 1951, at the time of his WMC recital on 9 January 1930 he was regarded as one of the great Russian composer-pianists, and was often compared to Rachmaninoff. In this recital Jeanne Dusseau sang four of his songs and he played a selection of his recent piano music. That same evening Medtner gave a second concert in the Conservatory of Music concert hall for music students.

The Canadian program on 18 February 1930 included a selection of Native North American songs that had been collected in the Nass and Skeena River regions of British Columbia by Ernest MacMillan and Marius Barbeau in the summer of 1927. According to the program, these were sung by Florence Glenn "in native manner." Included in the set was the lament "Hano," which nearly forty years later served as the inspiration for "Kuyas" from the opera Louis Riel by Harry Somers. The WMC members were evidently not terribly interested in novelties, however. In reply to a questionnaire asking them to list their favourite concert of the season, the members chose Claire Dux first, Harold Bauer second, Piatigorsky third, and the Aguilar Quartet fourth, with Medtner and the Canadian program in last place.

After the six regular concerts of the season, a special seventh open event was held to raise money for the WMC scholarship fund. This was an entertainment entitled "Episodes," given three times to packed houses at Hart House Theatre by the young U.S. performance artist Angna Enters on 9 and 10 April 1930. Enters enacted various amusing and poignant scenes from everyday life, to the accompaniment of music performed by Kenneth Yost on a piano hidden from sight. The critic Edward W. Wodson best captured the flavour of this unusual offering in his review in the *Telegram*:

> And who is Angna Enters — and what are her "Episodes?" Well, those who saw her last evening know, and will never forget. . . . She is dancer and statue and tragedy and comedy queen. She is the relentless and remorseless artist who creates and caricatures in the selfsame lightning flash. She is cynic and saint and chill alabaster and passionate flesh and blood in breathless alternations. She warms your heart with her pity and turns it icy cold with her ridicule, and her art never falters, because it is genius and intuitive. . . . [Y]et she never speaks a word, just "dresses up" and dances sometimes, walks, sits, stands, looks at you, leers at you, and all with an economy of gesture that is subtle and searching as the guilelessness of childhood. . . . A supreme artist is Angna Enters and everything she does is beautiful beyond praise.[6]

After the expenses for the Enters concerts had been met, over $700 in profit remained, with which the WMC started up a scholarship fund. Enters returned for a second WMC appearance on 7 February 1947 and was equally highly praised on that occasion. She might well have wondered why no scholarship had yet been awarded from the fund that her performances in 1930 had brought into existence. As it turned out, the money had been used to buy bonds, which were redeemed and reinvested over the years. The first scholarship, for $250, was finally awarded to the violinist Betty-Jean Hagen on 17 October 1950.

Only six recitals were held during the 1930–31 season, and for the first time ever none of them was open to the public. The membership committee had been doing extraordinary work, and had raised the WMC numbers from 284 at the beginning of the previous season to 626 at the end of it. Many of these new members stayed only for a season or two, and as a result there was a great deal of fluctuation during the decade in membership numbers. But still there were 512 members for the 1930–31 season, and as all six recitals were held at the Hart House Theatre, which seated only 459 people, for the time being the WMC could not afford to offer tickets to the general public. Nevertheless the season concluded without a deficit, which, given the lack of outside revenue and the general financial situation prevailing at the time, was quite an accomplishment.

The artists for the 1930–31 season included the Barrère Little Symphony, a chamber orchestra from New York conducted by the flutist Georges Barrère; Marion Kerby and John Jacob Niles, two U.S. artists who offered a program of "Negro Exaltations and Kentucky Mountain Songs" which had been collected by them and published by G. Schirmer and Co.; the Italian pianist Carlo Zecchi, a young former pupil of Busoni; the Compinsky Trio, a piano trio of two brothers and a sister who were born in Russia and raised in England; the eminent French mezzo-soprano Madeleine Grey in a recital of folk songs and modern French music; and, for the Canadian program, a piano recital by Ernest Seitz. All of these except Seitz were being presented in their local debuts, and Grey was being heard for the first time in Canada.

The most unusual program of the season was the one given by Kerby and Niles. Kerby was a singer but was better known as an actor, and Niles was a singer and pianist from Kentucky. A short while before their recital, the African American tenor Roland Hayes had appeared in Toronto singing similar material, and one reviewer noted that he had "stressed the musical content of the folk music, its reverence, and its purely artistic possibilities," whereas Kerby and Niles, Anglo-Saxon Americans, "brought out the surging, almost primitive force of the song."[7] Roland Hayes, who had once been a member of the famous Fisk Jubilee Singers, was one of the first classically trained singers to regularly include spirituals in his repertoire. Kerby, who had collected her material from black singers in the Mississippi delta, felt that the performance of this music should reflect its origins by preserving the use of dialect and a harsher vocal quality. As Rosalyn M. Story has pointed out, the debate about whether spirituals should be performed as high art or as primitive folk song continues to this day.[8]

The Rehearsal Club of the WMC began its activities in the fall of 1930, and had twenty members for the season. It held twelve meetings at which the members played for each other, and also gave an exchange concert with the Duet Club of Hamilton, just as the adult WMC members had done fifteen years earlier. The Rehearsal Club played at the Hamilton Conservatory, and in return the Duet Club performed at the Heliconian Club. In later seasons the Rehearsal Club continued these exchange visits with other women's musical clubs, including those in London and Brantford, and also gave public concerts in Toronto, both as part of the regular WMC series and also independently. At the WMC annual meeting on 27 April 1931, Margaret Brown, one of the Rehearsal Club members, performed some piano solos; she returned five years later to give a regular WMC concert on 10 December 1936.[9] In the meantime the WMC executive had voted to give $100 of the scholarship fund to her to assist in her London debut, which took place at Aeolian Hall on 15 June 1936.

At that same annual meeting Mary Osler Boyd was elected as the new WMC president. Although a proposal to limit the term of office to two or three years had been under consideration at the time, by the time she stepped down Mary Osler Boyd had served as president for eight seasons, from April 1931 until March 1939. Only Mary Henderson Flett Dickson served longer, and her term as president was not continuous. Mary Osler Boyd remained an active WMC committee member until 1942, when the club ceased functioning for the duration of the war. Upon the renewal of activities in 1946 she became the concert convenor once again, and held this position until illness forced her to retire in 1954.

Mary Osler was the youngest of the six children of Sir Edmund Boyd Osler, a well-known financier and politician who was the president of the Dominion Bank, a director of the CPR, and a member of parliament for Toronto from 1896 to 1917. Her uncle was Sir William Osler, the outstanding physician and educator. Mary Osler was educated abroad; a skilled pianist, she had many contacts with musicians throughout the world, which proved to be of great benefit to the WMC over the years. She married twice; her first husband was George Gibbons of London, and her second husband was Edmund Boyd, a Toronto physician who was a leading specialist in the treatment of ear and throat diseases. Upon her death at age sixty-nine on 9 January 1956, the *Globe and Mail* reflected on her career in an editorial:

> The late Mrs. Edmund Boyd exercised a leadership in Toronto's cultural life with less effort than usually is associated with recognized eminence. It was merely incidental to a life into which the finest principles of humanism had been incorporated that she became classified as a patron of the arts. She was an intelligent and charming connoisseur, whose education and daily life were devoted to an unassuming search for the highest standards.
>
> One result of her devotion to genuine values was that under her guidance the Women's Musical Club of Toronto brought many a musical artist to the city before fame had touched them. But fame followed . . . because they had superlative talent which Mrs. Boyd recognized before others perceived it.[10]

FIGURE 11

Eaton Auditorium, where WMC concerts
were held from 1931 to 1977.

Mary Osler Boyd was a member of the WMC for 35 years and she left $5,000 to the club in her will. The money was used to help finance an annual scholarship administered by the WMC, which shortly before her death had been named the Mary Osler Boyd Award.

The Barrère Little Symphony had proved so popular in the thirty-third season that it was asked back to open the WMC's thirty-fourth season with an open concert on 24 October 1931 at Eaton Auditorium. This was the first time that a WMC event was held in that theatre, which was used on occasion over the course of the next decade and then became the permanent home of the WMC when the club resumed its activities after the Second World War. The Eaton's College Street store had opened for business in 1930, but the first recital in the auditorium on the seventh floor did not take place until the spring of 1931. Eaton Auditorium provided excellent sight lines for the thousand-odd seats, which were divided between the main floor and a balcony. The hall's convenient downtown location was easily accessible by public transportation. Other factors which made it such an attractive hall for the WMC included a large foyer and two useful adjacent rooms: the Eaton's Round Room Restaurant, which was a convenient spot for pre-concert lunches or post-concert afternoon teas, and the Clipper Room, a smaller venue that could be used for more intimate receptions.[11] The only drawback, admittedly a major one, was that after it was renovated in the 1950s, the hall had less than ideal acoustics, a feature which came to be a leitmotif in reviews of WMC events held there in later years. The last WMC concert in Eaton Auditorium took place on 18 March 1977.

The artists who appeared at the regular Hart House Theatre venue during Mary Osler Boyd's first year as president included the French duo pianists Weiner and Doucet, the Dutch pianist Egon Petri, and the contralto Rosette Anday of the Vienna Opera, all of whom were featured in their local debuts. The Canadian concert was given by the violinist Audrey Cook, also in her local debut. Eaton Auditorium was used a second time for a public concert by the Rehearsal Club on 18 February 1932, which was given under the sponsorship of Lady Eaton (née Flora McCrea), the late Timothy Eaton's daughter-in-law and a longtime supporter of the WMC. Eaton Auditorium was available at a reduced rental rate for the WMC for many years thanks to her.

The WMC continued to experience financial difficulties during its thirty-fifth season. On 17 November 1932 the executive committee resolved to sell off the WMC's linen, china, and silverware to the Heliconian Club, a rather desperate measure that raised only fourteen dollars. In December the WMC executive decided to hold just five recitals that season instead of six "unless the finances of the club show an improvement."[12] Artists were still being engaged at the last minute as in the past, and a full slate of concerts had not yet been booked by December. As it turned out, however, the open concert on 9 January 1933, which was the local debut of the great German baritone Heinrich Schlusnus, resulted in a three-hundred-dollar profit for the club, allowing a sixth concert to be mounted. The extra concert was given by three members of the Rehearsal Club, the duo pianists Granatstein and Coles and the soprano Enid Gray, on 2 February 1933. Naomi Granatstein and Etta Coles were both pupils of longtime WMC member Mona Bates; they had a successful career as a two-piano team from 1929 until 1938.[13]

There were two Canadian concerts this season, the second one being a violin and piano recital given by Harry Adaskin and his wife Frances Marr Adaskin on 27 February 1933. The concert was beset by difficulties from all sides, as Lawrence Mason explained in his review:

What with the bombardment without and the conversationally inclined within, to say nothing of errant sheets of music, the nerve of less experienced players might well have been shaken: but the Adaskins came through the ordeal with flying colors, apparently less disturbed than was this listener.

Mason went on to give the Adaskins a rave review, but concluded his article with a rather peculiar diatribe:

Yet, truth to tell, this reviewer feels that these two artists do even finer work alone or in different combinations than with each other. He is heretic or bachelor enough to feel that married performers do not work well together, the success of the Lhevinnes and the Robertsons being, at most, merely the exception which proves the rule; and no one knows how much better they might have played if unmarried.[14]

Notwithstanding Mason's reservations, the Adaskins formed one of Canada's most successful and longest-lived duos; they performed together for over forty years, from 1923 until the 1960s.

The season closed with another local early music debut, this time by the Casadesus Society of Ancient Instruments, which had been founded in Paris in 1901 by the string player Henri Casadesus. The group performed a selection of French music for viol family and harpsichord from the eighteenth and early nineteenth centuries.

In an attempt to forestall some of the uncertainties experienced in seasons past and to gauge the mood of the membership, the WMC executive sent out another questionnaire before the last concert. The members were asked what they felt was the best way to deal with the club's financial difficulties: increase the membership fees, reduce the number of concerts, or hire less expensive artists. (The other way of improving the financial situation — increasing the membership numbers — was not really up to individual members, nor would it affect their personal enjoyment of the WMC.) The preferred choice, by far, was to hold membership fees at the same rate and reduce the number of concerts. In effect this was what had already happened, because in the previous two years the WMC had offered six concerts per season, whereas earlier seven or eight had been the norm. Five or six concerts were given each season until 1941–42, when wartime conditions reduced the number to three. Membership fees held steady at six dollars until 1937, when they were raised to eight dollars; during the war years they fell to five dollars and then to three dollars. Rather than declining, however, the expenditure on artists' fees jumped from about two thousand dollars for the 1932–33 season to three thousand the next year, and stayed at that level for the rest of the decade.

Mary Osler Boyd raised an interesting issue in response to a question posed by some of the members on this questionnaire:

Several members ask for more open concerts, or even that all our concerts should be open to guests, and there still seems to be some misunderstanding as to why a member may not always bring a visitor to our regular concerts. If this is allowed there is no advantage to joining the Club. Unless we have a loyal membership willing to pay the annual subscription to guarantee our entire season's programme even though they may be unable to attend every meeting, we would have no certainty or security as to our finances or the size of our audience. . . . If [all the concerts were] open, what would be the advantage of being a member of the Musical Club, and how would we differ from any series run for profit?[15]

It was to be expected that an identity crisis of this nature would occur as a result of the transition from a private to an open club. New members still had to be proposed and seconded by existing members and approved by the executive committee. But the issue of whether the WMC was a club at all or simply a concert-giving organization would continue to be debated in years to come.

The thirty-sixth season opened with the first non-Western performing ensemble to appear in a WMC event. Uday Shankar and his Company of Hindu Dancers and Musicians appeared in Eaton Auditorium on 30 October 1933. This was probably the first performing group from India to appear in Canada.[16] The company had been formed in Paris in March 1931, and, under the management of the impresario Solomon Hurok of New York, it toured throughout Europe and North America in the 1930s. Uday Shankar was an important role model for his younger brother Ravi Shankar. Ravi began his performing career as a musician and solo dancer in his brother's ensemble before going on to win even greater fame in the West as a sitar performer beginning in the 1950s.[17]

Even though this event was held on a Monday afternoon, the hall was full. The company consisted of Uday Shankar and a few other dancers, along with an instrumental ensemble that, according to WMC publicity and a review by Augustus Bridle, numbered over one hundred performers. (Ravi, who was only thirteen years old at the time, may have been one of the musicians in the entourage.) There were thirteen dances on the program, all created by Shankar, and the musical accompaniment was performed on sitar, sarod, tabla, and other Indian musical instruments. Bridle, the music critic for the *Toronto Daily Star*, took great interest in the event. The Saturday before the concert he wrote a column describing the various Indian musical instruments that would be heard,[18] and he wrote an enthusiastic, though not very insightful, review of the performance.[19] Evidently Shankar and his company made a great impact on the large audience that attended. Ticket sales for this event helped the WMC to record a profit of $1,000 for the season, thus temporarily solving its financial problems.

The rest of the season featured mainly European artists: the French soprano Ninon Vallin, the Paris Instrumental Quintet, the pianist Poldi Mildner from Austria, and the Russian-born violinist Nathan Milstein. Milstein closed the season on 6 March 1934; his recital, however, was overshadowed by the extensive celebrations on that same day of Toronto's centennial. The Canadian concert featured the local musicians Boris and Clement Hambourg. The proceeds from it were used to set up a trust fund to purchase the fine Guarnerius cello which Boris Hambourg had been given the use of for life. The idea behind this plan was to allow the instrument to be used without charge by a leading cellist after Hambourg's death. Over fifty years later this idea was imitated by another Canadian cellist, Denis Brott, who helped to establish the Canada Council's Musical Instrument Bank in 1985.

The Toronto debut of the Vienna Boys' Choir was the highlight of the thirty-seventh season. The choir performed to a full house in the only open concert of the season, given at Eaton Auditorium on 22 November 1934. The concert featured Italian Renaissance sacred music, some nineteenth-century Viennese pieces, and a performance of Schubert's one-act singspiel *Der häusliche Krieg* in a special arrangement for the choir. The twenty boys, aged eight to sixteen, were dressed in their trademark sailor suits and were a great hit with the audience, which was invited to meet them afterwards at a tea held in the Round Room. Other featured artists that season included the pianist Ossip Gabrilowitsch, another of the many Russian émigré musicians performing for the WMC during these years, and the great Polish violinist Bronislaw Huberman. The De Kresz Little Symphony provided the Canadian content for the season.

The success of Enters and Shankar inspired the WMC to host yet another out-of-the-ordinary dance recital on 7 March 1935. Alexandre and Clotilde Sakharoff of Lausanne performed a series of twelve solos and duets to the accompaniment of a hidden pianist, as in the Enters event. Augustus Bridle called it "the most intellectual dance recital ever given here," adding that it was "a fusion of pure beauty in costume — color, flawless rhythm, dramatic ideas and lovely music."[20] On the evening of their WMC performance, the Sakharoffs attended a local skating carnival with the intention of creating a new Canadian dance to add to their program.

For sheer talent and sensational debuts, the 1935–36 season was one of the greatest in the WMC's history. With the exception of the Canadian concert, which featured Jeanne Dusseau in her final WMC appearance on 25 November 1935, all of the musicians that season were making their local debuts. The open concert for the season was given by the Moscow Cathedral Choir in Eaton Auditorium on 28 October 1935. This was a nineteen-member mixed choir of Russian émigré singers, based in Paris; its program of Russian choral music ranged from folk songs to opera excerpts. The solo performers that season included two Polish-born musicians, the pianist Alexander Brailowsky and the cellist Emanuel Feuermann, as well as the Spanish guitarist Andrés Segovia and the African American singer Marian Anderson.

Segovia, whose scheduled WMC debut had been cancelled seven years earlier, appeared at Hart House Theatre on 6 February 1936. He performed eleven short works, including seven guitar pieces by Spanish composers and four arrangements of works by Handel, Bach, Haydn, and Grieg. In the course of his career, Segovia did for his instrument what Wanda Landowska did for the harpsichord, establishing the guitar as a respectable recital instrument in modern times. In light of this, it is interesting that Lawrence Mason in his review compared the guitar to the harpsichord:

> Few of us have taken the guitar seriously as an artistic medium. . . .
> It has remained for Andrés Segovia, however, to place the guitar definitely among the artistic solo instruments recognized by the contemporary musical world. . . .
> It is hopeless to attempt to describe Segovia's performance, since he has practically created a new musical world of his own. . . . His guitar sounded like an idealized harpsichord, equipped not only with three or four different keyboards, but with organ stops and piano pedals as well. The music he gave us was an unforgettable glimpse into a world of courtly grace, fragile loveliness, and subtle refinement far removed from the rush and turmoil, the loud assertiveness and violence of today.[21]

This was Segovia's only recital for the WMC. He was slated to return for a second appearance in a shared concert with the Spanish soprano Carmen Torres on 11 February 1949, but was forced to cancel at the last minute, and Torres did the entire recital herself.

The 1935–36 season was originally supposed to conclude with another dance performance, by the young Danish artist Nini Theilade. Theilade cancelled the engagement, however, and to make amends Solomon Hurok, her manager, offered a recital by Marian Anderson for the same fee of $600. The WMC executive quickly agreed to this suggestion, and phoned New York immediately to confirm the arrangement. And so it was that on 6 March 1936, Marian Anderson gave her local debut recital under the auspices of the WMC.

Although Anderson's public career had begun as a child in her native Philadelphia, it was only in 1935, after ten years of performing throughout Europe, that she was suddenly thrust into the limelight back home. The spark that ignited her career was a concert in Salzburg in the summer of 1935. Toscanini was in the audience, and upon meeting Anderson backstage at intermission, he proclaimed, "Yours is a voice such as one hears once in a hundred years."[22] News of her Salzburg triumph quickly reached the United States, and Solomon Hurok became her manager and arranged for a recital in New York's Town Hall on 30 December 1935. The success of that recital was so great that Anderson soon became one of the most sought after — and highest paid — artists in North America. It was the WMC's good fortune to obtain her services just at the point when her career was about to take off with unprecedented speed.

For the WMC recital, Anderson sang mostly German lieder, but concluded with four spirituals arranged by her friend Henry T. Burleigh (1866–1949), the eminent African American composer. Pearl McCarthy reviewed the event for the *Mail and Empire*:

> Talent is often spoken of as a gift. But endowment such as this young Negro woman used for the benefit of her audience yesterday was such a noble gift as to cause the listener to feel a bit of solemn awe even when the singer was giving a morsel of musical humor. . . .
>
> Every bit of her from her regal humility before her art, to her stage manner and her almost tailored ivory afternoon gown had to do with beauty as a unified whole. . . .
>
> Hart House Theatre was literally packed, and people who had not been able to arrive for the whole concert rushed in as they could, even until near the end, eager to hear even a little.[23]

Only one thing spoiled the event for McCarthy, as she noted at the end of her review: "The accompanist was, unfortunately, rather bad." The offending party was the Finnish pianist Kosti Vehanen, who was, in fact, one of the leading accompanists for eminent singers of the day. Vehanen later wrote an engaging book titled *Marian Anderson: A Portrait*.[24] The success of this recital was so great that Marian Anderson was quickly engaged for the WMC open concert at Eaton Auditorium the next season. She appeared there before another full house on 1 February 1937 in a similar program, once again with Vehanen as her accompanist. Pearl McCarthy did not review that recital,[25] but Augustus Bridle noted that "the pianist, accomplished Finlander Kosti Vehanen, was a wonderful co-artist." Bridle, on the other hand, found fault with Anderson, calling her a "wonderful, but not yet supreme, artist" and criticizing her spirituals for being "sung in the too-artistic lieder style."[26] Notwithstanding Bridle's criticisms, Marian Anderson was a favourite with Toronto audiences and returned to Eaton Auditorium many times under other auspices in later years.[27]

The thirty-ninth season began with the WMC's second foray into non-Western music. This time it was the Sinhalese baritone Devar Surya Sena, who gave a recital in Hart House Theatre on 29 October 1936, accompanied by his wife, Nelun Devi, at the piano. Sena, in his local debut, sang folk songs from many different regions of the Orient and also played a sitar solo, prefacing his selections with spoken introductions. Augustus Bridle in his review wrote that "He talked in cultured accents about Orient folksongs as though all his life he had been at

Oxford."²⁸ In fact, Sena had moved to England as a young man and was educated at Cambridge. He then returned to his native Colombo, where he set up the Surya Sena School of Singing in 1939 and went on to become one of the leading musicians in Ceylon.

The thirty-ninth season was another stellar one for the WMC, with the local debuts of the Kolisch Quartet and George Enescu, the return appearance of Marian Anderson, and to close the season, a concert by William Primrose, who carved out a place in the recital hall for the viola, just as Landowska did for the harpsichord and Segovia for the guitar. Primrose had performed in Toronto before, but this was his first local solo recital. The Canadian concert was given on 10 December 1936 by the pianist Margaret Brown.

The Kolisch Quartet was nearing the end of its spectacular career, but still commanded extraordinary respect from all who heard it. Rudolf Kolisch played the violin backwards, holding the instrument with his right hand and bowing it with his left, as a result of a childhood injury to his left hand. The quartet played without music, just as the Smetana Quartet later did. The Kolisch Quartet had premiered works by Schoenberg, Webern, Berg, and Bartók, but it offered more conservative fare in its WMC recital: Beethoven, Ravel, and Schubert. The concert was so well received that the quartet was invited back to give the opening concert of the fortieth season, on which occasion it performed works by Mozart, Beethoven, and Dvořák. The quartet disbanded two years later.

The great Rumanian violinist George Enescu had originally been booked by the WMC for the 1933–34 season, but that prospect fell through when he cancelled all of his contracts for that season due to the sudden illness of his lover (and later wife), the Princess Cantacuzino.²⁹ His delayed local debut took place at Hart House Theatre on 11 January 1937, and it was well worth the wait. Violin sonatas by Mozart and Lekeu opened and closed the program, surrounding a selection of shorter virtuoso pieces. According to Lawrence Mason, who could always be counted on for an eccentric turn of phrase, the "bewitched and enslaved audience still craved and begged for more, like veritable drug addicts,"³⁰ and Enescu obliged with two encores. The next month Enescu returned to Toronto in the triple role of composer, conductor, and violinist, when he led the Toronto Symphony Orchestra in a performance of his own *Rumanian Rhapsody No. 2* and then performed the Brahms Violin Concerto under the direction of Sir Ernest MacMillan on 9 February 1937.

The fortieth season of the WMC opened with the return engagement of the Kolisch Quartet at Hart House Theatre on 25 October 1937. Exactly

COUNTERPOINT TO A CITY

one week later, at Eaton Auditorium, the Salzburg Opera Guild gave Mozart's *Così fan tutte*, one of five operas given by that group in the course of a three-day stay in Toronto that marked its local debut. The WMC sponsored the Mozart performance, although it was not part of the club's regular series.

Other WMC events that season included the local debuts of the Spanish cellist Gaspar Cassadó and of two more Russian émigrés, the pianist Simon Barer and the great bass singer Alexander Kipnis. Mary Osler Boyd had heard Kipnis sing in Vienna and wanted to engage him for the WMC, but his fee was beyond the reach of the club. Nevertheless she got in touch with him and asked if he would appear for a reduced fee. To everyone's surprise he agreed to the WMC's terms; as the WMC executive minutes stated, "it was clear that the President had handled a difficult situation with her customary skill."[31] Simon Barer presented even greater difficulties, though of a different nature. He arrived at the border crossing in Buffalo on the morning of the day of his WMC recital without his passport. After a tense few hours on the phone with the Immigration Office, the WMC executive managed to arrange for his temporary admission to Canada. He was quickly motored to Toronto and taken immediately to the Hart House Theatre, where he began his concert just half an hour late, at 3:30 p.m.

Further problems attended the Canadian concert for the season, which was to have been given in Hart House Theatre on 3 February 1938 by the soprano Frances James and the violinist Adolph Koldofsky, with WMC member Gwendolyn Williams as accompanist. Three weeks before the recital date, Koldofsky and Williams informed the WMC that they would be unable to perform in Hart House Theatre, as it was blacklisted by the musicians' union, of which they were members. This placed the WMC in the awkward position of having to either cancel the concert, which would win them no friends among local professional musicians, or else find another concert venue. The executive swallowed deeply and booked the much larger and more expensive Eaton Auditorium for the event. Even if all 515 members turned out for the concert, the hall would still be half empty, so everyone was invited to bring a guest. The concert turned out beautifully, and, as is so often the case, most of the audience was completely unaware of the frantic manoeuvring that had gone on behind the scenes. The story had a happy ending for Koldofsky and Williams, as well: they were married in 1943.

The fourth decade of activities had certainly been the most turbulent one yet for the WMC. In the midst of the very worst of economic conditions in the world at large, it had struggled back from an almost hopeless position in 1929 to recover both financial and artistic strength and integrity in the course of the 1930s. Throughout it all, the concerts had continued — over sixty in all, many of them featuring outstanding talent and the local or Canadian debuts of eminent artists. The scope of the events had widened to include dance events and non-Western music, in addition to the standard concert fare of past years. The WMC had managed not just to survive, but to prosper in these difficult times.

NOTES

[1] WMC *Executive Committee Minutes*, 13 Sept. 1929.

[2] Georgina Russel was still alive and living in Pierrefonds, Quebec, at the time of the seventy-fifth anniversary of the WMC. In the fall of 1972 she wrote the WMC to thank the club for a copy of Goudge's *Look Back in Pride* which was sent to her at the suggestion of former president Eustella Langdon.

[3] WMC *Executive Committee Minutes*, 1 Oct. 1929.

[4] WMC *Executive Committee Minutes*, 1 Oct. 1929.

[5] WMC *Executive Committee Minutes*, 15 Nov. 1929.

[6] Edward W. Wodson, "Angna Enters Captivates," *Telegram* 10 Apr. 1930: 26.

[7] "Negro Folk Melodies Heard in Hart House," *Mail and Empire* 12 Dec. 1930: 10.

[8] Rosalyn M. Story, *And So I Sing: African-American Divas of Opera and Concert* (1990; New York: Amistad, 1993) 181.

[9] See William Schabas, "Brown, Margaret Miller," *Encyclopedia of Music in Canada*, 2nd ed., 1992.

[10] "Mary Osler Boyd," *Globe and Mail* 12 Jan. 1956: 6.

[11] Joan Parkhill Baillie, *Look at the Record: An Album of Toronto's Lyric Theatres 1825–1984* (Oakville: Mosaic, 1985) 201–12.

[12] WMC *Executive Committee Minutes*, 20 Dec. 1932.

[13] "Adaskin, Naomi Yanova," *Encyclopedia of Music in Canada*, 2nd ed., 1992. Naomi Granatstein later married John Adaskin, and after his death she married Reginald Godden.

[14] Lawrence Mason, "Adaskin Recital," *Globe* 4 Mar. 1933: 5.

[15] Mary Osler Boyd, "President's Report," WMC *Thirty-Fifth Annual Report 1932–33*, WMC Archives.

[16] Nazir Jairazbhoy, Nancy McGregor, and Regula Qureshi, "India," *Encyclopedia of Music in Canada*, 2nd ed., 1992.

[17] Kenneth Hunt, "Indian Summer: Ravi Shankar 75 This Year," *BBC Music Magazine* July 1995: 24–27.

[18] Augustus Bridle, "Next Week Toronto Music Brings World to Audience," *Toronto Daily Star* 28 Oct. 1933: 4.

[19] Augustus Bridle, "Hindu Music Dancers Are Mystic Magicians," *Toronto Daily Star* 31 Oct. 1933: 9.

[20] Augustus Bridle, "Zakharoffs [sic] Dance Marvel of Intellect," *Toronto Daily Star* 8 Mar. 1935: 28.

[21] Lawrence Mason, "The Guitar Sublimated," *Globe* 8 Feb. 1936: 10.

[22] Marian Anderson, *My Lord, What a Morning* (New York: Viking, 1956) 158.

[23] Pearl McCarthy, "Negro Contralto Makes Impression," *Mail and Empire* 7 Mar. 1936: 15.

[24] Kosti Vehanen, *Marian Anderson: A Portrait* (1941; Westport, CT: Greenwood, 1970).

[25] In November 1936 the *Mail and Empire* amalgamated with the *Globe* to form the *Globe and Mail*; Lawrence Mason stayed on as the regular music critic, with Pearl McCarthy contributing only occasional reviews.

[26] Augustus Bridle, "Exquisite Program by Negro Contralto," *Toronto Daily Star* 2 Feb. 1937: 5.

[27] Almost all doors previously closed to African Americans were open to Anderson, but she was still refused entry to the Granite Club in Toronto in 1944. Anderson died on 8 April 1993 at age 96.

[28] Augustus Bridle, "Several Music Tests Make Up Hectic Day," *Toronto Daily Star* 30 Oct. 1936: 7.

[29] Noel Malcolm, *George Enescu: His Life and Music* (London: Toccata, 1990) 190.

[30] Lawrence Mason, "Enesco Recital," *Globe and Mail* 16 Jan. 1937: 10.

[31] WMC *Executive Committee Minutes*, 13 June 1937.

7

The War and Its Aftermath

During the final year of Mary Osler Boyd's presidency, the WMC enjoyed an outstanding season from every point of view. A wide variety of performances was presented, the concerts were well attended, and the critical reception was for the most part very warm. The membership reached 540, a modest but noticeable increase over the previous year, and after the final audit there was a credit balance of $2,600 in the bank. The Rehearsal Club, then in its tenth season, enjoyed a full schedule of fortnightly meetings and took pride in the fact that many of its alumnae had gone on to enjoy successful careers as professional musicians. In her final report as president, Mary Osler Boyd was pleased to point out that during the past ten years the WMC had brought forty-four artists or ensembles for their first appearance in Toronto.[1]

There were three debuts during that season: the Trio of New York, the Ballet Caravan, and the Swiss soprano Ria Ginster. Alexander Kipnis made a return appearance for the WMC, and there were two Canadian concerts, featuring the Tudor Singers and Ida Krehm.

The season opened on 20 October 1938 with the Trio of New York, which consisted of the pianist Carl Friedberg, the violinist Danili Karpilowsky, and the cellist Felix Salmond. Salmond, whom the critic Augustus Bridle referred to jokingly as the "tallest living cellist,"[2] had made his local debut for the WMC fifteen years earlier. The club was not content to rest on its laurels with an illustrious line of Toronto and Canadian debuts; it now presented the first performance anywhere of this ensemble,[3] which went on to make its official debut at Town Hall in New York two days later.[4] The Trio of New York earned glowing reviews

COUNTERPOINT TO A CITY

for its WMC program, which featured trios by Brahms, Beethoven, and Schubert, along with the Handel-Halvorsen Passacaglia for violin and cello.

The WMC's reputation for sponsoring some of the most exciting dance events in Toronto was confirmed by the open concert of the season, which featured the Canadian debut of the Ballet Caravan on 15 December 1938. The dance impresario Lincoln Kirstein, whose mission was to seek out distinctively American themes for ballet and to showcase U.S. choreographers, designers, dancers, and composers, had formed the Ballet Caravan in July 1936.[5] In its Toronto appearance for the WMC, the Ballet Caravan performed three one-act ballets: *Promenade* (1936), choreographed by William Dollar and set to Ravel's *Valses nobles et sentimentales*, and two works choreographed by Eugene Loring — *Yankee Clipper* (1937), with music by Paul Bowles, and *Billy the Kid* (1938), with music by Aaron Copland. The musical accompaniments were performed on two pianos conducted by Elliott Carter, the musical director of the Ballet Caravan.

Billy the Kid had been premiered just over two months earlier, on 6 October 1938 in Chicago. The touring cast seen in Toronto was almost the same as that which had premiered the work, with Eugene Loring in the title role and Marie Jeanne in the dual role of his mother and sweetheart. Only some of the smaller roles were changed; Jerome Robbins, for instance, had danced a minor part in Chicago but did not travel to Toronto. Copland stated that "The reviews of the ballet *Billy the Kid* were consistently excellent. . . . I cannot remember another work of mine that was so unanimously well received,"[6] but the Toronto critics were only partly won over by the new ballet. Lawrence Mason, in his last review of a WMC event (he died less than a year later), referred to "the violently explosive dissonances of Aaron Copland," and wrote that "the general performance was not undeserving of commendation, if not over-brilliant intellectually."[7] Edward W. Wodson was also lukewarm towards *Billy the Kid*, writing, "Perhaps the music was to blame. Dissonant stuff — two pianos playing deliberately at times in two different and quite unrelated keys."[8] Nevertheless, the audience did enjoy the program, and, thanks to the WMC, Toronto had the opportunity to see and hear *Billy the Kid* five months before the ballet reached New York.

The two Canadian programs that season were of considerable interest. On 9 January 1939 Healey Willan's Tudor Singers gave a recital of Elizabethan madrigals and contemporary music (including Willan's *Hodie, Christus natus est*), sharing the platform with the local harpsichordist Florence Singer, who played Italian and French Baroque keyboard music. The Tudor Singers had been founded in 1933 but had recently been reorganized as a ten-member chamber choir, closely modelling its repertoire and performance style on the English Singers, which had been brought to Toronto by the WMC in 1927 and 1928. Like the English Singers, Willan's group dressed in period costume and sat behind a long oak table as it sang. Florence Singer performed on the Pleyel harpsichord which the T. Eaton Co. had bought in 1931 for use in Eaton Auditorium. She was no doubt influenced by Wanda Landowska, who had also been brought to Toronto by the WMC, in 1926. The second Canadian concert, on 2 March 1939, featured the pianist Ida Krehm, who had been born and received her early music education in Toronto, but had moved to Chicago in 1929. In the interim she had won several major prizes, including the Naumburg Foundation Award and a cash prize from the National Federation of Music Clubs, and had appeared in most of the major U.S. cities. The WMC concert marked her professional debut in her native city.

Notwithstanding these two successful Canadian concerts, the WMC was subjected to criticism in the *Globe and Mail* early in 1939 owing to a perceived lack of support for Canadian musicians. The affair arose as a result of a four-part article by Lawrence Mason titled "Case Histories of Canadian Artists."[9] The purpose of the articles, Mason wrote, was to show that deserving young Canadian musicians were not receiving professional engagements in Canada. In the first article, he cited the case of an anonymous violinist who had been unable to get a booking with various Toronto musical organizations, including the WMC. Mason wrote that "The Women's Musical Club was approached and was very nice about it, but stated, in effect, that only 'internationally known artists' were featured at the club's concerts."[10]

Mary Osler Boyd wrote a letter to Mason to defend the WMC's record in this matter by citing the Rehearsal Club and naming twenty-nine Canadian musicians or ensembles who had appeared for the club since 1925. In his reply to this letter, Mason praised the WMC for its work, but pointed out that the Rehearsal Club did not provide paid engagements and that the list of Canadians cited by Boyd included mostly established artists with international reputations, rather than deserving young professional artists.[11] He might also have pointed out that the Canadians hired by the WMC were vastly underpaid as compared to the international artists. During the 1938–39 season, for instance, the Tudor Singers and Ida Krehm were paid two hundred dollars each, whereas the next lowest amount paid was six hundred dollars to Ria Ginster. This pattern had been consistent for many seasons. In later years the WMC would rectify this discrepancy and also, through its various scholarships, provide important assistance to young Canadian musicians. It was not until 1989, however, that it addressed the heart of Mason's criticism, with the creation of the Career Development Award.

Despite this minor controversy, the future had rarely looked brighter for the WMC than it did at the time of the forty-first annual meeting on 17 March 1939. Under Mary Osler Boyd's leadership the club had built up a loyal membership, had presented concerts of consistently high quality, and had managed its finances well. The Rehearsal Club was providing a valuable service for aspiring young professional women musicians and was also proving to be a good training ground for the ranks of the WMC executive. Bertha Mason Woods, who became president at that meeting, had already served for two years as president of the Rehearsal Club. Indeed, of the four WMC presidents who followed Mary Osler Boyd, three of them succeeded to the position after at least one term as head of the Rehearsal Club.

Bertha Mason was the daughter of Lieutenant-Colonel Percival L. Mason of Toronto. She was educated at Havergal College and also studied piano at the Toronto Conservatory of Music. Her husband, W.B. Woods, was president of Gordon McKay Co. Ltd. Bertha Mason Woods was president of the WMC from 1939 until 1948, and in 1950 was named honorary president of the club, one of only a handful of women to be honoured in this way. She was actively involved in the WMC until she became ill about a year before her death on 3 May 1956 in Toronto at age seventy-one.

The Second World War began on 3 September 1939, and four days later the WMC executive held a preliminary meeting to discuss the policy of the club in wartime. Canada officially entered the war on 10 September 1939, and eleven days later the WMC executive held a second meeting to decide how the club could make itself relevant to a nation at war. It was decided to reduce the number of concerts from six to five, to reduce the membership fee from eight dollars to five dollars, and to make the open concert a benefit event in aid of the Red Cross. It was also necessary to change the season's program, cancelling contracts with musicians in enemy countries and finding replacement artists who could fit the club's reduced budget.

The opening concert of the season took place in Hart House Theatre on 17 October 1939. It featured Ossy Renardy, an eighteen-year-old violinist who was making his Canadian debut, accompanied by Gwendolyn Williams at the piano. Renardy was Viennese, and thus technically an enemy alien, but he was in the process of emigrating to the United

States. He went on to do a tour of western Canada after the WMC concert and to perform widely throughout the Allied nations during the war. He dazzled the Toronto audience and critics in a demanding program of Romantic virtuoso violin music; reviewers did not hesitate to place him in the same league as Heifetz, Elman, and Zimbalist. Tragically his career came to a premature end, for he was killed in a car accident in New Mexico at age thirty-three.

The next event was the benefit concert in aid of the Canadian Red Cross. The artist who was originally engaged to perform on this occasion was the soprano Jarmila Novotná. Novotná had emigrated to the U.S.A. from her native Czechoslovakia, but was busy with operatic engagements in the fall of 1939, and so a replacement had to be found. The WMC's good fortune in engaging Marian Anderson at the last minute as a replacement artist three years earlier was now repeated when the Novotná cancellation allowed it to engage the sensational young soprano Dorothy Maynor.

Maynor was born in Virginia in 1910 and studied at the Hampton Institute (now Hampton University) in that state under the Canadian-born musician R. Nathaniel Dett. Like Anderson, who came to widespread notice thanks to the endorsement of Toscanini, so too Maynor was catapulted to fame when she was "discovered" by Serge Koussevitzky in the summer of 1939; he called her "a musical revelation" that "the world must hear."[12] She scored a sensational triumph in her professional debut at Town Hall in New York in November and just eight days later came to Toronto for the WMC. Her recital at Massey Hall on 27 November 1939 before a capacity audience was only her second professional engagement. She was greeted by rapturous applause for a program that was almost identical to that of her New York concert; the numbers were about equally divided between spirituals and classical selections. Hector Charlesworth's review in *Saturday Night* reads in part:

> Because of her race, comparisons with the contralto Marian Anderson are inevitable, but these are as futile as would be a comparison between Lily Pons and Kirsten Flagstad because both are white. Miss Maynor's temperament is optimistic in contrast to the habitual solemnity of Miss Anderson; and she sings "Spirituals" better than any singer one has heard. . . . This is not art, it is genius.[13]

Interestingly, it is precisely for her singing of spirituals that Maynor has sometimes been criticized by other writers. Rosalyn M. Story, for instance, has stated that Maynor's "articulate speech and Italianate rolling of the r's while singing spirituals might have been considered less than authentic."[14]

The net proceeds for the Maynor concert were $1,265, and a cheque in that amount was promptly sent to the Canadian Red Cross. Maynor's career soared immediately after her Town Hall recital, but the WMC was able to invite her to give a return appearance the next season, and on 19 November 1940 she once again filled Massey Hall in the WMC's second Red Cross benefit concert. The program was similar to the previous one, and Arpad Sandor was an outstanding accompanist as on the earlier occasion. The performance brought tears to the eyes of many in the audience, and the reception was so warm that Maynor returned for four encores. The recital raised $954.07 for the Red Cross. Maynor continued to appear as a concert singer for the next two decades and more, but gave up performing after a heart attack in 1963. In 1964 she founded the highly successful Harlem School of the Arts, and in 1975 she became the first African American on the Metropolitan Opera's board of directors. She died on 19 February 1996.

Gwendolyn Williams served as the accompanist for the next two concerts in the 1939–40 season, which featured the cellist Raya Garbousova on 8 January 1940 and the tenor William Hain on 8 February 1940. Garbousova was born in Tbilisi (Tiflis) in the Caucasus, made her debut in Russia at the age of twelve, and then studied with Casals for several years. She emigrated to the United States in 1934 and was living in New York at the time of her Canadian debut for the WMC. Augustus Bridle, whose reviews were becoming increasingly eccentric, opened his account of her concert as follows:

In the "joy of living" Opus, Raya Garbousova's cello recital for the W.M.C. at Hart House yesterday is No. 1 for 1940. A color-harmony of soft-green gown, aureole of golden hair, [and] a glistening brown cello, was a romantic introduction to a program of almost perfect enchantment.[15]

Garbousova premiered the Barber Cello Concerto in 1946 and has continued to live in the U.S.A. William Hain was a young U.S. tenor, also from New York. He had been heard on radio broadcasts but the WMC event was his local debut recital. The reviews were lukewarm.

The season ended with the Canadian concert, a two-piano recital by Gordon Hallett and Clifford Poole at Hart House Theatre on 7 March 1940. Both young men were pupils of longtime WMC member Mona Bates and were members of her Ten-Piano Ensemble. They each played short solo selections, but the majority of the program was devoted to duo-piano repertoire. The reviews were very positive on the whole, but one critic pointed out that the annual Canadian concert of the WMC was always poorly attended and that only about half the usual audience turned out for this recital.[16]

Despite the wartime conditions that prevailed during the 1940–41 season, the WMC was able to carry on more or less as usual, with four concerts in Hart House Theatre and the return appearance of Dorothy Maynor in Massey Hall. The WMC executive wrote to the Trapp Family with a view to having them perform for the club this season, but unfortunately nothing came of this plan.

The season opened with a recital on 21 October 1940 by the Musical Art Quartet. The first violinist of this quartet was Sascha Jacobsen, who was a pupil of Franz Kneisel and upon the latter's death in 1926 had taken over his teaching position at the Institute of Musical Art (later the Juilliard School) in New York. For over a dozen years the quartet had been recognized as one of the most brilliant chamber music groups in the U.S.A., but the WMC recital marked its first appearance in Toronto. The members played four Stradivari instruments which had been bought for them by the music patron Felix Warburg. The local critics were entirely won over by the quartet, and Edward W. Wodson wrote that the group's sound brought to mind the Flonzaley Quartet.[17] By a twist of fate, the concert took place at the very same time as the funeral of Mary Henderson Flett Dickson, the WMC's first and longest-serving president.

The great French pianist E. Robert Schmitz appeared on 13 January 1941. Schmitz was born in Paris in 1889 and was a friend of Debussy's; he later emigrated to the United States and maintained residences in New York and San Francisco. He wrote an important book on piano playing,[18] and another one on Debussy's piano music which was completed just a few weeks before his death in 1949.[19] In the summer of 1939, Schmitz had visited Toronto to lecture and teach, and he returned annually thereafter. Among his Toronto pupils were Naomi Adaskin, Samuel Dolin, Reginald Godden, Weldon Kilburn, and Harry Somers.[20] In his WMC recital, Schmitz prefaced some of his selections with spoken commentary, prompting the following reaction from Augustus Bridle:

Robert Schmitz, mathematician, artillery expert, motor-speeder and linguist, gave his first public recital in Toronto yesterday for the Women's Musical Club at Hart House. Several in the audience had heard him for two summers as a piano pedagogue in recital. A few had read his book on pianistic art. But even these were startled by a different Schmitz as popular entertainer. . . . Who but a Frenchman born would have the buoyant humour to exhibit his penchant for war gunnery and higher mathematics in a piano recital?[21]

Schmitz performed works by Bach, Franck, Chopin, Falla, Debussy, and Borodin; the recital concluded with *Lezghinka* from Liapunov's *Études d'éxécution transcendante*, a crowd-pleasing selection that Ida Krehm had also played in her WMC recital two years earlier.

The Canadian concert on 10 February 1941 featured the Toronto debut of the violinist Arthur LeBlanc, accompanied by Gwendolyn Williams. LeBlanc had performed in his native Moncton and in Quebec as a child prodigy, but only came to widespread notice upon returning to Canada in 1938 after studies in Paris. He performed in New York at both Town Hall and Carnegie Hall in 1939, and was then signed by the U.S. agency Columbia Concerts. In reviewing his WMC recital, Augustus Bridle noted that he was the most important Canadian violinist since Kathleen Parlow,[22] while Edward W. Wodson called him "a Kreisler in the making."[23]

The season closed on 13 March 1941 with the first Canadian appearance of Ish-Ti-Opi, a Choctaw baritone from the United States. About one-third of his program was devoted to classical selections ranging from Scarlatti to Debussy, and the rest of it consisted of Native North American music of the Choctaw, Navajo, Shanewis, and Zuni nations. For the latter songs, Ish-Ti-Opi wore traditional Native clothing and headdress and sometimes accompanied himself on a Native drum. The review in *Saturday Night* called attention to the researches of the Canadian Geoffrey O'Hara into Native music, and also compared Ish-Ti-Opi to Pauline Johnson, who adopted the Native name Tekahionwake and also wore Native costume while giving recitations of her poetry.[24] A more exact parallel could have been drawn with the Mohawk baritone Os-ke-non-ton, who was born in Kahnawake, Quebec, circa 1890 and performed Native songs at the Canadian National Exhibition and in recital during the 1920s and 1930s.[25]

At the annual meeting, held in the Heliconian Club on 20 March 1941, Bertha Mason Woods reported that a mobile kitchen had been purchased with the money raised by the WMC for the Red Cross.[26] The kitchen was put into service in Bolton (near Manchester), England, and the WMC received a letter of thanks for this valuable gift from the National Fire Service commander for Bolton. Woods also mentioned that while the membership had not declined much since the previous year (there were 407 members), the attendance at the concerts had not been as good as

FIGURE 12

Ish-Ti-Opi, a Choctaw baritone from the United States who
made his Canadian debut with the WMC on 13 March 1941.

FIGURE 13

The Ten-Piano Ensemble under longtime club member
Mona Bates (centre) performed at the club's wartime benefit

usual. She added that "It is impossible to say anything about policy or programmes for next year ... ,"[27] but the executive committee minutes reveal that as a result of the gravity of the war, serious thought was being given to disbanding the WMC.[28]

In the event, the club managed to continue its activities for one more season. At an executive committee meeting on 25 June 1941, it was decided to further reduce the membership fee from five dollars to three dollars, to hold only three concerts for the season, and to have another benefit event for the Red Cross at Massey Hall.[29] The two "closed" concerts were both given at Eaton Auditorium. Only Canadian or British citizens were asked to perform this season, and British war refugees living in Toronto were invited to the last concert as guests of the WMC.

The opening concert on 3 November 1941 featured the lyric soprano Audrey Mildmay, who was born in England but came to Canada with her family when she was three months old and grew up in British Columbia. She later returned to England for vocal studies and in 1931 married John Christie. Together they established the Glyndebourne Festival in 1934, but with the onset of war in 1939 the festival was temporarily discontinued, and in the summer of 1940 Audrey Mildmay moved to Canada with her two children. The WMC recital was Mildmay's local debut, and before a large audience she sang classical selections and folk-song arrangements, accompanied by the indefatigable Gwendolyn Williams.

The open concert in aid of the Red Cross British Bomb Victims' Fund took place on 4 December 1941 and featured the Ten-Piano Ensemble conducted by Mona Bates. Less than half of the tickets had been sold by 17 November and it was beginning to look as if the whole purpose of the event would be undermined. But the WMC executive rapidly organized a phone campaign, and Mona Bates personally sold 701 tickets. As a result Massey Hall was filled and nearly $1,500 was raised for the Red Cross fund.

Mona Bates had organized the Ten-Piano Ensemble in 1931, recruiting the members from among her pupils. During the Second World War the ensemble became part of her Musical Manifesto Group, which was formed to raise money for the war effort. For the WMC recital there were twelve performers — four men and eight women, six whom were members of the Rehearsal Club. Augustus Bridle described this unusual event as follows:

The stage picture was imposing; four pianos in front, two of them dovetailed, four on a dais just behind and two at the back a foot higher. . . . [T]he picture of the young women in white and four young men in black and white performing on ten keyboards at once was itself a touch of Ziegfeld magnificence.

. . . At every group the players shifted their positions, with two extra players in reserve for particular numbers. Even that item of democracy was a complex thing to work out.[30]

The program opened with an Allegro by Mozart, in honour of the 150th anniversary of the composer's death. Other items ranged from Bach and Beethoven through Liszt and Tchaikovsky to the fiddle tunes "Arkansas Traveller" and "Turkey in the Straw," with "The Star Spangled Banner" and "O Canada" thrown in for good measure. Lighting effects were also used to enhance the effect of the selections. The concert was a great success and was greeted with thunderous applause from the capacity audience.

The final concert of the season, and as it turned out the last WMC event for over four years, featured the Toronto debut of the English pianist Betty Humby on 19 March 1942. She played short works by Mendelssohn, Debussy, Schubert, Holst, Chopin, and Tobias Mathay, who was her teacher. The recital earned favourable reviews from the local critics, especially Augustus Bridle, who compared Humby favourably to Myra Hess.[31] Humby had left England (and her husband) behind in 1940 to move to New York. By the summer of 1940 she was living in Vancouver with Sir Thomas Beecham. The two obtained divorces from their respective spouses and were married in 1943, after which they returned to England.

At the annual meeting on 26 March 1942 it appeared to be business as usual. The president congratulated the WMC members on having raised over five thousand dollars for the Red Cross during the previous three seasons. In her report Marjorie Counsell, the concert convenor, stated that "It is too early to announce the artists for next season but, with the obvious need we all have for music at this time and the even greater need Canada has for our patriotic help, we are looking forward to the future with enthusiasm and confidence."[32] The executive committee was reappointed, the secretary was reengaged, and the meeting concluded with a recital by two of the Rehearsal Club members.

When the executive committee met on 17 September 1942, however, there was a lengthy discussion about the advisability of continuing the activities of the WMC. Only six members were present, and the first vice-president, Nella Jefferis, chaired the meeting in the absence of the president. Ironically Marjorie Counsell, who had voiced such optimism at the annual meeting, was the one who moved that "owing to conditions in this, the fourth year of the war, the usual series of concerts for this season be discontinued."[33] Her motion was seconded by Pearl White-head, the president of the Rehearsal Club. As a counterproposal Nella Jefferis and Mildred Graydon moved that the WMC sponsor at least one concert to mark the forty-fifth anniversary of the club and to ensure continuity of membership, but the other four members present voted against this proposal, and so the original motion to discontinue the club was passed. At this time there were 362 regular members and 53 members in the Rehearsal Club.

Six years after the fact, Bertha Mason Woods provided her own explanation as to why the WMC had suspended operations after forty-four continuous seasons of musical activity. In 1948, as part of her final address as president of the WMC, she explained that "Owing to Government regulations, we were unable to continue our concerts for war relief and for that reason we temporarily discontinued our activities."[34] There is no mention of any such government interference in the executive committee minutes or in any other document in the WMC archives. In addition, Bertha Mason Woods was not present at the meeting which brought about the cessation of activities of the club. It seems more likely that the WMC decided to interrupt its normal activities because of the strain of the war effort and the demands that it made upon everyone's time and energy.

From September 1942 until February 1946 the WMC was inactive, sponsoring no musical activity of any kind during its forty-fifth through forty-eighth seasons. But early in 1946 plans began to be laid for the resurrection of the WMC. On 14 February 1946 a meeting was held at the Heliconian Club to discuss strategies for reorganizing the club and resuming operations in the changed musical world of postwar Toronto.[35] There was a disappointing turnout — only about forty people in all — but many of the former executive committee members were present, and their enthusiasm made up for the lack of numbers. The WMC still had nearly $3,400 in assets, consisting of a bank account, bonds, and the scholarship fund. Other than that, about all the club had to build on was its reputation and the dedication and energy of those of its members who were interested in starting over again from scratch.

At that initial meeting it was decided that the WMC could sponsor six concerts in Eaton Auditorium during the 1946–47 season if five to six hundred members could be signed up by the fall. The executive committee from 1942 agreed to stand until a new one could be elected at a general meeting. Some of the senior members of the WMC saw this new beginning as an opportunity to recreate the club according to their own personal vision. Mary Osler Boyd hoped to model the programs on those of the New Friends of Music concert series in New York. Pearl Whitehead, on the other hand, pleaded for more Canadian performers, arguing that the club should strive for fifty percent Canadian content in this area. As things turned out, both would have their way when concert-giving activity resumed.

By May the executive committee had decided to go ahead with a concert series in the fall and also to reactivate the Rehearsal Club. There were three articles in the local press that month, giving the club some good free publicity.[36] By September, the wmc had signed up 439 members at the new eight-dollar annual fee, and the series for the coming season was announced in the press. There would be three Canadian concerts and three with international artists, all to be held in Eaton Auditorium.[37]

The opening concert on 1 October 1946 did not augur well for the future. The Canadian-born mezzo-soprano Mona Paulee, who had been singing with the Metropolitan Opera for the previous five years, sang to a half-empty auditorium and the wmc lost $400 on the evening. But the important thing was that the wmc was back in the business of giving concerts, and by the end of October there were six hundred members, including forty-five in the Rehearsal Club. After the disappointing turnout for the first concert, which was an open one, Marjorie Counsell resigned as concert convenor. Later that year Mary Osler Boyd took over the job.

The other Canadian artists presented that season were the pianist Muriel Kerr on 11 December 1946 and the Little Symphony of Montreal under Bernard Naylor in its Toronto debut on 18 March 1947. The international artists were the Russian-American violinist Tossy Spivakovsky on 15 November 1946, the Griller String Quartet from England on 17 January 1947, and the mime artist Angna Enters in her second wmc appearance on 7 February 1947. The idiosyncratic Spivakovsky stood out as the favourite artist of the season and was invited for a return engagement on 17 November 1947.

At the annual meeting on 10 June 1947, held at the King Edward Hotel, Bertha Mason Woods reported that the wmc had 612 members but, because of the large capacity of Eaton Auditorium, it should aim to double that number (this was a goal that the club would never, in fact, reach).[38] Mary Osler Boyd in her report stated that the wmc should strive to emulate the Ladies' Morning Musical Club of Montreal, which had a membership of over a thousand and a long waiting list.[39]

THE WAR AND ITS AFTERMATH

As it turned out, the membership numbers dropped rather than increased the next season. Part of the reason for this was the dissolution of the Rehearsal Club in October 1947. Ironically the WMC executive had set aside $250 to award its first ever scholarship to a Rehearsal Club member, but before this could happen the Rehearsal Club was disbanded "as the need for it no longer existed," according to the executive committee minutes.[40] In place of the Rehearsal Club, the WMC initiated a student membership fee beginning with the fiftieth season at half the rate of the regular annual fee. With the disappearance of the Rehearsal Club, the last vestiges of the original purpose of the WMC — to provide an opportunity for young local women musicians to play for each other — disappeared.

The WMC executive committee decided to hold the fiftieth anniversary celebrations for the club at the first concert of the season, a recital by the Hungarian tenor Miklos Gafni on 17 October 1947. Gafni was only twenty-four at the time, but he was already being heralded as "the Hungarian Caruso." Mary Osler Boyd related that "In 1944 he and some fellow prisoners were lined up to march to the gas chamber. An s.s. officer jokingly told them to sing their last song. Gafni's singing so appealed to the officers that he was saved to entertain his captors."[41] Gafni survived the war, left Hungary to study in Italy, and went on to make his New York debut to rave reviews on 9 February 1947. At the time of his WMC recital, the tenor's remarkable life story was the subject of a planned motion picture titled *The Life of Miklos Gafni*, with the singer himself in the title role.[42] Given these circumstances and the fact that the WMC was celebrating its golden jubilee, the evening could hardly have been anything but a success. Of the local critics, only Augustus Bridle was lukewarm in his praise: he stated that Gafni's voice was "much too edgily caustic," and added that "This youth is only a 'novitiate.' "[43] Given the somewhat fragile health of the revived WMC, the fiftieth birthday celebrations were appropriately modest — each member was allowed to bring a guest to the recital, and afterwards Eaton's provided tea and a large cake to mark the occasion.

The Canadian cellist Zara Nelsova performed in the third concert of the season on 5 December 1947, accompanied by Leo Barkin. Despite a severe winter storm on that day, a large audience turned out to Eaton Auditorium. Nelsova was a local favourite, for she had been the principal cellist of the Toronto Symphony from 1940 to 1943 and had also been a member of the Canadian Trio with Kathleen Parlow and Sir Ernest MacMillan. The major work on her program was the Shostakovich Cello Sonata of 1934, a reminder that despite the initiation of the Cold War in

1946, the music of the leading Soviet composers remained popular with both audiences and performers in the West. Nearly twenty years later Nelsova would become the first North American cellist to tour the Soviet Union. She returned to the WMC on two occasions: on 7 February 1951 in recital with Leo Barkin again, and in the fall of 1991 as a jury member for the second Career Development Award competition.

On 21 January 1948 the pianist Rosalyn Tureck made her local debut for the WMC. Tureck had studied at the Juilliard School of Music with Olga Samaroff, who had also made her Toronto debut for the WMC, forty years almost to the day before Tureck's recital. Tureck had made her U.S. debut in 1936 and was already winning renown as a Bach interpreter par excellence. She included three works by Bach in her WMC program, as well as Brahms's *Variations on a Theme by Handel* and a few other short pieces. A fifteen-year-old Tureck fan and a budding Bach expert in his own right had given his own official debut recital in Eaton Auditorium earlier that same season — Glenn Gould.

The second Canadian concert of the fiftieth season marked a new departure for the WMC. The executive committee approached Arnold Walter about helping to mount a student opera production. In 1946 Walter had established the Opera School at the Toronto Conservatory of Music (which became the Royal Conservatory of Music of Toronto in 1947), and the school was preparing its third full production early in 1948 — a performance in English of Gluck's *Orfeo ed Euridice*.[44] The WMC's only previous foray into opera had been in 1937, when it sponsored a performance of Mozart's *Così fan tutte* by the Salzburg Opera Guild, and that event had not been part of the club's subscription series. The cost of the Opera School production, though modest for opera, was far beyond what the WMC usually allowed in its budget for one concert, but fortunately the Opera and Concert Committee of the Royal Conservatory, which was under the leadership of Jean Chalmers (who had been a WMC member in the 1930s), was able to provide further financial assistance.

The opera was performed in Eaton Auditorium on 6 February 1948. To help recoup the costs, the WMC made the event an open concert, and in the end the club netted a small profit on the production. Many of those involved in this performance went on to make important contributions to the cultural life of Canada. The cast included Louise Roy as Orpheus, Beth Corrigan as Amor, and Mary Morrison as Euridice; the young acting student Kate Reid was in the *corps de ballet*. Nicholas Gold-schmidt was the conductor, George Crum and Victor Feldbrill were the assistant conductors, Felix Brentano was the stage director, and Herman Geiger-Torel (on his first visit to Toronto) was the choreographer.

The third Canadian concert, and the final event of the season, was a recital by the soprano Johanne Moreland on 17 March 1948, accompanied by Leo Barkin. Moreland had once been a member of the Rehearsal Club and had since gone on to studies at the Juilliard School. The annual meeting was held on 15 June 1948 at the Women's Art Association on Prince Arthur Avenue. Bertha Mason Woods, who was retiring as president, was presented with an antique Sèvres box in appreciation of her work in guiding the WMC through a difficult period and in recognition of her role in bringing the club back to life after the war. In looking back over the previous decade, the WMC executive could point to the continued existence of the club as perhaps its greatest accomplishment. Only thirty-one concerts had been given over this period, about half the number given in the previous decade, but this was understandable in light of the fact that the club had been inactive for four of the ten seasons. The WMC's name and reputation were intact, and the club was well positioned to benefit from the postwar expansion of Toronto's musical life.

NOTES

[1] Mary Osler Boyd, "President's Report," WMC *Forty-First Annual Report* *1938–39.*

[2] Augustus Bridle, "Trio of New York Plays for Women," *Toronto Daily Star* 21 Oct. 1938: 8.

[3] Lawrence Mason, "Trio of New York: New Ensemble Makes World-Debut in Hart House Theatre," *Globe* 21 Oct. 1938: 7.

[4] G.G., "Trio of New York Opens Series Here," *New York Times* 23 Oct. 1938: 40.

[5] In 1961 Kirstein returned to Canada at the request of the Canada Council and wrote a highly critical report on the National Ballet of Canada, the Royal Winnipeg Ballet, and Les Grands Ballets Canadiens.

[6] Aaron Copland and Vivian Perlis, *Copland 1900 through 1942* (New York: St. Martin's Marek, 1984) 283.

[7] Lawrence Mason, "Ballet Caravan," *Globe and Mail* 16 Dec. 1938: 29.

[8] Edward W. Wodson, "Ballet Work of U.S. Group Is Original," *Telegram* 16 Dec. 1938: 33.

[9] Lawrence Mason, "Case Histories of Canadian Artists," *Globe and Mail* 14 Jan. 1939: 21; 21 Jan. 1939: 7; 28 Jan. 1939: 23; 11 Feb. 1939: 17.

[10] Lawrence Mason, "Case Histories of Canadian Artists: 1," *Globe and Mail* 14 Jan. 1939: 21.

[11] Lawrence Mason, "Case Histories of Canadian Artists[: 3]," *Globe and Mail* 28 Jan. 1939: 23.

[12] Story 79.

[13] Hector Charlesworth, "Dorothy Maynor, Legato Mistress," *Saturday Night* 2 Dec. 1939: 18.

[14] Story 180.

[15] Augustus Bridle, "Caucasian 'Cellist Plays Joy Program," *Toronto Daily Star* 9 Jan. 1940: 4.

[16] Isabel Turnbull, "Piano Duo Exemplifies Musical Co-ordination," *Globe and Mail* 8 Mar. 1940: 5.

[17] Edward W. Wodson, "Perfect Blend Marks Recital in Hart House," *Telegram* 22 Oct. 1940: 20.

[18] E. Robert Schmitz, *The Capture of Inspiration* (New York: Fischer, 1935).

[19] E. Robert Schmitz, *The Piano Works of Claude Debussy* (1950; New York: Dover, 1966).

[20] See Chapter 6, "The Schmitz Clan," in Reginald Godden and Austin Clarkson, *Reginald Godden Plays* (Etobicoke, ON: Soundway, 1990) 31–36.

[21] Augustus Bridle, "Artillery Expert Plays Good Piano," *Toronto Daily Star* 14 Jan. 1941: 17.

[22] Augustus Bridle, "Quebec Violinist Has Classic Style," *Toronto Daily Star* 11 Feb. 1941: 8.

[23] Edward W. Wodson, "Masters' Art Given Violin by Le Blanc," *Telegram* 11 Feb. 1941: 31.

[24] Hector Charlesworth, "Toronto Hears Red Man's Music," *Saturday Night* 22 Mar. 1941: 26.

[25] Edward B. Moogk, "Os-ke-non-ton," *Encyclopedia of Music in Canada*, 2nd ed., 1992.

[26] Bertha Mason Woods, "President's Report," WMC *Forty-Third Annual Report 1940–41*.

[27] Bertha Mason Woods, "President's Report," WMC *Forty-Third Annual Report 1940–41*.

[28] WMC *Executive Committee Minutes*, 14 Mar. 1941 and 20 June 1941.

[29] WMC *Executive Committee Minutes*, 25 June 1941.

[30] Augustus Bridle, "10 Keyboards at Once Play to Aid Bomb Victims' Fund: Mona Bates' Recital Has Touch of Ziegfeld Magnificence," *Toronto Daily Star* 5 Dec 1941: 50.

[31] Augustus Bridle, "Betty Humby Plays Exceptional Recital: English Pianist Surpasses All Previous Woman Performers Here," *Toronto Daily Star* 20 Mar. 1942: 9.

[32] Marjorie G. Counsell, "Concert Convener's Report," WMC *Forty-Fourth Annual Report 1941–42*.

[33] WMC *Executive Committee Minutes*, 17 Sept. 1942.

[34] Bertha Mason Woods, "President's Address," WMC *Annual Report Fiftieth Year 1947–48*.

[35] "Women's Musical Club Reorganized," *Globe and Mail* 15 Feb. 1946: 10.

36 "Coming Events: Women's Musical Club of Toronto," *Telegram* 4 May 1946: 15; "Will Feature Canadian Artist in Fall When Women's Musical Club Reopens," *Globe and Mail* 9 May 1946: 11; Bernice Coffey, "Artists of Future Encouraged by the Women's Musical Club," *Saturday Night* 11 May 1946: 34.

37 Colin Sabiston, "Women's Musical Club Announces Recital Series," *Globe and Mail* 20 Sept. 1946: 12

38 Bertha Mason Woods, "President's Report," WMC *Annual Report Forty-Ninth Year 1946–47.*

39 Mary Osler Boyd, "Programme for 1947–48," WMC *Annual Report Forty-Ninth Year 1946–47.*

40 WMC *Executive Committee Minutes,* 16 Oct. 1947.

41 Mary Osler Boyd, "Programme for 1947–48," WMC *Annual Report Forty-Ninth Year 1946–47.*

42 No commercial motion picture with that title was ever completed.

43 Augustus Bridle, "Troubadour Gafni Dynamic Neophyte," *Toronto Daily Star* 18 Oct. 1947: 4.

44 Kenneth W. Peglar, *Opera and the University of Toronto 1946–1971* (Toronto: n.p., 1971) 6.

8

Resplendent Recitals

At the conclusion of the WMC's golden jubilee season, longtime WMC
member Pearl Steinhoff Whitehead was elected as the new president. She had been the head of the Rehearsal Club for four years and was
one of the guiding lights in the reorganization of the WMC after the
Second World War. She was married to the lawyer Roy B. Whitehead,
who was a key figure in the founding of the United Church of Canada
in 1925 and served as the superintendent of insurance for Ontario from
1944 to 1961. Pearl Steinhoff Whitehead exercised considerable influence
in Toronto cultural circles; in addition to her activities with the WMC, she
was president of the Toronto Symphony Women's Committee from 1945
to 1948, and was one of the founders of the National Ballet of Canada in
1951. She was a woman of principle and acted on her beliefs. Although
one of the most active and industrious members of the TSO board of
directors, she resigned and cancelled her orchestra subscription in 1952
to protest the handling of the "Symphony Six" affair.[1] And not only did
she advocate fifty percent Canadian content for the WMC concerts, she
also saw to it that it was enforced during most of her term as president.

The WMC's Canadian content guidelines applied to performers rather
than compositions. In order to assist Canadian composers, an organization called the National Federation of Music Associations was formed
in Ottawa in 1948. This group recommended that a Canadian composition be performed at every concert given by its member organizations.
The WMC in the end declined the invitation to join the federation, but for
a time it did ask its guest artists to perform a Canadian work. This policy

initially met with some success as far as the Canadian performers were concerned. During the fifty-first season, one piece by Clermont Pépin, one by John Weinzweig, and two by Oskar Morawetz were featured in the WMC's regular series. In addition, Ray Dudley and John Beckwith played the latter's *Music for Dancing* (1948) for piano duet at the annual meeting in the Art Gallery on 5 May 1949.[2] Most foreign artists, however, did not have any Canadian compositions in their repertoire and evidently were unwilling to comply with the WMC's request. After that initial season, the number of Canadian compositions heard on WMC programs dropped off noticeably. The National Federation of Music Associations, for its part, seems to have been a short-lived and not terribly effective organization. Perhaps it was simply ahead of its time, for years later the Canada Council would revive the call for Canadian content in music programming and provide financial incentives to help ensure the success of the policy.

The fifty-first season opened with a recital on 19 October 1948 by the Parlow Quartet with Sir Ernest MacMillan as guest pianist. This concert marked MacMillan's last performance for the WMC; there cannot have been many in the audience who had witnessed his first appearance forty-four years earlier! Although he did not appear on stage again in a WMC event, MacMillan continued to be an honoured guest at WMC recitals into the 1960s. The Parlow Quartet had been formed in 1942 and had made its public debut in Eaton Auditorium in 1943. For the WMC recital, it performed Franck's Piano Quintet with MacMillan, and also Mendelssohn's String Quartet in E-flat major, Op. 12, and Clermont Pépin's String Quartet No. 1 in C minor. Pépin was a twenty-two-year-old student at the Royal Conservatory of Music of Toronto when he wrote this conservative but attractive quartet in 1948. The WMC concert featured the Canadian premiere of the work, which had been played by a student quartet from the Royal Conservatory at a students' conference in Rochester earlier that year.[3]

Benjamin Britten was originally supposed to have been the featured performer at the second concert of the season, on 19 November 1948. He proved not to be available, but the WMC audience was well pleased with his replacement, the Italian mezzo-soprano Ebe Stignani — so pleased, indeed, that the singer was invited to return for an open concert to inaugurate the next season. The third concert, on 1 December 1948, was given by the Canadian violinist Eugene Kash, accompanied by John Newmark. The program included a *Scherzo* by Oskar Morawetz.

The three final concerts of the season were each beset with problems. The open concert, featuring the return appearance of Rosalyn Tureck on the evening of 24 January 1949, unfortunately took place at the same time as the local debut of the Italian pianist Arturo Benedetti Michelangeli at Massey Hall. Consequently a much smaller audience than was expected turned out to hear Tureck, resulting in a revenue shortfall for the WMC. Next, Andrés Segovia was slated to give a joint recital with the Spanish soprano Carmen Torres on 11 February 1949. On the morning of that day, the WMC learned that Segovia was snowbound in Idaho and would be unable to appear. Torres saved the day by agreeing to give the entire program, and her accompanist Leo Barkin did yeoman's service by playing the added numbers at sight. And finally, the Viennese-born Toronto harpsichordist Greta Kraus became ill and was unable to give her scheduled recital on 23 March 1949. She was replaced by a local chamber orchestra conducted by Ettore Mazzoleni in a concert that included the *Divertimento No. 1* (1946) by John Weinzweig and the *Serenade for Strings* (1948) by Oskar Morawetz. This concluded what must surely have been one of Mary Osler Boyd's most trying seasons as the concert convener for the WMC.

It was Healey Willan's turn to make his farewell appearance before the WMC in the second concert of the 1949–50 season, on 8 December 1949. Greta Kraus shared the recital, playing Bach's *Chromatic Fantasia and Fugue* and a selection of shorter pieces on the harpsichord. Willan led the St. Mary Magdalene Singers in a program similar to the one he had given with the Tudor Singers ten years earlier — Elizabethan music and Willan's *Hodie, Christus natus est* were once again featured. It had been twenty-two years since Willan's debut with the WMC as the accompanist in a program of his own works.

The distinguished French team of the baritone Pierre Bernac and the composer-pianist Francis Poulenc appeared before a large audience on 24 January 1950. Included in their recital was Poulenc's *Banalités* (1940) to texts by the surrealist poet Guillaume Apollinaire; the work was well on its way to becoming the composer's most popular song cycle. A similarly large crowd turned out two weeks later for the English pianist Clifford Curzon, who had appeared with the Toronto Symphony Orchestra before but was making his local recital debut. For both of these events, a large number of local musicians turned out in addition to the WMC membership.

Two interesting Canadian events closed the season. Donna Grescoe, a young violinist from Winnipeg, gave a recital on 16 March 1950, accompanied by Leopold Mittman. Grescoe had been hailed as a child prodigy at age six and had made her New York debut at Town Hall in 1947 at age nineteen. Earlier in the same season as her WMC recital, she had appeared as a soloist with the Toronto Symphony Orchestra. Her WMC appearance was greeted with warm applause but tepid reviews.

The final event of the season, on 13 April 1950, featured the Volkoff Canadian Ballet with guest artist Melissa Hayden, who had begun her training in Boris Volkoff's Toronto studio. The company's mixed program, danced to piano accompaniment, included the "Barn Dance" from the ballet *Red Ear of Corn*, which had been premiered a year earlier with choreography by Volkoff and newly composed music by John Weinzweig. It was during this very period that Volkoff was involved in delicate negotiations with Pearl Whitehead and two other prominent Toronto women (Sydney Mulqueen and Aileen Woods) about the founding of a ballet company. On the advice of Ninette de Valois, however, the women chose Celia Franca instead of Volkoff to head up the new National Ballet of Canada in 1951.

The final dance event, and also the last non-Western performing group, sponsored by the WMC to date opened the fifty-third season on 17 October 1950. Dances of India and Tibet were performed by Sujata, a native of Bombay, and her European partner Asoka. Unlike Uday Shankar's company, which had brought a large entourage of Indian musicians for its WMC performance seventeen years earlier, Sujata and Asoka danced to the accompaniment of a small ensemble of western instruments. The critic Rose Macdonald was disappointed by this, but added that the "Sensuous beauty of the dances was heightened by the costumes, designed from such sumptuous materials as are rarely seen here in such profusion. . . ."[4]

The open concert on 17 November 1950 was given by the Virtuosi di Roma, a thirteen-member chamber orchestra that was on its first North American tour. The group was at the forefront of the Baroque revival that was then sweeping the concert world, and its WMC program was dedicated mainly to works by Vivaldi, including the rarely heard concerto for viola d'amore and strings. Mary Osler Boyd reported that "In the many years of my connection with the Musical Club, I do not remember any event for which we have received such enthusiastic acclaim, both from our members and from others in the audience who heard this unique programme."[5] The orchestra was invited back to give the open concert at the end of the next season, on 27 March 1952.

Two visitors from the Hamilton Conservatory of Music were featured in recital on 7 December 1950 — the Hungarian-born violinist Arthur Garami, who had come to Canada in 1949 with the help of Géza de Kresz and became the director of the conservatory's string department, and the Canadian pianist Reginald Godden, who was the principal of the conservatory from 1948 to 1953. Garami played the Bach *Chaconne* and, accompanied by George Brough, concertos by Mozart and Glazunov, while Godden played works by Franck, Prokofiev, Barber, and Debussy. Garami returned to the WMC on 3 November 1960 as the concertmaster of the McGill Chamber Orchestra and the soloist in two of Vivaldi's *Four Seasons*. The next concert, on 23 January 1951, featured the Toronto-born pianist Arthur Gold with Robert Fizdale, his duo-pianist partner, in a program that ranged from Bach to Stravinsky. The final two concerts of the season saw the return appearance of Zara Nelsova on 7 February 1951 and the Toronto debut of the Belgian soprano Suzanne Danco on 15 March 1951.

A new departure in the printed programs this season was the inclusion of a newsletter. The idea originated with Pearl Whitehead, who suggested that the letter could feature items about the guest artists as well as news about promising young Canadian musicians. The first issue followed this plan, with articles on Sujata and Asoka and on two young Canadians, the violinist Betty-Jean Hagen and the composer John Beckwith. After this promising start, however, the newsletter dropped the Canadian content in favour of advertising the coming artists in the WMC series, and the newsletter itself was discontinued the following season. Another short-lived WMC newsletter was begun in 1970, and a longer-lived one was started by Jack and Ruth Brickenden in 1991.

A significant innovation was that the first WMC scholarship was awarded on 17 October 1950, during the first concert of the fifty-third season. [6] A scholarship fund had been listed as part of the WMC's annual financial report since 1930, and twice the executive had made a small award from this fund in order to assist young Canadian musicians (the pianist Margaret Brown received $100 in 1936, and the soprano Margaret Brett received the same amount in 1942). In 1947 an award of $250 was planned for a member of the Rehearsal Club, but that club was disbanded before the award could be given. By 1950 the WMC executive felt that it was in a sufficiently sound financial position to begin awarding a scholarship on a regular basis, and upon receiving a recommendation from the Royal Conservatory of Music, the first award in the amount of $250 was given to the violinist Betty-Jean Hagen, a pupil of Géza de Kresz. (Hagen won the Naumburg Award and made her New York recital debut that same year.) With an endowment of $5,000 from the estate of Mary Osler Boyd in 1956, together with a gift of $1,000 from Mary Osler Boyd's sister at the same time, the scholarship was put on a more secure financial footing, and it has been awarded every year but one from 1950 to the present.

FIGURE 14

Pearl Steinhoff Whitehead presents a WMC scholarship
to nineteen-year-old pianist Ray Dudley in 1951.

The fifty-fourth season was Pearl Steinhoff Whitehead's last as president. Her waning influence may be inferred from the fact that only one of the six recitals that year featured Canadian performers — a chamber concert of Baroque music given on 6 December 1951 by Greta Kraus with Hyman Goodman, violin, and Gordon Day, flute. Instead of using Eaton Auditorium's twenty-year-old Pleyel harpsichord, Kraus performed on a new harpsichord which had recently been built for her in Vienna. Leo Smith singled the instrument out for praise in his review in the *Globe and Mail*.[7]

The season opened on 15 November 1951 with the first Toronto appearance of the soprano Irmgard Seefried, who had been a member of the Vienna State Opera since 1943. At the piano was Paul Ulanowsky, who was a favoured accompanist for the leading singers of the day; for the WMC he appeared with Ebe Stignani, Suzanne Danco, Ernst Häfliger, and Hermann Prey, in addition to Seefried. Poor scheduling plagued the WMC once again, for on the evening of the Seefried recital, the German soprano Erna Berger also gave a concert in Eaton Auditorium. This did not detract from Seefried's local debut, however, and she was invited back to give the open concert of the next season on 27 October 1952.

The premiere of Arnold Walter's Sonata for Pianoforte was featured on 17 January 1952 as part of a recital by the Hungarian-born pianist Béla Böszörményi-Nagy. Walter had come to Toronto in 1937 to teach at Upper Canada College and worked his way up the ladder at the Royal Conservatory and the University of Toronto, finally becoming director of the Faculty of Music in 1952. His piano sonata was completed in October 1949 and was published by Gordon V. Thompson in 1951. Böszörményi-Nagy had moved to Toronto with his wife and family in 1948, also with the help of Géza de Kresz. He taught at the Royal Conservatory of Music until 1953, then moved to the United States.[8] His Canadian pupils over the years included Paul Helmer, Gordon Macpherson, Paul McIntyre, Earle Moss, Bruce Vogt, and Lorne Watson.

Two leading French musicians appeared early in 1952: the baritone Gérard Souzay (8 February), a pupil of Pierre Bernac who was then just at the start of an important career, and the cellist Paul Tortelier (13 March). Souzay was featured in his Toronto debut. Tortelier performed a newly composed work of his own titled *Tableau de Famille*; the four movements were "Paul (37)," "Maud (24)," "Pascal (4)," and "Pau (1)." The first two were portraits of Tortelier and his wife, and the last two were musical sketches of their children — Yan Pascal (b. 1947), who later became a violinist and conductor, and Maria de la Pau (b. 1950), who became a concert pianist.

Tortelier was invited back to give another recital the next season on 11 December 1952. On both occasions he was accompanied by John Newmark, who replaced Leo Barkin as the unofficial WMC house accompanist. Between 1937 and 1951 Barkin accompanied William Primrose, Zara Nelsova, Johanne Moreland, Ebe Stignani, and Carmen Torres for the WMC, while Newmark played for Eugene Kash, Paul Tortelier, Maureen Forrester, Donald Bell, Consuelo Rubio, John Boyden, John Shirley-Quirk, Norma Lerer, and Anna Chornodolska between 1948 and 1978. Both men were consummate professionals, able to step in at a moment's notice with minimum rehearsal (and sometimes with no rehearsal at all!) and yet still perform at the highest level. The WMC has been fortunate over the years in being able to draw on the services of skilled musicians like Barkin and Newmark, as well as local pianists such as Gwendolyn Williams, George Brough, Mario Bernardi, Jane Coop, Stephen Ralls, Bruce Ubukata, and William Aide, among others, to perform the underpaid and undervalued but extremely important role of accompanist.

Doris Godson Gilmour became the new president of the WMC at the end of the 1951–52 season. She was born in South Africa, studied voice in London with Liza Lehmann, and made her debut at Aeolian Hall circa 1919. In 1921 she married a Canadian, Major Adam Harrison Gilmour (1885–1955), and she moved with him in 1922 to Winnipeg and in 1933 to Toronto, where he became a director of the investment company Nesbitt, Thomson in 1934. The Gilmours founded the Opera Guild of Toronto, an opera company which mounted a full season at the Royal Alexandra Theatre in 1936 and gave sporadic productions for a few years thereafter. Doris Godson Gilmour sang several roles with the Opera Guild of Toronto, including Elizabeth in *Tannhäuser* and Elsa in *Lohengrin*, and she also sang Aïda with the St. Paul Civic Opera Association. She had joined the WMC executive as third vice-president in 1948 and worked her way up the ladder, finally serving as president for three seasons (1952–55). She was also active in the Women's Committee of the TSO and other volunteer groups. She died in Toronto on 11 March 1959; a brief tribute to her was printed in the program for a WMC recital by Leontyne Price on 2 April 1959.

The Irmgard Seefried concert which opened the fifty-fifth season saw another important WMC debut — that of the music critic John Kraglund, who succeeded Leo Smith as the staff writer for the *Globe and Mail*.[9] Over the course of the next thirty-five years, Kraglund reviewed almost every WMC recital, until his retirement in April 1987; the club has had few more faithful supporters in the course of its one hundred years.

In addition to the return appearances of Seefried and Tortelier, the fifty-fifth season saw concerts by the Reginald Kell Players in their Toronto debut (Kell was a distinguished English clarinettist who had moved to the U.S.A. in 1948), the local husband-and-wife duo-piano team of Margaret Parsons (a former Rehearsal Club member) and Clifford Poole, the Belgian violinist Arthur Grumiaux (also in his Toronto debut), and the English pianist Moura Lympany, who had twice been soloist with the Toronto Symphony Orchestra but was featured in her first Toronto recital.

An innovation this year was that the annual meeting was held on the stage of Eaton Auditorium preceding the Lympany recital, which was the final concert of the season. By holding the annual meeting during a regularly scheduled event in Eaton Auditorium, the club was saved the expense of renting another facility on a different date. This was one of a series of cost-cutting measures introduced that year because of mounting costs in every area of operations. Postcards were no longer sent to remind members about the individual concerts; instead the information was printed on the back of the membership card. The quantity and quality of paper in the programs was reduced, and a printed annual report was done away with. Perhaps the most Draconian move was to reduce the amount of the WMC scholarship from $250 to $100. These measures allowed the WMC to balance its budget for the year. One further change — moving the concert time from 2:30 p.m. to 2:00 p.m. — was not to save money; rather it was to enable the WMC members to return home before the afternoon rush hour, which was already an annoying factor of life in Toronto.

For the first time since the resumption of concerts in 1946, all of the artists in the 1953–54 season were new to the WMC. The Italian bass Cesare Siepi opened the series on 26 October 1953. He had appeared in Toronto the previous season in the Metropolitan Opera's touring production of *La Forza del destino*, but the WMC concert was his first local recital. Siepi sang Italian, German, and French songs and two Italian opera arias. Hugh Thomson reported that "At the close of his printed program the house broke into cheers . . . and he obliged with a flock of encores."[10] From the financial point of view, though, the event was not a success, because it was the open concert of the season and poorly attended. A second singer, the African American soprano Helen Phillips, appeared on 11 February 1954, making her Canadian debut for the WMC. Despite an obvious cold, she won over the audience in a varied and interesting program that ranged from Vivaldi through Clara Schumann to the African American composer William Grant Still and concluded with four spirituals. She, too, was called back for several encores, and was engaged for a return concert the next season on 28 October 1954.

There were also two pianists during the fifty-sixth season, Glenn Gould on 19 November 1953 and Grant Johannesen on 21 January 1954. Gould had done a few out-of-town concerts and enjoyed a growing reputation in Canada, but the sensational Town Hall debut, Columbia recording contract, and international fame were still more than a year in the future. For the WMC, Gould played works by Gibbons, Bach, Schoenberg, and Beethoven, with the Berg Sonata, Op. 1 as a generous encore. John Kraglund wrote that Gould "gave evidence . . . that Canadian pianists can take their place among the top artists generally heard here," and praised Gould's Bach and Schoenberg performances, but of the pianist's approach to the Beethoven Sonata, Op. 110, he wrote that "greater depth of emotional interpretation can be expected with a fuller maturity."[11] Just over two years later, Gould recorded the last three Beethoven sonatas, and his interpretation of these works on disc was widely regarded as idiosyncratic at best; Gould's biographer Otto Friedrich called the recording "a botch."[12] Johannesen in his Toronto debut presented a more traditional program and was greeted by a lukewarm review from Kraglund. Nevertheless, in her address at the end of the season, Doris Gilmour singled out Johannesen and Phillips as the outstanding young artists presented that season, and did not even mention Gould![13]

Géza de Kresz, who had first appeared in a WMC recital in 1925, made his final appearance on 10 December 1953 to conduct the De Kresz Chamber Orchestra, with his former pupil Betty-Jean Hagen as soloist in concertos by Haydn and Vaughan Williams. De Kresz had lived in Budapest from 1935 to 1947, but then returned to Toronto to start his career over again virtually from scratch at age sixty-five. The De Kresz Chamber Orchestra had been formed in 1952, and the WMC event seems to have been its second and final concert.[14] Hagen, who had been given the first WMC scholarship three years earlier, had won several important awards in the meantime, including the 1953 Carl Flesch Medal. She received good reviews for the WMC concert, notwithstanding the fact that, as John Kraglund reported, she lost her place in the Haydn concerto and had to stop to consult the score before continuing.[15] On 19 March 1987, Hagen again appeared in a WMC recital, this time with the Hart Piano Quartet. There had been a great many changes in the musical life of Toronto in the intervening thirty-four years, to be sure, but one thing had remained constant — John Kraglund was still the *Globe and Mail* music critic. His review of the concert was his last of a WMC event, for he retired in April 1987.

On 18 March 1954 the season closed with an excellent recital by the Albeneri Trio. The name of the group was derived from the first letters of the names of the founding members: the violinist Alexander Schneider, the cellist Benar Heifetz, and the pianist Erich Itor Kahn. Schneider had been replaced five years earlier by the Italian violinist Giorgio Ciompi, but the group retained its original name. The trio had appeared in Toronto before in the Friends of Great Music series, one of several rival concert-giving organizations which had sprung up in Toronto after the war. At the annual meeting, which was held on stage just before the Albeneri Trio concert, there was bad news and good news to report. The bad news was that membership had fallen by 120, a dramatic twenty-percent drop from the previous year. The executive had considered moving the WMC series to the smaller Crest Theatre, but in the end decided to stay put in Eaton Auditorium. The good news was that an exciting roster of artists had been signed for the coming season, including the German baritone Dietrich Fischer-Dieskau who, after a year of negotiations, had finally agreed to make his Canadian debut with the WMC the following spring.

The fifty-seventh season got off to a good start on 7 October 1954 when Gerald Moore presented his lecture-recital "The Accompanist Speaks" to a near-capacity audience. Moore was no stranger to Toronto. With his parents and two brothers he had moved to the city from England as a teenager in 1913, and he stayed until 1919, when he left for piano lessons with Mark Hambourg in London. The rest of the Moore family remained in Toronto, and the middle son, Trevor F. Moore, became a highly successful man of affairs and later the president of the Toronto Symphony Orchestra Association. Gerald Moore had returned to Toronto to give classes on the art of accompanying for the Royal Conservatory of Music summer school sessions in 1948 and 1949. In his 1954 WMC recital, Moore offered some humorous asides and many insights into the role and duties of the accompanist who, as he pointed out, "takes half the responsibility, but never half the fee."[16] Indeed, later in the WMC season Moore returned as the accompanist for Dietrich Fischer-Dieskau's recital; Fischer-Dieskau received $750 for the engagement, while Moore was paid just $150.

The WMC was indirectly responsible for the creation of an important chamber orchestra in 1954. In February of that year, Mary Osler Boyd asked Boyd Neel to give an orchestral concert in the WMC series. (Neel had moved to Toronto from England in 1953 to become the dean of music at the University of Toronto.) Neel agreed to consider this offer, and in July 1954 he formed the Hart House Orchestra, which was modelled on the successful Boyd Neel Orchestra that he had founded in England in 1932.[17] The official debut of this new group took place before an enthusiastic WMC audience on 25 November 1954. The orchestra played symphonies by Abel, Haydn, Britten, and Mozart to glowing reviews; John Kraglund reported that the event marked "a significant step forward in the city's growing musical life."[18]

Neel later spearheaded the campaign for a new home for the Faculty of Music. That initiative resulted in the construction of the Edward Johnson Building, which officially opened in March 1964. The building housed a 500-seat concert hall, which was named Walter Hall in 1974 in memory of Arnold Walter; in 1985 the hall became home to the WMC series.

Two further Toronto debuts followed in the next two concerts: the first by the Dutch pianist Daniel Wayenberg on 27 January 1955, and the second by the young French violinist Gérard Jarry on 3 March 1955. But these events were overshadowed by the last concert of the season, the Canadian debut of Dietrich Fischer-Dieskau on 21 April 1955. The young baritone, who was still a month shy of his thirtieth birthday, was already a leading singer with the opera companies in Berlin, Munich, and Vienna, had appeared at the Bayreuth and Edinburgh Festivals, and had made several highly praised recordings. There was intense excitement in the press and musical circles leading up to the concert, and the audience was not disappointed. On the program were the six Heine songs from Schubert's *Schwanengesang* and a complete performance of Schumann's *Dichterliebe*. The critic Hugh Thomson wrote that "the members forgot their club manners and let fly with a lusty cheering ovation," and he gave credit to Gerald Moore by adding that "there were two stars on stage, singer and accompanist."[19] Kraglund called the recital "one of this year's truly outstanding concerts," and stated that it was "never less than superlative."[20]

Fischer-Dieskau himself has given an account of the WMC recital in his memoirs, in which he pays tribute to Gerald Moore's talents as a pianist:

In Toronto my recital was scheduled for two o'clock in the afternoon, at that time the usual hour for the women's clubs, where by definition no men were allowed to be in attendance. The friend with whom we were staying stopped her car at a department store. When she saw our bewilderment, she told us simply to go in and find the elevator. We were to take it to the seventh floor, where we would have no trouble finding the concert. And so, forge ahead into the noontime crowd to celebrate the *Dichterliebe* somewhere. At the indicated floor the loudspeaker announced, "Children's wear."

We got off anyway. A silent man in livery was waiting and led us to a greenroom whose door opened onto the stage. And what a surprise: a pretty auditorium with about eight hundred seats and good acoustics. Before we started on the Schubert, Gerald went on the stage alone. I was about to follow him, but he gestured me to remain behind. His fabulous touch coaxed the British national anthem from the piano; clearly he had practiced it often and had long since become used to performing it.[21]

An article in the *Globe and Mail* revealed what was going on on the other side of that elevator door before the concert started:

Voices and rustlings, at first murmorous and indistinct, increased and merged in a resonant hum from the audience at Eaton Auditorium. Backstage, executive members of the Women's Musical Club of Toronto listened with growing dismay.

The concert, sponsored by the club, should have been a rare moment for the executive. But something was missing — the artist, a famous German baritone. . . .

The clock was ticking off the final minutes to curtain time when an elevator door slid open and a figure jiggled from behind a crowd and came out at a half-run: The missing artist. He hoped they hadn't worried. He had come upon an old friend and had spent the day at his Port Credit home. The artist stepped before his audience and burst into song ("I, Atlas, the cursed, have to bear the burden of the world . . ."). Backstage, members of the Women's Musical Club silently added one more unsettling memory to an already abundant score.[22]

Despite the worries he caused, Fischer-Dieskau was quickly hired for a return engagement, an open evening concert on 25 October 1956. On that occasion he sang Schubert's *Winterreise*, accompanied by Leo Taubman. The cycle was sung without intermission or applause before a spellbound standing-room-only crowd. Kraglund summed it up simply: "It was an evening long to be remembered."[23]

The annual meeting of the WMC was held in Eaton Auditorium on 28 April 1955, one week after the Fischer-Dieskau concert, and it marked the close of an era for the club. Doris Godson Gilmour ended her term as president, and longtime members Judith Grant Howse Finch, Mary Osler Boyd, and Pearl Steinhoff Whitehead all resigned from the executive committee. Bertha Mason Woods was the sole member of the old

FIGURE 15

Kathleen Irwin Wells (at the piano), the nineteenth
president of the WMC, and Pauline Mills McGibbon,
a vice-president of the club, in 1955.

guard to remain, and within a year she too had stepped down because of ill health. These five women between them had held the presidency of the WMC from 1929 on, and with their resignations more than a quarter of a century of the club's history came to an end. But the strength of the WMC has always been that as one group retires, another is ready to take its place, and so on this occasion, as always, the club continued on its path without skipping a beat.

The newer members of the executive had already made their impact. During the past year, a special committee under Pauline Mills McGibbon, who was the third vice-president of the WMC at the time, had revised the Constitution of the club with the assistance of Mr. Justice Dalton Wells of the Supreme Court of Ontario and Mr. D.J. Ongley. Aside from some minor changes made by Mary Osler Boyd in 1949, the Constitution had not been altered since 1923. According to the revised Constitution, which was ratified at a special meeting held on 3 March 1955 before the Gérard Jarry concert, at least one new member had to be added to the executive committee each year, and no member of the executive could hold the same position for longer than three years. These measures had first been proposed twenty-five years earlier, but were only now brought into effect. The regular infusion of new blood into the WMC executive committee ranks was now constitutionally guaranteed. At the annual meeting in 1957 an amendment to Article III of the Constitution was approved, which stated, "General membership in the Club shall be restricted to women."[24] Interestingly enough, there had been nothing in the Constitution up to that time that would have forbidden men from joining the WMC, should any have chosen to do so.

The new president of the WMC was Kathleen Irwin Wells, whose husband had helped to revise the Constitution. Kay Wells was a pianist who had performed in a duo with Winifred MacMillan (Ernest MacMillan's sister and pupil) in the 1930s. She had joined the WMC when it was revived in 1946, had been head of the Rehearsal Club when it disbanded in 1947, and had subsequently filled various positions on the executive committee. Among those who joined the WMC executive during her term as president were Amy Fleming Timmins and Margaret Young Snell, both of whom later became the president of the club. By a clever and convenient new plan that Kay Wells arranged, WMC members could join by phoning Eaton's and putting the membership fee on their charge account. A less popular plan of hers, no doubt, was to raise the membership fee from eight dollars to ten dollars.

In the sixtieth season, Jessie Macpherson, who was the dean of women and a professor of ethics at Victoria College, University of Toronto, and

148

had earlier been head of the women's committee of the Mendelssohn Choir, became the new president of the WMC. Kay Wells and Jessie Macpherson both remained on the WMC executive after their two-year term as president was over; Wells served until 1964 and Macpherson stayed on until 1962. Both women also wrote short articles outlining the history of the WMC.[25]

The fifty-eighth season got off to a shaky start when the originally scheduled artists for the first two concerts had to be changed. The Ukrainian-born U.S. pianist Shura Cherkassy was to have opened the series, but that plan fell through, and the Cuban-born U.S. pianist Jacob Lateiner was the substitute artist on 20 October 1955. An even bigger disappointment occurred when the Berlin Chamber Orchestra, which was to have given an open concert on 2 November 1955, cancelled its North American tour with only a week's notice after the orchestra's conductor, Hans von Benda, decided that he was too old to face the rigours of an extended tour. (Benda, who had founded the Berlin Chamber Orchestra in 1939, was only sixty-six years old in 1955 and lived to age eighty-three!) This cancellation cost the WMC nearly $250, as the tickets and programs for the concert had already been printed. In place of this event, an extra concert was added on at the end of the season. The substitute group was the Mozarteum Orchestra of Salzburg, which was featured in its Canadian debut on 20 April 1956. The orchestra was conducted by Ernst Maerzendorfer and appeared with two vocal soloists, the soprano Emmy Loose and the baritone Ralph Herbert. The program was entirely devoted to works by Mozart, as it was the bicenntenial of that composer's birth in Salzburg. The artists' fees for this concert amounted to $2,500, a far larger sum than had ever been spent before on a single concert. Accordingly the concert venue was switched to Massey Hall, which seated over twice as many people as Eaton Auditorium, and with a vigorous advertising campaign the WMC managed to attract a large enough audience to cover its expenses. The concert was dedicated to the memory of Mary Osler Boyd, who had died just over three months earlier.

The WMC caught a rising star when it presented the local recital debut of the twenty-five-year-old Montreal-born contralto Maureen Forrester on 9 February 1956. The singer was on a coast-to-coast tour of Canada with her accompanist John Newmark; the two had recently completed a two-and-a-half-month tour of eight countries in Europe for the Jeunesses Musicales organization. The newspapers reported that Forrester was the first Canadian singer to make an extended tour of Europe in more than twenty years, and the engagement earned her the honorary title of "Canada's Singing Ambassadress."[26] The excitement in the local press was even greater than it had been for the Fischer-Dieskau debut the previous season; the papers obviously took great pride in the accomplishments of this young Canadian artist. The violist Otto Joachim of Montreal assisted in the WMC recital, playing a viola sonata by Milhaud and accompanying Forrester in a song cycle by the U.S. composer Norman Peterkin for contralto and viola and in the two Brahms songs, Op. 91, for contralto, viola, and piano. Also on the program were three early German songs and works by Schumann and Britten. Hugh Thomson wrote that "Miss Forrester showed herself no common singer, but a truly great young artist," and accurately predicted that "some day [she] will be famous!"[27]

Maureen Forrester has remained grateful for the opportunities that came her way from women's musical clubs in Canada. Early in her career she won a prize and a concert engagement from the Ladies' Morning Musical Club in Montreal, and she went on to perform for women's musical clubs in centres large and small across Canada. This provided a useful intermediate stage between student recitals and professional engagements. In her memoirs, Forrester lamented the decline of the women's musical club movement:

> It's a shame that there isn't a circuit of clubs and concert societies like it today for young singers to gain experience. Now women work or play golf and go off to Hawaii; they don't go to daytime concerts. As a result, there aren't the outlets for a young generation of musicians to apprentice in quite the way that I did. In those days you could build a career step by step, but today you graduate from a conservatory, you give a recital, and right away you're on the firing line. . . . In a sense my career came at the end of an era.[28]

Forrester may have overstated the case somewhat. Women's musical clubs in Canada were already less numerous in the late 1950s than they were during the heyday of the movement forty years earlier, but the decline has been very gradual, and a significant number continue to offer performance opportunities to the young artists of today.

Other Toronto debuts during the WMC's fifty-eighth season featured the Czech-born soprano Eva Likova on 1 December 1955 and the Swiss pianist Karl Engel on 19 January 1956. Likova, who was based in New York City at the time, gave the first concert performance of the song cycle *Dissidence* by the young Quebec composer Pierre Mercure as part of her recital. Engel played works by Mozart, Schubert, Schumann, and

Ravel to glowing reviews. The season also featured a recital by the violinist Alexander Schneider, accompanied by Artur Balsam, on 15 March 1956. Schneider, who was an outstanding musician and musical activist, cannot have regarded the recital as one of the highlights of his career. He played to a small house and was greeted with largely hostile reviews in the local press.

The fifty-ninth season opened with the return of Fischer-Dieskau, which was followed by a series of outstanding debuts: the pianist Louis Kentner (8 November 1956), the Hungarian String Quartet (29 November 1956), the Vienna Octet (24 January 1957), and the pianist Kendall Taylor (14 February 1957). The season closed with a recital by the African American soprano Adele Addison on 21 March 1957. Then the sixtieth season offered the debuts of the soprano Leontyne Price (7 November 1957), the Barylli Quartet (21 November 1957), the Quartetto di Roma (30 January 1958), the mezzo-soprano Christa Ludwig (13 February 1958), and the pianist István Nadas (20 March 1958), as well as concerts by I Solisti di Zagreb with Antonio Janigro as conductor and cello soloist (24 October 1957) and the Toronto pianist Raymond Dudley (5 December 1957). Taken together, these two seasons represent arguably the greatest concentration of musical talent in the entire history of the WMC.

The popular Hungarian-born English pianist Louis Kentner was featured in his Toronto debut three weeks before he made his U.S. debut in New York. The Hungarian Quartet performed works by Haydn, Beethoven, and Schubert. John Kraglund was particularly enthusiastic about its leader, Zoltán Székely, writing, "Rarely have we heard such purity of tone, accuracy of intonation and a willingness to maintain a precise balance with the other players."[29] The Hungarian Quartet returned for a second WMC recital on 22 October 1959, when it played works by Mozart and Beethoven. Székely, who became a Canadian citizen in 1979, had a significant influence on string playing in Canada; he moved to Canada in the early 1970s and taught at the Banff Centre for the Arts beginning in 1975.

The Vienna Octet was made up of Vienna Philharmonic Orchestra members. It was formed in 1947 and was led by the violinist Willi Boskowsky; all of the members were first-desk players in the orchestra. The concert, which featured the Beethoven Septet and the Schubert Octet, drew a crowd of over one thousand people, including many Toronto Symphony Orchestra members and other local musicians. Hugh Thomson wrote that "Eaton Auditorium looked for all the world like a musicians' convention."[30] The octet was invited back for a second concert on 27 November 1958 and a third one on 3 March 1966.

Kendall Taylor's concert took place during a heavy snowstorm, which reduced the attendance. His performing style had at least one thing in common with that of Glenn Gould: he continually made unpleasant vocal sounds as he performed, according to one local critic.[31] Taylor returned to Toronto later in 1957 under better weather conditions to teach at the Royal Conservatory's summer school.

Adele Addison's recital took place on the same date as an evening concert in Eaton Auditorium by another soprano, Blanche Thebom. Addison took the honours on this occasion. She was a protégée of Dorothy Maynor, and was widely admired as a lieder recitalist. Her program for the WMC began with classical selections and concluded with four spirituals. Addison had appeared only once before in Toronto when, early in her career, she had been a last-minute replacement for Lotte Lehmann in 1951.[32] John Kraglund wrote that her WMC recital was "another triumph for the singer" and "a superlative concert."[33]

I Solisti di Zagreb, which opened the sixtieth season, was on its first North American tour when it was presented by the WMC. The Yugoslav chamber orchestra would return twenty years later for its second WMC recital on an historic occasion — the last WMC concert to be held in Eaton Auditorium.

The other instrumentalists heard during the sixtieth season were also well received. Raymond Dudley was a pupil of Alberto Guerrero, and István Nadas was a pupil of Béla Bartók. Dudley had won the second WMC scholarship in 1951 and was teaching at Indiana University at the time of his WMC recital. The Barylli Quartet, like the Vienna Octet, was made up of Vienna Philharmonic members; it had been founded during the war by Walter Barylli, who was the concertmaster of the orchestra at the time. The Quartetto di Roma attracted a large crowd for its program of piano quartets by Beethoven, Brahms, and the modern Italian composer Ennio Porrino.

The appearance of Leontyne Price generated an excitement in the local press comparable to that aroused by the appearances of Fischer-Dieskau and Forrester. Price had sung with the Toronto Symphony Orchestra, but this was her first local recital. With David Garvey as her accompanist, she sang classical selections ranging from Handel to Britten, and concluded with six spirituals. The thirty-year-old Price was just then coming into her own as an opera diva, thanks in no small measure to her idol Marian Anderson, who had broken the colour barrier at the Metropolitan Opera in 1955. Price's WMC recital fell in the midst of an engagement with the San Francisco Opera, for she was called in unexpectedly to sing

FIGURE 16

Leontyne Price on the day of her Toronto recital debut
for the WMC (7 November 1957) with Jessie Macpherson,
the president of the WMC at the time.

FIGURE 17

Margaret Young Snell presents WMC awards to
Walter Buczynski and Teresa Stratas in 1958.

Aïda in place of Antonietta Stella, who had developed appendicitis.[34] Price flew into Toronto from San Francisco on the day of her recital, and had to fly out later the same day, but she graciously agreed to stay for a reception and tea held in her honour at the Toronto Ladies Club. The WMC was fortunately able to engage her again for an open concert at the end of the next season on 2 April 1959. That recital included the first performance of *Cantata Sacra* by the young African American composer John Carter; each movement of the work was based on a different spiritual.

Three months after the Price recital, the German singer Christa Ludwig was featured in her North American debut. Although still a month shy of her thirtieth birthday, Ludwig had already established herself as one of the leading mezzo-sopranos of the day through her appearances on stage in Europe. As the local German newspaper pointed out, she would have already been known to many in Toronto from her performance as Octavian in a recently issued recording of *Der Rosenkavalier* conducted by Herbert von Karajan.[35] For the WMC, Ludwig sang lieder by Schubert, Brahms, Wolf, Strauss, and Mahler, accompanied by Henry Jackson. Among those in the audience, interestingly, was Gerald Moore, who had recently accompanied Ludwig in a Wigmore Hall recital that featured many of the same works as those on the WMC program. Hugh Thomson reported that in the opening Schubert group, Jackson sounded "almost amateurish" but "picked up as the recital went on."[36] Perhaps his style was a little cramped when he learned that Moore was in the audience!

It was fitting that at the end of a season which had featured recitals by Leontyne Price and Christa Ludwig, the Mary Osler Boyd Award should be presented to a nineteen-year-old local music student who showed considerable promise as a singer herself — Teresa Stratas. A second award was made that year, in memory of Mrs. J.G. Fitzgerald, a longtime WMC member who died suddenly on 31 January 1958. This second award was won by the pianist and composer Walter Buczynski.

In addition to Fitzgerald, two other longtime members died that season: Mrs. Tower Fergusson, a contralto who had sung in a WMC recital as early as 1908 (the club received some valuable early programs from her estate); and Mrs. Douglas Ridout (the mother of the composer Godfrey Ridout), who had served on the executive committee for many years. The WMC had suffered the loss of many of its senior members within a short period, but nevertheless had enjoyed a period of great stability on the whole. The membership consistently hovered at just under six hundred women, and six concerts had been given every year from the fiftieth through the fifty-ninth seasons, with a modest increase to seven concerts in the sixtieth season. There had been so many sensational debuts during the past ten years that the reputation of the WMC as a discoverer of new talent was at an all-time high. Other women's musical clubs may have been on the decline by the late 1950s, but for the WMC the best was just beginning.

NOTES

[1] Schabas 233.

[2] *Music for Dancing* was Beckwith's first commissioned piece; it was premiered by Beckwith and Dudley at the Royal Conservatory of Music on 15 January 1949 (John Beckwith, letters to the author, 3 and 19 Nov. 1995).

[3] The Parlow Quartet recorded the Pépin work for Radio Canada International on RCI 12, 1950, reissued on *Anthology of Canadian Music*, vol. 5, 1980.

[4] Rose Macdonald, "Sensuous Far East Dances Give Beauty of Ice and Fire," *Telegram* 18 Oct. 1950: 7.

[5] Mary Osler Boyd, "Concert Convenor's Report," WMC *Annual Report Fifty-Third Year 1950–51*.

[6] Unfortunately the WMC *Executive Committee Minutes* for the fifty-second through fifty-fifth seasons (1949–53) were inadvertently destroyed, and so the discussions leading up to the decision to begin awarding the scholarship have been lost.

[7] Leo Smith, "Music in Toronto: Harpsichord, Violin and Flute Heard at Second Concert of Women's Musical Club," *Globe and Mail* 7 Dec. 1951: 8.

[8] Mária Kresz and Péter Király, *The Violinist and Pianist Géza de Kresz and Norah Drewett: Their Life and Music on Two Continents* (Toronto: Canadian Stage and Arts, 1989) 166, 171.

[9] John Kraglund, "Music in Toronto: Audience Cheers Seefried Concert, Begs Encores," *Globe and Mail* 28 Oct. 1952: 23.

[10] Hugh Thomson, "Cesare Siepi Opens for Women's Club," *Toronto Daily Star* 27 Oct. 1953: 53.

[11] John Kraglund, "Music in Toronto: Pianist Gives Evidence Canadians Can Take Place among Best Artists," *Globe and Mail* 20 Nov. 1953: 12.

[12] Otto Friedrich, *Glenn Gould: A Life and Variations* (Toronto: Lester, 1989) 69.

[13] Doris Gilmour, "Address of the President," WMC *Annual Reports Season 1953–54*.

[14] Kresz and Király 172.

[15] John Kraglund, "Music in Toronto: Betty-Jean Hagen Heard in First Toronto Appearance since Winning Medal," *Globe and Mail* 11 Dec. 1953: 32.

[16] George Kidd, "Clap, Laugh as U-K Pianist Gives 'Lesson,' " *Telegram* 8 Oct. 1954.

[17] Boyd Neel, *My Orchestras and Other Adventures: The Memoirs of Boyd Neel*, ed. J. David Finch (Toronto: U of Toronto P, 1985) 159–60.

[18] John Kraglund, "Music in Toronto: Hart House Orchestra Is Reality," *Globe and Mail* 26 Nov. 1954: 1.

[19] Hugh Thomson, "Fischer-Dieskau Debut Greeted with Cheering," *Toronto Daily Star* 22 Apr. 1955: 13.

[20] John Kraglund, "Music in Toronto," *Globe and Mail* 22 Apr. 1955: 9.

[21] Dietrich Fischer-Dieskau, *Reverberations: The Memoirs of Dietrich Fischer-Dieskau*, trans. Ruth Hein (New York: Fromm, 1989) 320–21.

[22] Brian Magner, "Impresarios with a Mission," *Globe and Mail* 17 Oct. 1959, Globe Magazine: 14. Fischer-Dieskau is not mentioned by name in the article, but he is the only German baritone to have begun his WMC recital with Schubert's "Der Atlas" from *Schwanengesang*.

[23] John Kraglund, "Music in Toronto," *Globe and Mail* 26 Oct. 1956: 14.

[24] "General Business: Changes in the Constitution," WMC *Annual Reports Season 1956–57*. Article III was changed in 1989 to open the general membership to both women and men.

[25] Kathleen Irwin Wells, "The Women's Musical Club of Toronto," *BSS Bulletin* Apr. 1956: n.p.; Jessie Macpherson, "Women's Musical Clubs," *Canadian Music Journal* 5.4 (1961): 45–47.

[26] Maureen Forrester with Marci McDonald, *Out of Character: A Memoir* (Toronto: McClelland, 1986) 109.

[27] Hugh Thomson, "Maureen Forrester Said 'Tops' in Eaton's Debut," *Toronto Daily Star* 10 Feb. 1956: 4.

[28] Forrester and McDonald 100.

[29] John Kraglund, "Music in Toronto," *Globe and Mail* 30 Nov. 1956: 15.

[30] Hugh Thomson, "Women's Club Sponsors Debut of Vienna Octet," *Toronto Daily Star* 25 Jan. 1957: 4.

[31] George Kidd, "Technical Brilliance Displayed by Pianist — But No Vocals, Please," *Telegram* 15 Feb. 1957: 27.

[32] George Kidd, "An Autograph to Remember," *Telegram* 17 Mar. 1957: 1D, gives a charming account of Addison's first Toronto concert in 1951.

[33] John Kraglund, "Music in Toronto," *Globe and Mail* 22 Mar. 1957: 9.

[34] Story 108.

[35] "Christa Ludwig gastiert in Toronto," *Toronto Courier* 6 Feb. 1958. The recording was Richard Strauss, *Der Rosenkavalier*, cond. Herbert von Karajan, Philharmonia Orch. and soloists, Angel 3563, 1957.

[36] Hugh Thomson, "Vienna's Christa Ludwig Sings Debut at Eaton's," *Toronto Daily Star* 14 Feb. 1958: 13.

9

A Decade of Growth

B uoyed by the wonderful slate of artists who had appeared during the 1950s, the WMC soared to new heights in the 1960s and reached its highest membership levels ever. In addition to building on its long-standing reputation for bringing promising young solo recitalists to Toronto, the WMC won new esteem during this period as a presenter of chamber music groups — the number that appeared in its series doubled compared to the previous decade. With a well-nigh infallible sense of what was good for the club and what Toronto audiences wanted to hear, the WMC executive guided the organization to a golden era.

The 1960s were a golden era for Toronto also. The metropolitan area came into its own as a major urban centre of one and a half million inhabitants (1961 census), but did not yet suffer from the high crime rate, overcrowding, and other attendant evils that plagued most cities its size. The growing cosmopolitan mix of the city is illustrated by the fact that by the end of the decade fifty percent of the city was of non-Anglo-Celtic origin.[1] The new City Hall, completed in 1965, became the city's most famous landmark and symbolized Toronto's outlook at the time — modern, bold, and confident. Further excitement was generated by the celebrations of Canada's Centennial in 1967. Throughout the decade a wide range of outstanding musical performances was on offer, from the premiere of *Camelot* at the new O'Keefe Centre for the Performing Arts in 1960, through the Beatles at Maple Leaf Gardens in 1964, to concerts of the Toronto Symphony under its exciting young Japanese conductor Seiji Ozawa from 1965 to 1969. The WMC could only benefit from the energy and enthusiasm that were in the air during this era.

An important innovation for the WMC occurred on 22 April 1958, when the executive committee decided to allow men to become members. This was an interesting development, especially in light of the fact that the Constitution had been changed only the previous year to restrict general membership in the club to women. The executive committee got around that article of the Constitution by creating a new category of associate membership for men. This granted the male members no privileges other than concert attendance, which cost them the same fee as the women members. The associate members would have no say in the running of the club and could not serve on the executive committee, but for the first time ever, any man could attend all of the concerts in the WMC series simply by paying the ten-dollar fee for the season.

A second change in the membership structure occurred two months later. On 20 June 1958 a group membership for the Royal Conservatory of Music and the Faculty of Music was created. For a small annual fee of one hundred dollars, music students and staff were allowed to attend any of the afternoon concerts in the WMC series. The Royal Conservatory withdrew from the plan in 1966, but the Faculty of Music continued to hold a group membership with the WMC into the 1970s. The group plan increased the audience numbers for the WMC's concerts, but it also drew the club unwittingly into the Faculty of Music's card-punching fiasco.

In 1965 the Faculty of Music Council decided that students would be required to attend at least eighty percent of the university's Thursday afternoon lecture and concert series. Each student received a card, which had to be punched at the door of the event and turned in at the end of term. The WMC series was listed in the Faculty of Music's calendar of events, and so its concerts counted towards the eighty percent attendance requirement for music students. John Beckwith has described how the card-punching idea was received by those involved:

> Students found the rule a drastic one, but they also invented various ways to get round it: by having the card punched at the main entrance to the hall and then exiting by another door, or by having someone else present the card for punching. There were student-organized protest meetings and petitions, an editorial in the student press, and at length on 2 October 1969 a weary Dean and Acting Director posted a notice: "The Faculty Council held a meeting on Thursday . . . at which it was decided to abolish the punching of cards at Thursday afternoon events."[2]

The abolition of the card-punching routine had an immediate and drastic effect on student attendance at WMC events. Whereas previously an average of two hundred music students had attended each WMC recital, after card punching was abolished about one-third that number turned up.

There were two further categories of membership in the early 1960s: professional musicians could subscribe for five dollars (half the regular fee), and students in disciplines other than music could join for three dollars.[3] It must have been confusing to administer and control five different categories of membership (regular, associate, group, professional, and student), but perhaps in the end it was worth it, for during this period the WMC numbers grew steadily each year to reach their highest levels ever. Eaton Auditorium was regularly filled to capacity, and tickets for the general public to the open concerts were in short supply. The WMC concert series, in short, was one of the most coveted tickets in Toronto.

During the sixty-first season, the second year of Jessie Macpherson's presidency, the WMC concerts featured a combination of new faces and old friends. The Vienna Octet (27 November 1958), Rosalyn Tureck (4 December 1958), and Leontyne Price (2 April 1959) all made return appearances, while the singers Donald Bell (16 October 1958) and Ana Raquel Satre (12 February 1959), along with the pianist Gary Graffman (30 October 1958), were introduced to Toronto audiences. In addition there was an appearance by the Toronto Woodwind Quintet (19 March 1959), the first of four woodwind quintets that the club would feature over the next seven years.

Rosalyn Tureck, who had not yet found widespread fame at the time of her two WMC concerts a decade earlier, was now much better known, having won success in Europe in the meantime. Perhaps inevitably, comparisons were made this time around with Glenn Gould, who in the intervening ten years had become the other great Bach pianist of the day. The comparisons even extended to the subject of idiosyncratic mannerisms. John Kraglund devoted a whole column to Tureck's custom-made elbow-length mittens and her use of a hot water bottle to warm up the keyboard on cold days.[4] On the occasion of her return appearance with the WMC the next season on 29 February 1960, the local papers again revelled in Tureck's eccentricities. The *Globe and Mail* revealed her concert-day ritual (a massage, several hours at the piano, a special meal, and a nap) but judged that she was not quite as eccentric as Wanda Landowska, who used to travel with her own black silk sheets.[5] The *Telegram* made much of the fact that Tureck practised yoga to relax, and both papers commented once again on her special mittens.[6] Despite this fascination with Tureck's offstage mannerisms, it was her playing that mattered, and on both occasions she drew a capacity audience for two all-Bach programs that earned her glowing reviews.

The recital by Donald Bell recalled the exciting debut of Fischer-Dieskau three years earlier. The twenty-four-year-old baritone from South Burnaby, B.C., was virtually unknown in Toronto but had already scored some significant triumphs in Europe. He had studied for two years in Berlin with Hermann Weissenborn, who had been Fischer-Dieskau's teacher, and a few months before his WMC recital Bell had made his debut at Bayreuth as the Night Watchman in *Die Meistersinger von Nürnberg*. Bell's recital accompanist was John Newmark, who flew from Montreal to rehearse with the young singer in Germany. Expectations were high for the WMC event, which was billed as Bell's North American professional debut. Bell rose to the occasion and gave an outstanding performance of lieder by Schubert, Brahms, Wolf, and Loewe. The critic Hugh Thomson predicted, "Here is an artist who should gain the international fame of Glenn Gould, Lois Marshall and Maureen Forrester. You wait and see!"[7] Bell returned twice more to give recitals for the WMC, on 5 November 1959 and on 9 February 1967, accompanied by Newmark on both occasions. The 1967 recital included the premiere of Oskar Morawetz's *Four Songs on Poems by Bliss Carman*, which was a Centennial commission written especially for Bell.

In her outgoing address as president, delivered at the annual meeting on 16 April 1959, Jessie Macpherson voiced satisfaction in all aspects of the year just passed except for the financial report, which showed a deficit that, though small, was still large enough to wipe out the bank balance left over from the previous year and put the club $120 into the red at the end of the season. Eustella Burke Langdon was elected at that same meeting as the new WMC president. Before moving to Toronto with her husband John E. Langdon, an investment dealer with McLeod, Young, Weir and Ratcliffe, Eustella Langdon had been president of the highly successful Ladies' Morning Musical Club of Montreal. In addition to serving as president of the WMC for two years, she was concert convenor for ten years. With advice from an enormous circle of musical friends, she was able to attract stellar performers to the WMC at fees that did not exceed the club's limited budget. The headline of a newspaper article about Eustella Langdon said it all: "Amateur Impresario Outguesses the Pros."[8]

Before the sixty-second season started, a fairly lengthy article about the WMC appeared in the *Globe and Mail*,[9] which may have helped to boost the membership numbers that season (the total increased from 564 to 662). Eustella Langdon, who had been interviewed for the article, pointed out that the WMC was no longer a closed organization — "For this club that day is gone, just as the day of the amateur performance is gone," she stated.[10] The article mentioned that the WMC concert series filled a fully professional role in Toronto's musical world, despite the fact that the club operated on a shoestring budget with no outside financial support. The article also stated that a performer on the theremin, an electronic musical instrument invented in the U.S.S.R. in 1922, once appeared in a WMC recital. Unfortunately no corroboration of this event has yet come to light.

The sixty-second season, like the sixty-first, featured three return appearances, three debuts, and one local ensemble. The Hungarian String Quartet, Donald Bell, and Rosalyn Tureck were the returnees, while the new artists were the U.S. pianist Richard Goode (19 November 1959), the Swiss tenor Ernst Häfliger (21 January 1960), and the Saidenburg Chamber Players from New York (24 March 1960). The local group was the Toronto Baroque Ensemble, led by Greta Kraus in a well-received concert on 3 December 1959.

Richard Goode was one of the youngest performers ever to be presented in a WMC recital. He was only sixteen years old at the time of his Canadian debut for the club, and his concert of works by Mozart, Beethoven, Brahms, and Schubert led John Kraglund to write that "we have frequently heard less thoughtful interpretations by artists of long-established fame. . . . the young artist left nothing to be desired in matters of nuance and phrasing."[11] Goode returned for two further WMC solo recitals on 26 October 1961 and 7 November 1963, and was the accompanist for a joint recital by Benita Valente and Harold Wright on 23 January 1964. Each appearance was greeted by warm reviews in the local papers.

Towards the end of the 1959–60 season it was reported in the WMC executive committee minutes that "there is a possibility of Eaton Auditorium being closed in the not too distant future."[12] The rumour was unfounded as it turned out, but it was a foretaste of the uncertainty about the fate of Eaton Auditorium that would plague the WMC for years before the auditorium was actually closed in 1977.

Controversies over modern music surfaced for the first time in the WMC during the 1960–61 season. In the earliest years, WMC recitals had not infrequently featured music by living composers, but over the years the programs had come to reflect the increasing conservatism of the concert music world at large. Since the time of the reorganization of the WMC in 1946, very little music by living composers, and none by those representing the avante-garde movement, had been heard in club recitals. Then, in the course of one season, the members were introduced to Aaron Copland's Piano Variations, Alvin Etler's Quintet for woodwinds, and two works for violin and piano — Anton Webern's *Vier Stücke*, Op. 7, and Igor Stravinsky's *Duo Concertant*. Only the Etler work was a recent one, but the other works provided a good sampling of prewar avant-garde styles. Some of the wmc members were clearly not impressed that such music was being included in the concert series, and they let their feelings be known to the executive committee. In her final address as president, delivered at the annual meeting on 13 April 1961, Eustella Langdon spoke out in defence of modern music:

> Of all the music presented at the Club this season, that which has aroused most interest and most controversy is the Contemporary, which is only normal and also a very good thing.
>
> After all, it isn't important whether we *love* contemporary music or *hate* it or are merely bored by it. The point of real importance is to hear it, and hear it authoritatively performed by musicians of deep conviction. We feel quite definitely that this policy has been carried out in a highly successful manner this season. . . . Let it be known then, that the Women's Musical Club of Toronto gives outstanding contemporary music an open-minded hearing. After all, the music most of us love and which is so familiar now, was once contemporary music, and some of the best of it, had a very poor reception at the start.[13]

The local music critics were also divided on the question of the merits of contemporary music. At the *Toronto Daily Star*, the duties of music critic were split between two composers, John Beckwith and Udo Kasemets, and both were enthusiastic about the inclusion of contemporary music in the wmc programs. Kasemets wrote, "Not only does this vital club introduce first class artists to the local public — it also offers programs which contain a respectable amount of 20th century music," and he added that the wmc series was "on its way to becoming one of the most outstanding musical events in this city."[14] George Kidd at the *Telegram* and John Kraglund at the *Globe and Mail* were more reserved about contemporary music; they did not write anything negative about the pieces featured in the wmc series, but neither did they wax enthusiastic about them, as Beckwith and Kasemets did.

The musicians responsible for programming the above-mentioned contemporary works were the U.S. pianist William Masselos, who played the Copland *Piano Variations* in his Canadian debut on 20

October 1960; the New York Woodwind Quintet, which featured the Etler quintet in its Toronto debut on 1 December 1960; and Paul Lee, piano, with Paul Makanowitzky, violin, who performed the Webern and Stravinsky pieces along with works by Beethoven and Franck on 2 March 1961. Masselos returned the next season for a WMC recital on 1 February 1962 that included the first local performance of the First Piano Sonata by Charles Ives, a work that he had recorded. Four of the sonata's five movements were included on the program. Kasemets found the sonata to be "a marvellous kaleidoscope of life,"[15] but Kraglund's initial impression was that the work "seemed a disjointed jungle of irrelevant dissonance."[16] Lee and Makanowitzky returned for a second WMC recital on 13 February 1964. They performed violin sonatas by Bach, Beethoven, Debussy, and Bartók on that occasion.

Other featured artists during the sixty-third season were the McGill Chamber Orchestra under Alexander Brott (3 November 1960), the Spanish soprano Consuelo Rubio in her Canadian debut (17 November 1960), the Hungarian pianist Annie Fischer in her Toronto debut (2 February 1961), and the young Canadian baritone John Boyden (13 April 1961).

At the end of the season Eustella Langdon stepped down as president but retained her duties as concert convenor. The new president was Margaret (Peggy) Young Snell, who was a member of the WMC executive from 1956 to 1967 and, as of 1995, was the earliest living president of the club. She was also one of the founders of the National Youth Orchestra in 1960. One of Peggy Snell's first acts as president was to strike a Constitution Committee that was chaired by Pauline Mills McGibbon, who had served in the same position for the previous revision of the WMC Constitution in 1955. The revisions to the Constitution this time around were fairly minor and involved details about the election of the executive committee. The most important change was that the maximum term of office for any elected officer of the WMC was reduced from three to two years. These changes to the Constitution were ratified at the next annual meeting on 5 April 1962. That same month, Pauline McGibbon resigned from the executive, but it was by no means her last contact with the club. Indeed, during her term as the lieutenant governor of Ontario she hosted two receptions for the WMC, one in April 1974, and one in February 1978 that was attended by over two hundred members.

In addition to return appearances by the pianists Richard Goode and William Masselos, the sixty-fourth season featured the Toronto debuts of two sopranos, Miriam Burton (23 November 1961) and Rita Streich (1 March 1962), and concerts by two chamber groups, the Quintetto

Chigiano (9 November 1961) and the Beaux Arts Trio (5 April 1962). Greta Kraus also made her fourth WMC appearance at the harpsichord, leading a group of local musicians in a concert of baroque music on 7 December 1961. Just as she had ten years earlier, Kraus used the occasion to introduce another new harpsichord from her personal collection.

The Quintetto Chigiano, described at the time as the only permanent ensemble of its kind in the world, was a piano quintet from Siena that had been founded in 1939 under the patronage of Count Guido Chigi Saracini. The Count was an Italian nobleman who had personally revived the musical life of Siena by spending over a million dollars of his personal fortune to found the Accademia Musicale Chigiana (a music school) in 1932 and the Settimana Musicale Senese (an annual music festival) in 1939. The Quintetto Chigiano played on priceless musical instruments from the count's own fabulous personal collection. The instruments have recently been restored and are still in use by pupils at the Accademia Musicale Chigiana.[17]

The sixty-fourth season closed on a high note with peerless performances of works by Haydn, Ravel, and Beethoven by the Beaux Arts Trio, which had been formed in 1955 and was still performing with its original violinist, Daniel Guilet. George Kidd called it "a performance to remember,"[18] and John Beckwith stated, "It is concerts like this that renew one's faith in music."[19] The trio made a welcome return appearance on 21 November 1963 and gave two further recitals for the WMC in the early 1970s.

By the time of the 1962–63 season, concert activity in Toronto was beginning to intensify. Musical events were featured six or seven nights a week, often with two or more attractions on the same evening. Three organizations offered recital series similar in nature to that of the WMC. The big-ticket performers appeared in the International Artists series at Massey Hall, which was run by the impresario Walter Homburger. Among the musicians appearing in that series during the 1962–63 season were Artur Rubinstein, Daniel Barenboim, Wilhelm Kempff, Victoria de los Angeles, Birgit Nilsson, and Maureen Forrester. Local performers, including Teresa Stratas, the Canadian String Quartet, Greta Kraus, and the Hart House Orchestra, were highlighted that season in the Faculty of Music's concert series in the Edward Johnson Building. An eclectic new series dedicated to rarely heard music ranging from the Middle Ages to the present was offered for the first time that season by Ten Centuries Concerts, whose programs, like those of the WMC, were for the most part open only to subscribers.[20] When the performances by the Toronto Symphony, York Concert Society, Canadian Opera Company, National

Ballet of Canada, Toronto Mendelssohn Choir, and Festival Singers of Toronto are added into the mix, it can be appreciated that the competition for audiences and artists was beginning to grow intense. The WMC was able to hold its own for a number of reasons: the loyalty of its members, the wisdom of its executive, a careful choice of artists, and the fact that it was the only group sponsoring afternoon concerts.

The only evening concert and the only open event during the sixty-fifth season featured the German baritone Hermann Prey in his Toronto recital debut on 31 January 1963. The recital had been scheduled for a year earlier, but other commitments prevented Prey from keeping that engagement and his place was taken by Rita Streich. Although he was only thirty-three at the time, Prey had already performed widely in recital and had appeared in most of the leading opera houses in Europe and North America. His recital of lieder by Beethoven, Schubert, and Strauss provided further confirmation of the WMC's reputation for introducing the most exciting young singers of the day to Toronto audiences.

Other artists making their Toronto debut for the WMC that season were the U.S. soprano Carolyn Stanford (25 October 1962), the Kroll Quartet (8 November 1962), the U.S. pianist Lillian Kallir (22 November 1962), and the Trio di Bolzano (28 February 1963), which Eustella Langdon had heard while on vacation in Italy and had signed up on the spot. In addition Anton Kuerti was featured in his local recital debut (21 March 1963), and the Toronto Woodwind Quintet gave its second concert for the WMC (6 December 1962).

The violinist William Kroll had appeared in a WMC recital in 1923 with the Elshuco Trio, but he was still at the top of his form in 1962. John Kraglund called him "the dream violinist,"[21] and Udo Kasemets wrote that all four members of his quartet were "ideal chamber musicians."[22] Kraglund cited the WMC concerts by the Kroll Quartet and the Beaux Arts Trio as two of the highlights of 1962 in his year-end review of musical activity in Toronto.[23]

Anton Kuerti had first performed in Toronto in 1961, when he was a last-minute substitute for Myra Hess, who had cancelled her appearance with the Toronto Symphony. Then in 1963, Peter Serkin was taken ill and cancelled his WMC appearance on short notice. Eustella Langdon, the WMC concert convenor, decided to ask Kuerti to substitute, and after calling a dozen U.S. cities she finally caught up with him just as he was about to go off on a skiing trip. Kuerti agreed to put off his vacation and travel to Toronto instead. John Kraglund in his review of Kuerti's recital remarked, "let us hope his future appearances are frequent and planned, rather than accidental."[24] Peter Serkin and Kuerti were both pupils of the former's father, Rudolf Serkin, and both appeared in recital for the WMC during the 1964–65 season. Kuerti moved to Toronto in 1965 as the pianist-in-residence at the University of Toronto.

At the annual meeting on 21 March 1963 it was reported that the total membership for the 1962–63 season had reached 811, the highest level ever in the history of the WMC. A concerted campaign now began in earnest to raise the number to 1,000, at which point the plan was to close the membership and start a waiting list, just as the Ladies' Morning Musical Club of Montreal had done. At that same meeting Amy Fleming Timmins, a contralto and formerly a well-known Canadian concert singer, was elected as the new president. She had joined the WMC executive in 1955 and remained actively involved in the club until the 1970s.

The sixty-sixth season saw return appearances by the Beaux Arts Trio, the Lee-Makanowitzky duo, and Richard Goode, who appeared both in solo recital and as the accompanist for the season's open concert, which featured the soprano Benita Valente and the clarinettist Harold Wright. The new artists that season were the Quintetto Boccherini (24 October 1963), a cello quintet from Italy led by the violinist Pina Carmirelli; the Canadian baritone John Boyden (5 December 1963), who was accompanied in a recital of German, French, and English songs by the Canadian pianist Donald Hassard; and the German-born U.S. pianist Claude Frank (19 May 1964). The Quintetto Boccherini and Frank were appearing in their Toronto debuts; Frank made a return appearance on 21 October 1965.

This season was Eustella Langdon's last as concert convenor; she was succeeded by Trudy Graf, a German-born architect who had only recently joined the WMC. Kathleen Irwin Wells, who was head of the membership committee and had done much to raise the membership numbers to the highest level in the club's history (920 members as of 1 April 1964) also retired at the end of the season, as did Angela Watson Langlands, who had been the secretary-treasurer for the past twelve years. This season once again marked an occasion when many of the "old guard" retired and new faces, among them Muriel Gidley Stafford and Helen Christilaw Goudge, stepped in to replace them.

During the second season of Amy Fleming Timmins's presidency, Anton Kuerti was the only artist in the series who had performed previously for the WMC. The other artists that season were the Drolc Quartet from Germany (22 October 1964), the Sinhalese cellist Rohan de Saram (5 November 1964), the seventeen-year-old pianist Peter Serkin in his delayed Toronto debut (19 November 1964), the Festival Singers of Toronto (3 December 1964), the U.S. mezzo-soprano Grace Bumbry

(21 January 1965), and the Danzi Woodwind Quintet from Holland (11 March 1965). Serkin's recital on a Thursday afternoon in Eaton Auditorium for the WMC was followed the very next day by an evening concert given by his father for the International Artists series at Massey Hall.

Great interest in the press was occasioned by the Toronto debut of the flamboyant diva Grace Bumbry in the only evening open event of the season. Bumbry had created headlines around the world when she became the first African American singer to appear at Bayreuth, after she was cast by Wieland Wagner as Venus in a 1961 production of *Tannhäuser*. At age seventeen she had sung for and won the praise of Marian Anderson, and seven years later, after her success at Bayreuth, she had signed a five-year, $250,000 contract with Solomon Hurok, Anderson's former manager.[25] Now, at age twenty-eight, she was taking the world by storm, and enjoying every minute of it. Arriving in Toronto on the day of her WMC recital, she met with the press in the afternoon wearing "a huge, turban-like orange hat, a suit and knee-length leather boots."[26] She won over the local critics with her vivacious, fun-loving manner in the press conference, and impressed them no end that evening in her recital, singing a generous selection of lieder and opera excerpts ranging from Beethoven to Barber.

According to press reports, the WMC reached its goal of one thousand members on 3 December 1964, the day of the Festival Singers concert.[27] It was decided, therefore, to temporarily put an end to the evening open concert. All seven events were held in the afternoon during the 1965–66 season, making it the first season in thirty-five years with no open concert. In fact, the long-standing tradition of an evening open concert was quietly done away with at this time, to be revived only on special occasions in future. For a number of years thereafter, WMC members and their guests were numerous enough to fill Eaton Auditorium for most concerts. Later, as the WMC membership fell, the restrictions on the purchase of guest tickets was eased until eventually all of the WMC concerts became, in effect, open events.

At the annual meeting on 21 April 1965, members were advised that they had until 31 May to renew, after which the membership would be open to the general public again. As it turned out, a waiting list was not needed, for the WMC never again reached the one-thousand-member cutoff point. At that same annual meeting, Muriel Gidley Stafford became the twenty-fourth president of the WMC.

Muriel Gidley had studied at the Toronto Conservatory of Music from 1925 to 1927, taking organ lessons with G.D. Atkinson and theory with Ernest MacMillan. She was the organist at Park Road Baptist Church from 1927 to 1958, and served as national president of the Royal Canadian College of Organists from 1957 to 1959. In 1950 she married for the first time, becoming the second wife of Merrill C. Stafford, who was the president of the Turnbull Elevator Company. By a charming coincidence, Merrill Stafford was born in 1899, the same year that the WMC was founded, and, like the club, he continued to enjoy a vigorously active life in 1997.

Muriel Stafford joined the WMC executive in 1963 and served on it until 1970, continuing as a regular member of the club thereafter. The administrative experience she gained in running the RCCO was put to good use during her term as president of the WMC. She regards the changes she made to the financial affairs of the club (upgrading the portfolio of investments and moving the WMC account from a bank to a trust company which offered a better interest rate) as her major initiative as president.[28] These improvements to the club's financial affairs allowed her to keep the membership fee at the same rate during her two years as president, despite rising costs in every area of operations. She also brought many new women into the WMC executive committee ranks to replace those who had retired. Shortly before she herself retired from the WMC executive, she made several changes to the Constitution, which were adopted at the annual meeting on 16 April 1970. Aside from her continuing participation in the WMC, Muriel Stafford has also served as the treasurer of the Heliconian Club, and she is an avid and expert gardener, as the breathtakingly lovely grounds of her North Toronto home demonstrate.

The sixty-eighth season was not one of the high points of the WMC's history from an artistic standpoint, if one can judge from the reviews. It opened with the return appearance of Claude Frank on 21 October 1965, which "left mixed impressions," according to John Kraglund.[29] The second concert was given on 4 November 1965 by the Canadian contralto Marilyn Duffus, accompanied by Garth Beckett, and they received the first genuinely bad reviews in the history of the WMC.[30] The Stanley Buetens Lute Trio (9 December 1965), in a recital of music from the thirteenth to eighteenth centuries, "prompted many of the ladies at Eaton Auditorium to depart at intermission,"[31] and the Belgian pianist Frans Brouw (20 January 1966), who would later settle in Quebec City, "lacked the necessary communication as well as personality."[32] The German violinist Edith Peinemann (10 February 1966) was found to be "lacking in excitement,"[33] and even the usually reliable Vienna Octet (3 March 1966) was judged on this occasion to be "haughty and pedantic."[34] The one event that provided a memorable musical experience for the

WMC was "an exciting and near-flawless concert"[35] by the Juilliard String Quartet on 18 November 1965.

The sixty-ninth season did not begin well either, for a comedy of errors plagued the opening concert on 20 October 1966 by the Sestetto di Bolzano, a woodwind quintet with piano. Some of the sextet's luggage went missing, as a result of which the flutist had to appear in a business suit and use someone else's instrument, and the group had to play from borrowed music.[36] In addition, the regular pianist was ill and his place was taken by a substitute who did not have much time to rehearse with the other members. And finally, the choice of repertoire was unfortunate. The group played Hindemith's *Kleine Kammermusik*, Op. 24, No. 2, which had rather worn out its welcome through recent performances in WMC recitals by the New York Woodwind Quintet, the Toronto Woodwind Quintet, and the Danzi Woodwind Quintet. Also on the program was Poulenc's *Sextet* for piano and winds, which had been done by Mario Bernardi with the Toronto Woodwind Quintet. Not surprisingly, the local critics were not impressed by the Sestetto di Bolzano's Toronto debut performance.

No untoward incidents marred the second recital of the season on 3 November 1966, which featured the U.S. cellist Paul Olefsky and the pianist Walter Hautzig, both in their local debuts. Of the Canadian performers that season, the husband-and-wife duo-pianists Renée Morisset and Victor Bouchard (17 November 1966) and the Montreal pianist Ronald Turini (19 January 1967) did not fare well at the hands of the critics, but Donald Bell (9 February 1967) was greeted with rave reviews. Two other recitals were judged outstanding in every respect — that by the French flutist Jean-Pierre Rampal, with Robert Veyron-Lecroix accompanying on harpsichord and piano (15 December 1966), and the return appearance by the Juilliard Quartet (9 March 1967). At the annual meeting at the end of the season, Helen Christilaw Goudge became the twenty-fifth president of the WMC. She is best known to WMC members as the author of *Look Back in Pride*, a history of the club written in 1972 for its seventy-fifth anniversary.

Further bad reviews plagued the WMC during the seventieth season. The Marlboro Trio (26 October 1967) was "uninspired,"[37] and the U.S. soprano Helen Vanni (9 November 1967), who was perhaps best known locally for her recording of Schoenberg lieder with Glenn Gould, was "too severely monochromatic with her sound."[38] The U.S. pianist Edward Auer (23 November 1967) gave a recital which was "remarkably dull,"[39] the Zagreb String Quartet (18 January 1968) provided "able rather than virtuosic string playing, punctuated by minor fluffs and slips in intonation,"[40] and the twenty-one-year-old U.S. violinist James Oliver Buswell IV (7 March 1968) was "lightweight."[41] Only a mixed recital of rarely performed works on 7 December 1967 given by four local musicians (the soprano Mary Morrison, the clarinettist Stanley McCartney, the flutist Robert Aitken, and the pianist Marion Ross), and the Toronto debut of the English baritone John Shirley-Quirk on 1 February 1968 received entirely favourable reviews.

After three seasons of middling talent with only the occasional outstanding performance, the lustre of the WMC recital series was in danger of becoming tarnished. This was a serious matter, as the main business of the club is to sponsor concerts, and if the reputation of the concert series suffers, the fortunes of the WMC can only wane as a result. It is for this reason that the position of concert convenor is of an importance rivalling that of the president, for the concert convenor decides which artists will appear in the WMC series. (See appendix 2 for a list of the WMC's concert convenors over the years.) The executive committee decided at this time that one way of addressing the problem was to spend more money on fewer (and thus hopefully better) artists, and so beginning with the 1968–69 season the WMC series was reduced from seven to six concerts.

A second cause for concern was the state of Eaton Auditorium itself. The hall had once been renowned for its excellent sound — William Glock in the late 1940s had deemed it one of the two finest concert halls in Canada[42] — but renovations and a redecoration with plush velvet platform hangings in the 1950s had reduced its acoustic vitality drastically. Critics frequently complained that the auditorium was no longer a suitable venue for the intimate chamber music and solo recitals which were the mainstay of the WMC concert series, and some club members were beginning to agree with that point of view. In the spring of 1968, the WMC asked a professional consultant for advice about the acoustics of the auditorium. In his report, the consultant stated that the hall itself had good acoustics, but the stage setup was poor; he suggested the addition of screens and drops to reflect the sound into the audience. John P. Heffernan, the manager of Eaton Auditorium, advised the club that the cost of these items would be nine hundred dollars, and as neither Eaton's nor the WMC was willing to spend that amount of money, nothing was done.

The fact that Canada's Centennial year had passed without any recognition or special ceremony by the WMC to mark the occasion was another matter of disappointment for some members. Various plans had been put forward in executive committee meetings at one time or another — an all-Canadian season of performers, the commissioning of a Canadian composition, and a history of the WMC were three of the suggestions — but none of these came to fruition.

Meanwhile another problem related to patriotism had been brewing beneath the surface for some years — the issue of the playing of "God Save the Queen" before WMC concerts. The policy in the past had been to ask the featured accompanist to play the anthem on the piano before the concert began. If the person involved was willing, this was fine. Sometimes, for example when Gerald Moore performed the task, it could even be a moving musical experience. Some pianists, though, would not perform this duty, and of course sometimes there was no pianist; on these occasions a recording was used. This too resulted in problems. Complaints about the poor quality of the club's recording of "God Save the Queen" appear periodically in the executive committee minutes, and on one occasion the sound technician got the record tracks mixed up and "Rule Britannia" was played by mistake.[43] During the Centennial year, the WMC switched to "O Canada," but this drew criticism from some members, and so a compromise solution was worked out: "O Canada" would be played at the first concert of the season, and "God Save the Queen" at the last. Ironically, the Toronto city bylaw which stipulated the performance of a national anthem at the start of all concerts was abolished in 1967, before the compromise solution could be enacted.[44] As it was now legally permitted to do so, on 25 January 1968 the WMC executive committee voted to cease the practice of playing a national anthem altogether, except for special occasions in the future when it would be deemed desirable to revive it.

Notwithstanding these problems, the WMC was still enjoying exemplary health in the spring of 1968. The membership, although it had fallen slightly from the high of one thousand reached in 1964, was still large enough to fill Eaton Auditorium almost to capacity for most concerts. The WMC finances were in sufficiently good shape that in the 1966–67 season the club had begun awarding three scholarships instead of one each year. Although the general artistic level of the recitals may have fallen off somewhat in recent years, the club could still point with pride to many outstanding musicians who had appeared in the seventy concerts that had been sponsored during the previous ten years.

NOTES

1 J.M.S. Careless, "Toronto," *The Canadian Encyclopedia*, 1985 ed.

2 John Beckwith, *Music at Toronto: A Personal Account* (Toronto: U of Toronto P, 1995) 37–38. Boyd Neel was the dean and acting director. According to the WMC *Executive Committee Minutes*, the decision to abolish card punching had been reached by 11 September 1969.

3 The professional musician membership category was discontinued in 1963.

4 John Kraglund, "Music in Toronto," *Globe and Mail* 4 Dec. 1958: 35

5 "Pianist Has Designed Own Concert Frocks," *Globe and Mail* 25 Feb. 1960: 18.

6 Edna Usher, "Dig This Yoga-Practising Pianist," *Telegram* 1 Mar. 1960: 24.

7 Hugh Thomson, "Baritone Donald Bell Heard in Eaton Debut," *Toronto Daily Star* 17 Oct. 1958: 26.

8 [Blaik] Kirby, "Amateur Impresario Outguesses the Pros," *Toronto Daily Star* 26 Jan. 1963: 22.

9 Magner 14, 25.

10 Magner 14.

11 John Kraglund, "Care, Clarity Mark Debut of Pianist, 16," *Globe and Mail* 20 Nov. 1959: 2.

12 WMC *Executive Committee Minutes*, 3 Mar. 1960.

13 Eustella F. Langdon, "Report of Committee," WMC *Annual Reports Season 1960–61.*

14 Udo Kasemets, "Ensemble Superb," *Toronto Daily Star* 2 Dec. 1960: 31.

15 Udo Kasemets, "Ives Beethoven of Tomorrow," *Toronto Daily Star* 2 Feb. 1962: 21.

16 John Kraglund, "Pianist Easily Handles Demanding Program," *Globe and Mail* 2 Feb. 1962: 4.

17 Juliet Love Giraldi, "Instruments Saved from Decay in Siena," *BBC Music Magazine* Oct. 1995: 15.

18 George Kidd, "Beaux Arts a Splendid Trio," *Telegram* 6 Apr. 1962: 35.

19 John Beckwith, "New York Trio Has 'Virtuosity to Spare,' " *Toronto Daily Star* 6 Apr. 1962: 26.

20 R. Murray Schafer, "Ten Centuries Concerts: A Recollection," *On Canadian Music* (Bancroft, ON: Arcana, 1984) 21–35.

21 John Kraglund, "Dream Violinist Leads Quartet," *Globe and Mail* 9 Nov. 1962: 37.

22 Udo Kasemets, "Kroll Quartet," *Toronto Daily Star* 9 Nov. 1962: 21.

23 John Kraglund, "Hopes High for '63 after Exciting Year," *Globe and Mail* 29 Dec. 1962: 14.

24 John Kraglund, "Skiing Pianist Returns to Fill Another Gap," *Globe and Mail* 22 Mar. 1963: 10.

25 Story 151.

26 Ralph Thomas, "Made Name in Europe: 'No Hope in U.S.,' Says Opera Star," *Toronto Daily Star* 21 Jan. 1965: 35.

27 John Kraglund, "Festival Singers Top Obstacle," *Globe and Mail* 4 Dec. 1964: 15, and George Kidd, "Festival Singers Charm Music Club," *Telegram* 4 Dec. 1964: 41, both report that the goal of one thousand members was achieved on the day of the Festival Singers concert.

28 Muriel Gidley Stafford, personal interview, 26 July 1995.

29 John Kraglund, "Pianist's Technique Wins Out," *Globe and Mail* 22 Oct. 1965: 15.

30 John Kraglund, "Even in Her Entrance, Singer Disappointing," *Globe and Mail* 5 Nov. 1965: 13, and George Kidd, "Contralto Fails to Convince," *Telegram* 5 Nov. 1965: 41.

31 John Kraglund, "Lutes and Recorders Seen but Not Heard," *Globe and Mail* 10 Dec. 1965: 15.

32 George Kidd, "Interest Lags at Piano Recital," *Telegram* 21 Jan. 1966: 39.

33 John Kraglund, "Violinist Peinemann Lacking in Excitement," *Globe and Mail* 11 Feb. 1966: 13.

34 Douglas Hughes, "An Over-Cautious Show by Famed Vienna Octet," *Toronto Daily Star* 4 Mar. 1966: 24.

35 George Kidd, "Students Flock to Juilliard Quartet," *Telegram* 19 Nov. 1965: 40.

36 William Littler, "Smooth Uneventful Debut," *Toronto Daily Star* 21 Oct. 1966: 24. Littler became the *Star*'s music critic in 1966; this was his first review of a WMC event.

37 John Kraglund, "Club Concert Is Uninspired," *Globe and Mail* 27 Oct. 1967: 13.

38 Kenneth Winters, "Soprano Helen Vanni: Bit Too Brisk and Brittle," *Telegram* 10 Nov. 1967: 47. Winters had succeeded George Kidd as the *Telegram* music critic early in 1966.

39 John Kraglund, "Despite Assets, Auer Produces Dull Recital," *Globe and Mail* 24 Nov. 1967: 15.

40 William Littler, "The Zagreb Quartet: Able Enough, but a Bit Pale," *Toronto Daily Star* 19 Jan. 1968: 24.

41 William Littler, "He Treats Violin Like a Racing-Car," *Toronto Daily Star* 8 Mar. 1968: 28.

42 Marjorie Hale, "Eaton Auditorium," *Encyclopedia of Music in Canada*, 2nd ed., 1992.

43 Betty Lee, "Getting the Musical Best for a Bargain," *Globe and Mail* 7 Sept. 1971: 10.

44 Helmut Kallmann, "National and Royal Anthems," *Encyclopedia of Music in Canada*, 2nd ed., 1992.

10

Look Back in Pride

A new phase in the WMC's history was initiated during the second year of Helen Goudge's term as president, when the club asked the federal government for the right to have donations to the WMC made tax deductible. The application was made in September 1968, and charitable organization status was granted in January 1969. The WMC immediately created a new category of "sustaining member" for anyone who made a donation to the club. For the first time in its history, the WMC was actively soliciting funds instead of relying solely on membership fees and guest tickets as its source of income. The move was an important first step in creating a more businesslike approach to the handling of the club's finances. The plan did not get off to a very successful start, however. The minimum donation required for a charitable receipt was initially set at one dollar, and only two dollars in donations were received by the end of the 1968–69 season. The minimum level was then increased to ten dollars, and sustaining members were offered the chance to have their names published in the concert programs. From that point on the sustaining membership category began to help improve the club's finances. At the same time, the membership fee was raised from $10 to $12.50 beginning with the 1969–70 season, to help offset an increase in the rental fee for Eaton Auditorium from $60 to $75 per event. Subsequent increases saw the membership fee reach $22 by the 1976–77 season, a sign of the inflationary economic times.

A less fortunate initiative was the decision to have a new logotype designed to replace the club's existing one — the intertwined letters WMCT, which had been in use at least since 1900. The old logo, with its overlapping ornately shaped letters, is admittedly somewhat Victorian in look, but it nonetheless has a certain dignity and charm, and had served the club well for seventy years. The new logo was certainly no improvement on the old one. It was created by Anne Grotian, who donated her design to the club. Grotian's lettering was amateurish compared to the beauty of the Victorian original, and in trying to appear trendy and modern, her logo ended up looking even more irredeemably dated than the older one. Extraordinarily enough, the executive committee was at first well pleased with the new logo, and even used it on the annual brochure for the 1969–70 season. This uncharacteristic lapse in good taste was quickly repaired, however, and for the next two seasons no logo at all appeared on the annual brochures, while the old logo continued to be used on the concert programs. The original logo was revived for the seventy-fifth anniversary season brochure and has been used ever since.

The seventy-first season opened with a recital by the Orford String Quartet on 24 October 1968. The quartet had only been formed three years earlier, but it was already installed at the University of Toronto as the unofficial quartet-in-residence, and it had extensive touring and a successful New York debut to its credit. The local critics greeted the Orford's performance of quartets by Haydn, Berg, and Mendelssohn warmly but nonetheless with a certain reserve, as if they were not yet quite ready to admit that a local quartet could be accorded the same accolades as the best visiting ensembles.

The recital by the Irish contralto Bernadette Greevy on 14 November 1968 represented another new initiative for the WMC. The club agreed with the Ladies' Morning Musical Club of Montreal to jointly sponsor Greevy's Canadian concerts as part of the artist's first North American tour. It was an isolated gesture that brought to mind the failed initiative in the 1920s, when the WMC had hoped to create a federation of Canadian women's musical clubs to facilitate just such collaborations. Greevy's recital prompted one of William Littler's more peculiar reviews, in which he fantasized about proposing marriage to Greevy but called off the idea because of reservations about her singing.[1] The review reads as though Littler were trying to live up to the eccentric style of his predecessor Augustus Bridle.

The Toronto debut recital of the sixty-two-year-old eminent French cellist Pierre Fournier took place on 23 January 1969. Despite his outstanding international career, Fournier had only appeared in Toronto once before with the Toronto Symphony. Local musicians turned out in force for the recital, as Kenneth Winters reported: "Everywhere you looked in the packed hall you saw a musician. An eminent singer. The members of a professional string quartet. Section leaders of the Toronto Symphony. Composers. Teachers. The lot."[2] The program was the same one that Fournier and his accompanist Leon Pommers had prepared for their Carnegie Hall recital in February; it included works by Locatelli, Bach, Brahms, Honegger, and Tchaikovsky. The unanimous verdict was that it was one of the finest recitals heard in Toronto that year.

The other artists that season were the Israeli pianist David Bar-Illan (5 December 1968), the Brahms Quartet (6 February 1969), and the Danzi Woodwind Quintet (6 March 1969). Memories of the Sestetto di Bolzano fiasco surfaced at the Brahms Quartet recital. The cellist's instrument was damaged in transit, so he had to use a borrowed instrument for the recital, and at his insistence the program was changed, with a Mendelssohn piano quartet substituted for the originally scheduled Beethoven Quartet, Op. 16. Despite these problems, however, the concert itself went ahead smoothly in the end.

The season as a whole was one of the more successful ones in recent memory for the WMC, and did much to repair the club's reputation, which had been somewhat tarnished by a preponderance of weak programs in the preceeding three years. In reviewing the WMC's seventy-first season, Kenneth Winters judged that the series represented "probably the best dollar-value in live music in Toronto."[3] The WMC had good reason to congratulate itself at the annual meeting, which took place at the Heliconian Club on 16 April 1969. Elizabeth Lodi Mittler, a professional violinist, was elected at that meeting to succeed Helen Goudge as president.

The seventy-second season, like the seventy-first, opened with an outstanding young ensemble, the Guarneri String Quartet. The upper three instrumentalists of this quartet had all trained at the Curtis Institute in Philadelphia, and they met their cellist at the Marlboro Music Festival in Vermont. Two of the group's members, Michael Tree and David Soyer, had already been featured in a WMC recital in 1967 as members of the Marlboro Trio. The Guarneri Quartet, though only four years old at the time of its WMC recital on 23 October 1969, was already well known and highly respected from its recordings and previous local appearances, and its concert started the season off on a very high level indeed.

The pianist Anton Kuerti matched the standard set by the Guarneri Quartet in his recital on 11 December 1969. Before a packed auditorium Kuerti gave electrifying performances of works by Mozart, Chopin, Beethoven, and the *Suite for Piano* (1968) by Oskar Morawetz, which he had premiered a few days earlier in Montreal. He was greeted with four curtain calls at intermission and over half a dozen at the end of the recital. Kenneth Winters reported that Kuerti "refreshed his status . . . as one of the best pianists before the public," but he was less impressed by the members of the audience:

> They were armed with jangly charm-bracelets, thin, brittle paper bags which rattle like snare-drums if you breathe near them, snap-catch handbags which open and close with a report like a small rifle, and cellophane-wrapped sweets for hair-trigger coughs. They included all kinds of left-over conversation from their meeting at the last concert and invariably chatted until the pianist had begun to play.[4]

Evidently the WMC should have revived the admonition that had first appeared on a club program in 1906: "SILENCE is requested during the numbers."

Another outstanding recital was offered on 22 January 1970, when the Dutch soprano Elly Ameling was featured in her Canadian debut, accompanied by Irwin Gage. Ameling had come to notice in the mid-1960s through recordings for the nascent period-instrument movement, notably in cantata performances with the Collegium Aureum and in recitals accompanied by Jörg Demus on the fortepiano. She had since appeared widely in Europe and South America as an oratorio and lieder singer. President Elizabeth Mittler, who was of Dutch origin, was able through friends in Holland to invite Ameling to Toronto. Thus began what developed into a warm relationship between Ameling and Toronto, which over the years would see many return appearances (including one for the WMC in 1973) and the development of many close ties. Ameling's WMC recital of songs by Purcell, Mozart, Schumann, Debussy, and Wolf was greeted by rave reviews in the local papers. The acclaim was repeated a week later when Ameling made her New York recital debut at Lincoln Center.

The high standards of the season were maintained by the Beaux Arts Trio, which made its third WMC appearance on 5 February 1970. Isidore Cohen, who had appeared in a WMC recital in 1965 as the second violinist of the Juilliard Quartet, now came as the trio's new violinist, replacing Daniel Guilet. William Littler reported that "If anything, Cohen plays with greater security and more dependable intonation than his predecessor and the ensemble sounds as close-knit as ever."[5]

There were only two recitals that season that were less than first rate, one by the U.S. bass Thomas Paul on 20 November 1969 and the closing recital by pianist Murray Perahia on 5 March 1970. Paul's voice was lacking in colour and volume, and he was overshadowed by his accompanist, Martin Katz. The twenty-two-year-old Perahia was featured in his Canadian debut, but unfortunately he was convalescing from a serious illness and could barely get out of bed on the day of his concert. After cutting one of the numbers on the first half of the program, he contemplated cancelling the rest of the concert at intermission, but marshalled his energy and completed the show. The recital, needless to say, was not up to his standard.

In January 1970 the WMC began an occasional newsletter to inform members about upcoming events and other issues of interest. The first newsletter asked the members to vote on whether the concert time should be moved from 2:00 p.m. to 1:30 p.m. to avoid the afternoon rush hour traffic (the same concern that had caused the move from 2:30 p.m. to 2:00 p.m. in 1953). The members voted in favour of the earlier hour, which has remained the concert time ever since. The change in time was confirmed at the annual meeting at the Heliconian Club on 16 April 1970. At the same meeting, changes to the Constitution that had been suggested by Muriel Stafford were also ratified.

By 1970 the issues of feminism and women's rights were being much debated in Canada. Many women's groups had been forming across Canada in the late 1960s, and in 1967 the federal government set up the Royal Commission on the Status of Women, which tabled a 488-page report in the fall of 1970. The commission's 167 recommendations all had, as a philosophical basis, the principle that "equality of opportunity for Canadian men and women was possible, desirable and ethically necessary."[6] The issue of the women's liberation movement was raised by Kenneth Winters in his review of the first concert of the 1970–71 season. The review was headlined "Lib Shows in Women's Musical Club," and began as follows:

Women's liberation is old. Symbolically at least it was achieved years and years ago in Toronto when a few women decided to arrange their own musical life, set up their own annual concert series, attend it in the daytime when most men are out of the way, and just generally enjoy music without help or interference from the unfair sex.

They weren't militant about it, of course, or even evangelical. But they put the thing together, got it going, kept it solvent, and today, the Women's Musical Club of Toronto offers about as high a level of non-star-system, youth-oriented, astutely selected concert fare as you'll find anywhere.[7]

In fact, the WMC had little if any point of contact with the women's liberation movement. Like other long-standing women's groups in Canada, the WMC was a child of the women's reform movement of the late-nineteenth century. It had lived through several campaigns for women's rights over the years, the most recent of which was the women's liberation movement. If the WMC had aligned itself with any national organization — and it did not — it would most likely have been the National Council of Women of Canada (founded in 1893), with its emphasis on duty and service, rather than the National Action Committee on the Status of Women (founded in 1971), with its emphasis on rights and reform.

The concert which occasioned the above-quoted remarks by Winters was a recital by the pianist Agustin Anievas. Both the recital and the concert season that followed it lived up to the average standard of the WMC, without in any way surpassing it. The season saw the Toronto debuts of Anievas and of the French violinist Jean-Jacques Kantorow (19 November 1970), a return appearance by John Shirley-Quirk (10 December 1970), concerts by the Lenox String Quartet from Binghampton, New York (21 January 1971) and the Japanese cellist Tsuyoshi Tsutsumi, who was on the faculty of the University of Western Ontario (4 February 1971), and Robert Aitken's first solo recital for the WMC, accompanied by Erica Goodman, harp (4 March 1971). None of these concerts was a disappointment, but none aroused any especial enthusiasm either.

The seventy-fourth season was on an entirely different plane. The season opened and closed with return visits from two of the finest chamber ensembles ever to grace the WMC series: the Beaux Arts Trio (21 October 1971) and the Juilliard String Quartet (16 March 1972). The other artists that season were all featured in their local debuts: the Hungarian violinist György Pauk (18 November 1971), the Argentinian contralto Norma Lerer (9 December 1971), the Warsaw Quintet (a piano quintet, 13 January 1972), and the Jamaican pianist Nerine Barrett (3 February 1972). The only Canadian artist for the season was the pianist John Newmark, who appeared as Lerer's accompanist. Nerine Barrett drew measured but cautious praise, while the reviews for the rest of the concerts ranged from enthusiastic to ecstatic. It was a good year for the WMC to put its best foot forward, because a competing chamber music and solo recital series under the direction of Franz Kraemer started that year at the new St. Lawrence Centre for the Arts.

The annual meeting at the end of the seventy-third season was held at the Heliconian Club on 1 April 1971, and at that time Juliette Abreu del Junco was elected as president. An amateur flutist, she came to Canada

FIGURE 18

From left, Elizabeth Lodi Mittler, Juliette Abreu del Junco,
and Françoise Dreyfus Sutton at the 75th anniversary concert.

from France in 1959. While she was president the plans to celebrate the WMC's seventy-fifth anniversary were drawn up and carried out. But before that could be done, however, there was a loose end to clear up with regard to one of the WMC's awards.

Five years earlier the WMC had received a letter from Joan Hume, the daughter of Irene Simons Hume, a soprano who had performed in Toronto during the 1920s (she had appeared in a WMC recital on 22 January 1920) and had died on 9 January 1966. Joan Hume asked the WMC to administer an annual scholarship in memory of her mother; the award was to be in the amount of $100 and open only to singers. It was intended that the award would be paid for with the interest of a $2,000 bequest that would be forthcoming from the estate. In the meantime, Joan Hume sent in $100 so that the first award could be given. By the spring of 1971, five Irene Simons Hume Awards had been given out, but still no bequest had been received from the estate. When the WMC looked into the matter, it discovered that Irene Simons Hume had died intestate, and the award was terminated.

With that matter cleared up, the WMC executive turned its full attention to the seventy-fifth anniversary celebration. Elizabeth Mittler, the past-president, was in charge of planning the events. A commemorative booklet was proposed at an executive committee meeting on 28 January 1971 (it was actually the resurrection of an idea that had first been planned for Canada's Centennial year). However it was not until February 1972 that WMC past president Helen Goudge agreed to write the booklet. In response to a request for WMC memorabilia, several members sent in old concert programs, some of them dating back to 1900. These were added to the WMC archives and helped Goudge to research the early activities of the club. Goudge worked quickly, and by September 1972 she had completed a fine thirty-two-page history of the club, titled *Look Back in Pride*. The booklet was not only a treasured commemorative keepsake for WMC members, but also served to make the club's activities known to a wider audience, and it was of great use in preparing the present history of the organization.

Look Back in Pride was rushed into print and copies were ready for the special opening concert of the seventy-fifth season. Unfortunately the blue ink on the cover of the booklet did not dry properly, and as a result the festive audience was subjected to stained hands, gloves, and evening clothes. The remaining copies of the booklet were processed through special drying ovens to correct this problem.

In February 1971, Eleanor Koldofsky Sniderman joined the WMC executive and agreed to take charge of publicity for the club.[8] Even before joining the executive committee, she had assisted the WMC by getting her then husband, Sam "the Record Man" Sniderman, to underwrite the cost of printing the concert programs. Now, as the PR director for the club, she went into high gear. First, she got each of the three major local daily newspapers to run a long article outlining the history and present activities of the WMC in the fall of 1971.[9] Next, she coerced the record companies whose artists were featured in the WMC concert series into helping to underwrite the cost of the seventy-fifth anniversary celebrations. Some of this money was used to produce a more attractive annual brochure for the seventy-fifth season, and a special contribution from Nonesuch Records paid for a champagne reception after the opening concert of that season. Eleanor Koldofsky was on the WMC executive for less than two years, but her commitment, energy, and connections were a major factor in ensuring the success of the club's seventy-fifth anniversary.

The gala celebration of the WMC's seventy-fifth anniversary took place during the opening event of the 1972–73 season, which was an evening concert on 19 October 1972 by the Toulouse Chamber Orchestra in Eaton Auditorium. The celebration was not without its difficulties and disappointments, in addition to the already mentioned problem of the smudging ink from the cover of *Look Back in Pride*. The first setback came in March 1972, when Governor General Roland Michener declined an invitation to be the patron of the event. This problem was remedied when the Honourable William Ross Macdonald, the lieutenant governor of Ontario, lent his name to the event as patron and agreed to attend the concert. Then in September, a little over a month before the concert, the WMC learned that Louis Auriacombe, the founder and conductor of the Toulouse Chamber Orchestra, was too ill to travel with the group. The orchestra was willing to go ahead with the tour and play without a conductor, but the critics felt that it did not play as well in Toronto on its own as it might have if Auriacombe had been conducting. Indeed, some felt that the orchestra was not the best choice for a gala concert. The truth of the matter is that it was not specially chosen for the event, but rather came as part of a package deal from Mariedi Anders Artists Management. By choosing four groups from the Anders agency for its concert season that year, the WMC was given a twenty percent reduction in the artists' fees. It made good economic sense, but did not perhaps result in the highest artistic standards for the gala concert.

To add a further stroke of bad luck, the Israel Philharmonic gave a concert under Zubin Mehta in Massey Hall on the same evening as the WMC concert. This not only drew away potential audience members, but also attracted more attention in the press. John Kraglund attended the Massey Hall event and sent a substitute to review the Toulouse Chamber Orchestra, while William Littler attended half of each concert. Kaspars Dzeguze, reviewing the WMC concert for the *Globe and Mail*, wrote as follows:

[T]he Toulouse Chamber Orchestra, . . . while not abetting the celebration in any brilliant or extravagant fashion, managed to provide solid and decorous grounds for the festivities.
    Indeed, the whole evening was somewhat muted: when Lieutenant-Governor W. Ross Macdonald arrived, he was greeted by the organist's chopped up version of God Save the Queen and highlights from O Canada.
    One expected that a football game rather than a concert would follow such an opening, but no such excitement ensued.[10]

What the organist (who was Earle Moss) played was the Canadian Vice-Regal Salute, which is no doubt most familiar from its use at major sporting events, but is also, according to protocol, to be performed as the lieutenant governor reaches his seat.[11] It is an admittedly odd potpourri consisting of the first six bars of "God Save the Queen," followed by the first four and last four bars of "O Canada."[12] What the Toulouse Chamber Orchestra played was a concert of works by Couperin, Bach, Corrette, Mozart, and Stravinsky. Littler, who heard only the second half of the program, wrote that the orchestra's playing "had all the bite of a pair of toothless gums."[13] In reply, one audience member wrote a letter to the *Star* to say that Littler's review was in poor taste and to defend the orchestra's playing.[14] Despite the problems on stage and behind the scenes that evening, it was a happy occasion for the WMC, and a chance to celebrate a long and distinguished history of concert giving and service to the community.
    The second concert of the season was given by the Smetana Quartet on 16 November 1972. The quartet had been formed in 1945, and still had all of its founding members except for the violist. The Smetana Quartet, like the Kolisch Quartet, played its entire repertoire from memory. For the WMC concert it performed works by Beethoven, Janáček, and Smetana. Ronald Hambleton in his review wrote that "the playing was near perfection."[15]
    The Canadian concert of the season was to have featured the baritone Louis Quilico in recital on 7 December 1972. After agreeing to this date, however, Quilico was asked to replace Tito Gobbi as Iago in the

Metropolitan Opera's production of Verdi's *Otello*, which starred fellow
Canadian Jon Vickers in the title role. Despite an attack of pneumonia,
Quilico wore himself out by commuting between previously booked
performances on the west coast and rehearsals with the Met in New York.
The date of the WMC recital fell two days after an *Otello* performance,
and two days before a live Saturday afternoon broadcast of the opera.
On one day's notice, Quilico informed the WMC that he would have to
cancel his recital, for on doctor's orders he had to stay in bed if he was
to do the radio broadcast. The programs had been printed, and Martin
Smith, who was to have been Quilico's accompanist, was already in
Toronto. Late on Wednesday, the U.S. baritone Robert Goodloe flew
into Toronto and rehearsed an entirely different program with Smith.
The next afternoon he sang at Eaton Auditorium in place of Quilico.
Ironically Goodloe was also singing in the same production of *Otello*,
but in the minor role of Montano. Quilico, incidentally, gave up a $2,000
fee from the WMC, which was the highest amount the club had offered a
solo artist up to that time.

The last three concerts of the season were all very successful. They
featured Secolo Barocco, a French chamber ensemble led by the flutist
Michel Debost in its Canadian debut on 18 January 1973, the Spanish
soprano Pilar Lorengar in her Canadian debut on 22 February 1973,
and the Austrian pianist Walter Klien in his Toronto debut on 8 March
1973. Lorengar was accompanied by the pianist Donald Hassard, who
as a result of the Quilico cancellation was the only Canadian musician
featured that season.

The anniversary season provided the opportunity not only to reflect
on the past history of the WMC, but also to plan for its future. The number
of members had been dropping steadily since the mid-1960s, and now
stood at about 750, which meant that Eaton Auditorium was rarely filled
to capacity. The WMC executive committee considered changing the
concert day to Sunday afternoons and thought of switching the venue to
a different location — the MacMillan Theatre, Ryerson Theatre, and St.
Lawrence Centre were among the venues considered — but in the end
decided not to make any changes for the time being. Shortly after this
decision was reached, however, the sale of the Eaton's College Street
store was announced, casting the future of Eaton Auditorium into doubt.
The WMC participated in a vigorous campaign to keep Eaton Auditorium
open, but the spectre of being forced out of its long-standing home hung
over the club like a dark cloud for the next four seasons.

At the seventy-fifth annual meeting on 19 April 1973, Françoise Dreyfus Sutton was elected as the new WMC president. An amateur pianist,

she was born in Paris and moved to Toronto in 1955 to marry Marshall Sutton, a Canadian whom she had met at the Edinburgh Festival. At the invitation of Muriel Stafford, she joined the WMC executive in January 1967 and served as the concert convenor and first vice-president before being elected as president. At the same meeting Božena Brajsa Naughton became the concert convenor. She held the position for four seasons, during which time she developed a good working relationship and close personal friendship with Françoise Sutton. Naughton and Sutton, like all of the WMC members interviewed in the course of writing this book, stressed that making good friends through sharing musical experiences and working with others to help run the club was one of the main benefits that they received from their association with the WMC.[16]

The seventy-sixth and seventy-seventh seasons are two of only three seasons in the entire history of the WMC to have featured no Canadian performers at all (the other such season was the fifty-ninth). The seventy-sixth season was to have opened with the Tatrai Quartet from Hungary, but when that group was forced to cancel its North American tour, the Prague Madrigal Singers were featured instead in their Canadian debut on 15 October 1973. The highlight of their program was a performance of selections from *Madrigali guerrieri et amorosi*, Claudio Monteverdi's eighth book of madrigals. Elly Ameling in her return appearance on 8 November 1973 attracted a near capacity audience for her recital of German and French songs. Two Japanese chamber ensembles were featured in their local debuts that season, the Japan Trio on 6 December 1973 and the Tokyo String Quartet on 7 March 1974. The cellist of the Japan Trio was Tsuyoshi Tsutsumi, who had been featured in a WMC solo recital in 1971. The trio and the quartet were both greeted with warm reviews; the quartet in particular was praised for its polished playing and the warm sound of its matched set of Amati instruments, on loan from the Corcoran Gallery in Washington. The other artists heard that season were the Texan cellist Ralph Kirschbaum (24 January 1974) in his Toronto debut and the Israeli pianist Daniel Adni (7 February 1974) in his Canadian debut. Adni greatly impressed one local critic, who called the twenty-two-year-old musician "one of the greatest pianists of our time, or, for that matter, of any time."[17]

The first two concerts of the seventy-seventh season occasioned some anxious moments for the executive committee. The Dimov Quartet from Bulgaria was featured in its Toronto debut on 17 October 1974 and the London Virtuosi chamber ensemble gave its Canadian debut on 14 November 1974. Both groups arrived later than anticipated, the latter less than three hours before concert time and the former with just

minutes to spare. The WMC has always tried to encourage its artists to
arrive on the day before the concert, but it has no power to enforce the
request, and so can do nothing else but smile bravely and hope for
the best when faced with situations such as these.

Christmas came early for the WMC when the King's Singers included
seasonal selections in its recital on 28 November 1974. Global TV featured excerpts from the concert in its Christmas program for the year.
Aside from the festive selections, the recital was eclectic in a way that
only a King's Singers program could be, ranging from sixteenth-century
Spanish secular music to a potpourri of popular songs in barbershop-
style arrangements, all carefully prepared and presented with panache
and humour.

Michel Debost, who had appeared two years earlier with Secolo
Barocco, gave a highly praised solo recital on 9 January 1975. The French
String Trio was next in the series, giving its local debut on 13 February
1975. The trio's violinist was Gérard Jarry, who had first performed for
the WMC in a solo recital twenty years earlier. Both Debost and the trio
were popular with WMC audiences. Debost made four appearances with
the club, and the trio was featured three times, including a concert
with Debost as guest artist in 1978.

The final concert of the season was given on 6 March 1975 by the
pianist Katharina Wolpe, who had recently completed a two-year stint
as a pianist-in-residence at the University of Toronto's Faculty of Music.
She had attracted a fair amount of attention during her stay in Toronto,
both for her effectiveness as a teacher and for her performances of
contemporary music. For the WMC program, however, she settled on
standard fare — Haydn, Schubert, Brahms, and the Chopin Sonata in B
minor, Op. 58. Wolpe had asked the WMC for a Bösendorfer piano, but
when that request was denied, she agreed to perform on a Steinway
instead. The recital was adequate but unremarkable until the close of the
slow movement of the Chopin sonata, when the pianist apologized and
left the stage. Most of the audience waited politely for the pianist to
reappear and finish the program, but when Wolpe returned to the stage
she announced that she would be unable to perform the final movement
of the sonata because of a cramp in her right hand. John Kraglund in his
review of the recital elaborated upon the problem:

It will surprise no one that the problem stemmed from the piano at
her disposal. Even the city's best pianos have failed to delight some
of the leading soloists to visit the city in recent seasons. Miss Wolpe,
of the sturdy school of piano playing, was left with the piano with

the softest action, no time to have anything done about it and so with the necessity to restrain her technique.[18]

It is an occupational hazard of professional pianists that they are subjected to a completely unfamiliar instrument when performing on tour, but the result rarely turns out as regrettably as it did for Wolpe.

At the annual meeting held on 10 April 1975 at the Heliconian Club, Françoise Sutton in her final remarks as president of the WMC reported that "the problem of Eaton Auditorium's future existence was being carefully investigated with the one assurance to date being, that the seven storey structure, housing the auditorium, will not be demolished but retained as a 'multi-use' building."[19] At that same meeting Elizabeth McCowan Thomas became the new president of the WMC. A further change occurred in the fall of 1975 when Ottilie (Mrs. H.A.) Gunning stepped down as the secretary-treasurer of the WMC, which was still the only paid position in the club. She had served in that role for nine years, and her involvement with the WMC continued until the time of her death in 1992. The WMC established the Ottilie M. Gunning Piano Scholarship in her memory with a generous donation from the Gunning family. Gunning's successor as secretary-treasurer was Sylvia (Mrs. D.G.) MacMillan, who held the position until April 1989. An honorarium was paid to the secretary-treasurer, but it was really a labour of love, and Sylvia MacMillan in effect worked without pay, as she returned her honorarium to the club each year. Both Gunning and MacMillan ran the business affairs of the WMC out of their homes.

The seventy-eighth season was to have begun with a recital by the Glinka Quartet of Moscow, but that group was forced to cancel its North American tour with only ten days' notice, leaving the WMC to find a replacement. One of the difficulties of dealing with East European musicians during the Cold War was that their travel documents could be taken away at a moment's notice, and it was the WMC's bad luck to have this happen to two string quartets (the Tatrai and the Glinka) within the space of two years. The Vághy String Quartet, which had been formed in New York in 1965 and became the quartet-in-residence at Queen's University in 1968, came to the rescue on this occasion. The quartet performed works by Haydn, Prokofiev, and Ravel. William Littler made the interesting observation that "there is about the quartet something of a trans-Atlantic quality, combining a measure of European mellowness with North American drive. It makes for interesting listening."[20]

Other chamber ensembles in the WMC series that season were the French group Secolo Barocco in a return appearance on 22 January 1976, and the Trio di Trieste, a piano trio that had been formed in 1933 and had been touring for over three decades but had never been heard in Toronto before its WMC recital on 25 March 1976. The season also saw the Canadian debuts of two young English artists, the mezzo-soprano Anne Howells on 6 November 1975 and the pianist Howard Shelley on 4 December 1975, and a recital by the German violinist Christiane Edinger on 12 February 1976. It was a season of solid, if unspectacular, music making.

The question of the future of Eaton Auditorium was raised again at the annual meeting on 29 April 1976. Betty Thomas reported that the club was assured of the use of the auditorium for the coming concert season, but had received no commitment for anything further. It was her hope that the hall would be refurbished in time for the opening of the WMC's eightieth season in the fall of 1977.[21] It quickly became apparent, however, that this was not going to be the case. A WMC committee was formed in May 1976 to search for an alternative concert venue, and after finding the existing concert halls unsuitable for one reason or another, it eventually settled on St. Andrew's Presbyterian Church at the corner of King and Simcoe streets. Meanwhile the seventy-ninth concert season took place, as usual, in Eaton Auditorium.

The season opened with the Toronto debut recital of the Hungarian pianist Peter Frankl on 21 October 1976. In his review of the concert, John Kraglund noted in an ironic aside that "the smile . . . he frequently turned on the audience indicated he was enjoying himself much more than I was enjoying him."[22] The next concert featured another Toronto debut, that of the young U.S. cellist Lynn Harrell. Harrell presented the WMC with an unusual request: he wanted a tennis match before his concert.[23] This was duly arranged, and Harrell acquitted himself with honour both on and off the court on that day. Two accomplished young Canadian musicians appeared in recital on 9 December 1976, the baritone Ingemar Korjus and his accompanist, the pianist Jane Coop. Coop had won the Mary Osler Boyd Award from the WMC for the 1970–71 season. This recital was to have been the first WMC event broadcast by the CBC, but a disagreement over the fee led to a cancellation of the arrangement.

Avant-garde music reared its head again at the recital by the outstanding U.S. clarinettist Richard Stoltzman on 13 January 1977. Appearing with Stoltzman was the Canadian musician William Douglas, who was featured as piano accompanist, bassoonist, and composer on this occasion. Douglas had written a piece called *Collage* for clarinet and piano, which consisted of five movements titled "Playtime," "Dawn Mirage," "Rock Etude," "Flower," and "Sky." John Kraglund reported that "the juvenile puppet-pianist presentation of Playtime seemed aimed at an audience slightly younger than the members of the WMC,"[24] and William Littler noted that "in a so-called Rock Etude he [Douglas] and Stoltzman abandoned their instruments entirely to scat-sing and thigh-slap themselves silly."[25]

The audience was not amused by these antics, and at least one WMC member left and resigned her membership in the club as a result of this concert.[26] The WMC's concert programming, which had featured a fair amount of contemporary music in the 1960s, had by now reverted to more conservative fare. Modern music had increasingly become the exclusive preserve of specialist societies such as New Music Concerts and Arraymusic, both of which had begun giving concerts in Toronto in 1972. With the rise and proliferation of such groups locally, the mainstream concert organizations felt released from any obligation to living composers. The resulting ghettoization of contemporary music, especially of the avant-garde stream, has remained an unfortunate fact of concert life.

The Eaton's College Street store was closed on 5 February 1977, and the final two concerts of the WMC season took place under rather gloomy circumstances, with the members having to make their way to the seventh floor auditorium through a darkened building. About the only other person making use of the auditorium at that time was Glenn Gould, who was engaged in intense recording sessions there after learning that he too was soon to be evicted from the premises. In the spring of 1979, Gould was allowed to use Eaton Auditorium again briefly for more recording sessions. His record producer, Andrew Kazdin, has described what the hall looked like at that time:

Basically, it looked as if a bomb had hit the place. Walls were missing, doors were boarded up. There were no lights. There was no heat. Our favorite "Green Room" no longer existed. Thick layers of dust covered everything — mostly due to the destruction of so much plaster.[27]

Nevertheless, the hope that the WMC might one day return to Eaton Auditorium was kept alive into the 1980s after the new owner's proposal to demolish the hall was prevented by a 1987 Supreme Court of Canada decision. The financial support to refurbish the auditorium has not materialized, however, and so the hall has remained in limbo.

The penultimate WMC concert in Eaton Auditorium was given by the French String Trio with guest pianist Georges Pludermacher on 17

February 1977, and the last concert there featured the return appearance by I Solisti di Zagreb on 10 March 1977, twenty years after their first WMC concert. In 1931 another chamber orchestra — the Barrère Little Symphony — had given the very first WMC concert held in Eaton Auditorium. In the intervening forty-six years, over two hundred WMC concerts had been held there. For most people, Eaton Auditorium *was* the WMC, and vice versa. The members had no experience of, and could scarcely imagine, the one without the other. The concerts, the receptions, the fiftieth and seventy-fifth anniversary celebrations, indeed almost all memories of anything to do with the WMC were inextricably bound up with Eaton Auditorium. In the spring of 1977, the WMC could certainly look back with pride, but the pride was mingled with nostalgia and more than a little sense of regret, for it was clear that an era had come to a close. It was not just a question of moving to a new concert venue next season, but of beginning a new chapter in the history of the WMC.

NOTES

1 William Littler, "Love Isn't Necessarily Blind," *Toronto Daily Star* 15 Nov. 1968: 29.

2 Kenneth Winters, "Cellist Pierre Fournier: A Musician's Musician," *Telegram* 24 Jan. 1969: 42.

3 Kenneth Winters, "All Hits, No Misses in Women's Musical Club Series," *Telegram* 7 Mar. 1969: 24.

4 Kenneth Winters, "Kuerti Once Again Shows His Class," *Telegram* 12 Dec. 1969: 48.

5 William Littler, "Masterly Nicanor Zabaleta Makes Harp Speak for Itself," *Toronto Daily Star* 6 Feb. 1970: 23; the second half of this review is devoted to the Beaux Arts Trio concert.

6 Cerise Morris, "Status of Women in Canada, Royal Commission on the," *The Canadian Encyclopedia*, 1985 ed.

7 Kenneth Winters, "Lib Shows in Women's Musical Club," *Telegram* 30 Oct. 1970: 52.

8 Eleanor Koldofsky Sniderman was the sister-in-law of Gwendolyn Williams Koldofsky, who had been the regular WMC accompanist during the late 1930s and early 1940s.

9 Betty Lee, "Getting the Musical Best for a Bargain," *Globe and Mail* 7 Sept. 1971: 10; John Fraser, "Name's Victorian Scent Keeps This Myth Lingering On," *Telegram* 23 Sept. 1971: 56; and William Littler, "The Musical Teacup Brigade of Toronto," *Toronto Daily Star* 30 Oct. 1971: 69. A fourth article appeared in the spring of 1972 — Carl Morey, "Toronto Women's Musical Club," *Performing*

Arts in Canada 9.1 (1972): 19. See the preface for a brief discussion of these four articles.

[10] Kaspars Dzeguze, "Toulouse Ensemble Shows Certain Style," *Globe and Mail* 20 Oct. 1972: 14.

[11] *A Few Fundamental Rules on Entertaining the Lieutenant Governor's Party*, Article 8, WMC Archives, Metropolitan Toronto Reference Library.

[12] Helmut Kallmann, "National and Royal Anthems," *Encyclopedia of Music in Canada*, 2nd ed., 1992.

[13] William Littler, "Half a Concert by Israeli Orchestra Whets the Appetite for More," *Toronto Daily Star* 20 Oct. 1972: 30.

[14] A.H.L. Baudot, "Music Review Was in Poor Taste," *Toronto Daily Star* 3 Nov. 1972: 7.

[15] Ronald Hambleton, "Quartet Given Rare Silent Tribute," *Toronto Daily Star* 17 Nov. 1972: 26.

[16] Božena Brajsa Naughton and Françoise Dreyfus Sutton, personal interview, 27 July 1995.

[17] Rick Kardonne, "Pianist Demonstrates 'Flawless Ability' for Appreciative Capacity Audience," *Canadian Jewish News* 15 Feb. 1974: 16.

[18] John Kraglund, "Piano Action Much Too Soft for Volpe [sic] Touch," *Globe and Mail* 7 Mar. 1975: 14.

[19] *Minutes of the Annual Meeting of the WMC*, 10 Apr. 1975.

[20] William Littler, "Chamber Music Audience Grows with Players," *Toronto Star* 17 Oct. 1975: E6.

[21] *Minutes of the Annual Meeting of the WMC*, 29 Apr. 1976.

[22] John Kraglund, "Peter Frankl Not Quite the Pianist His Publicity Claims," *Globe and Mail* 22 Oct. 1976: 16.

[23] Françoise Sutton, personal interview, 27 July 1995.

[24] John Kraglund, "Stoltzman Right at Home from Bach to Berg and Back," *Globe and Mail* 14 Jan. 1977: 14.

[25] William Littler, "Clarinet Literature Thwarts a Fine Player," *Toronto Star* 14 Jan. 1977: E8.

[26] Božena Naughton, personal interview, 27 July 1995.

[27] Andrew Kazdin, *Glenn Gould at Work: Creative Lying* (New York: Dutton, 1989) 149.

11

Finding a New Home

Mildred Levagood Toogood was elected as the WMC president at the annual meeting on 28 April 1977. It would be her job to guide the club into the post–Eaton Auditorium era. The first difficulty she had to face was a lack of money caused by declining membership dues. It was decided that the number of concerts would have to be reduced, from six to five. As a further economizing measure, the WMC again accepted a package of four concerts from the Mariedi Anders agency at a twenty percent reduction in artists' fees. The next issue to be dealt with was the move to a new concert venue. It seemed at first that the WMC had made a good choice in selecting St. Andrew's Presbyterian Church. The church was even older than the WMC, having been completed in 1875, but was fresh from restorations undertaken during its centennial celebrations. Its downtown location was convenient to public transportation routes, and the church interior had a warmer, more intimate atmosphere and better acoustics than Eaton Auditorium.

But the drawbacks of the church as a concert venue soon became evident. The lighting was inadequate, the sightlines were poor, there was no foyer or other space for receptions or intermission gatherings, and the artists had to put up with a makeshift greenroom. For concerts requiring a piano, there was the added expense and inconvenience of renting an instrument and having it lifted up a flight of stairs into the church. The sightlines were improved for the 1978–79 season with the addition of a platform, but by then a further problem had materialized. Across the street from the church, construction on Roy Thomson Hall began in 1978, and the resulting noise and dirt proved to be the last straw.

After two seasons in St. Andrew's Presbyterian Church, the WMC series moved to Christ Church, Deer Park.

The first WMC event in St. Andrew's featured the Deller Consort from London in a concert of Renaissance vocal music on 3 November 1977. The Consort had last appeared in Toronto eleven years earlier. In the meantime Alfred Deller had retired, but his place had been taken by his son Mark, who was also a countertenor. The recital seemed to prove the wisdom of the WMC's choice of concert venue, for the program of motets, madrigals, and lute solos would have been ineffective in Eaton Auditorium but was perfectly suited to the acoustics and ambience of St. Andrew's.

Two chamber ensembles were featured in return appearances that season, the Orford String Quartet on 8 December 1977 and the French String Trio, with guest artist Michel Debost, on 2 February 1978. The Orford Quartet was a replacement for the Chilingirian String Quartet from England, which was to have been featured in its Toronto debut. A recent Canadian work was included on the Orford Quartet's program, Srul Irving Glick's *Suite Hébraïque No. 3*, which had been premiered in Montreal in 1975. John Kraglund wrote that Glick's work was "effective music, easy to listen to and, in this case, brilliantly and seriously performed."[1] It was a busy day for the Orford members; after finishing the WMC recital they travelled to Buffalo for an all-Beethoven concert that same evening. The French String Trio and Debost were warmly received for their concert of flute quartets by Viotti and Mozart, and trios for flute, violin, and viola by Reger and Beethoven.

The Japanese pianist Mitsuko Uchida was scheduled to make her Canadian debut for the WMC on 12 January 1978, but illness forced her to cancel the engagement with only two days' notice. Taking the news in stride, the WMC acted quickly and managed to make its second impressive substitution of the season, offering the Toronto debut of the U.S. pianist Abbey Simon in place of Uchida. The fifty-five-year-old Simon had won much international acclaim in concert and through his recordings, and needless to say the local critics were highly impressed that the WMC could secure an artist of his magnitude on only forty-eight hours' notice. To top things off, the WMC still managed to secure the Canadian debut of Uchida two years later.

The eightieth season ended with a recital on 30 March 1978 by the Bulgarian violinist Stoika Milanova. Milanova had studied at the Moscow State Conservatory in the 1960s with David Oistrakh and had performed extensively throughout the Soviet Union. In Toronto she was the house guest of Laura Kenton Muir, a cellist and the WMC's concert convenor at the time. The Muir home was kept under surveillance by the KGB during Milanova's stay, for it was suspected that the Bulgarian artist might want to defect. No doubt the KGB was determined to avoid another embarrassing incident like the one in 1974 when the great dancer Mikhail Baryshnikov had literally slipped through its fingers following a reception after the Bolshoi troupe's final performance at the O'Keefe Centre. Milanova did in fact manage to elude the KGB after her recital; not to defect, but rather to make an unscheduled visit to Niagara Falls.

The second season in St. Andrew's opened and closed with chamber ensembles from England — The Music Group of London on 26 October 1978 and the Allegri String Quartet on 29 March 1979. In between came two Canadian concerts, the first by the Montreal soprano Anna Chornodolska accompanied by John Newmark on 7 December 1978, and the second a return appearance by Robert Aitken and Erica Goodman on 18 January 1979. The season also featured the Toronto debut of the Israeli pianist Joseph Kalichstein on 22 February 1979.

Ontario Lieutenant Governor Pauline McGibbon was among the large audience in attendance for the recital by Aitken and Goodman, which included the premiere of *Trance* for flute and harp by Barbara Pentland and a generous sampling of other modern music. (In addition to his activities as a flutist, Aitken was also a composer and the founding artistic director of New Music Concerts.) John Kraglund wrote of Pentland's piece that "There was that cool remoteness which conjures wide-open spaces and is probably as close to a national sound as anything Canadian composers have achieved."[2] The Allegri String Quartet concert featured a recent work also — Benjamin Britten's String Quartet No. 3, the last major work the composer completed before his death in 1976. The work had been performed only once before in Toronto.

At the annual meeting, held in Heliconian Hall on 26 April 1979, Isabel Laidler Jackson became the new president. She had joined the executive committee in 1973, and in the course of over twenty years of dedicated service to the WMC to date she has filled most of the positions on the executive, in addition to chairing the committee for the ninetieth anniversary celebrations and cochairing the history committee for the club's centennial. In an interview with the *Toronto Star* shortly after becoming the president of the WMC, Isabel Jackson reported that she was nurtured on music and said, "Music is my life. Music is the most important thing to me."[3] Her husband, Alan T. Jackson, is the Ontario representative for the distinguished Canadian organ-building firm Casavant Frères of St-Hyacinthe, Quebec.

The only good news reported at the annual meeting was the fact that

COUNTERPOINT TO A CITY

the WMC was given $1,000 by the J.S. McLean Foundation, the first outside support that the club had received in its eighty-one years of activity. On the down side, Mildred Toogood in her outgoing report as president noted that membership numbers had dropped "owing to a drawback in the location of the church and the number of younger women working and unable to attend."[4] In fact, the membership numbers were not just in decline, they were in a free-fall, and would be for several years to come. Almost from the moment it was forced to leave Eaton Auditorium, the WMC began losing members in record numbers. Between 1977 and 1983, the total shrank by almost sixty percent. By the end of the 1982–83 season, the WMC had just over three hundred members, even fewer than it had had in the crisis year of 1929, when the club had almost disbanded. However, in 1929 the WMC managed to bounce back and recruit over three hundred new members within a year, whereas this time the recovery would be much more gradual and modest.

Mildred Toogood's contention that the number of women in the work force contributed to the decline in membership numbers does not really bear up under closer scrutiny. The WMC was now fully open to both men and women, and the greater percentage of women who were working was offset by other factors, such as a greater flexibility in work schedules and the growing number of people who were self-employed (not to mention unemployed). The fact that there was still a significant audience available for weekday afternoon concerts was proven when the Toronto Symphony entered the market in 1984 with its highly successful Monday afternoon concert series.

The identity crisis caused by the loss of the WMC's long-standing home was certainly one of the main reasons for the decline, but the problem was compounded by the unsuitability of the two churches chosen as the concert venue during these seasons. Christ Church, Deer Park was an improvement over St. Andrew's in some respects, but in one important matter it was a step backward — the acoustics were much poorer. Complaints about its too-resonant acoustics would become a constant theme in reviews of WMC concerts. With the decline in membership, however, the WMC finances were in poor shape and so the club could not afford to shop around for a better concert venue. As a result, the WMC was forced to stay put in Christ Church for six seasons.

The first concert in Christ Church was given on 25 October 1979 by two musicians who had won WMC scholarships, the bass John Dodington and the pianist Jane Coop, who appeared both as soloist and as accompanist. The next event, given on 6 December 1979, featured the Canadian debut of the Aulos Ensemble, a group of six musicians from New York that introduced the WMC members to eighteenth-century music performed on period instruments. Unfortunately the soft-toned instruments were no match for a neighbourhood chain saw which intruded its sonic sewage into the concert proceedings periodically. The third concert of the season on 10 January 1980 saw the Toronto debut of the young U.S. cellist Kristi Bjarnason, a pupil of Pierre Fournier.

The season concluded with the Canadian debuts of Mitsuko Uchida on 21 February 1980 and the Sydney String Quartet on 13 March 1980. Among the awards which the thirty-year-old Uchida had won was second prize in the 1970 International Chopin Competition in Warsaw, and the WMC recital featured her in an all-Chopin program. Although she was often praised for her sensitive, delicate musicianship on other occasions, Uchida in her WMC recital was accused of a heavy-handed approach that was lacking in poetry and lyricism.[5] The acoustics of Christ Church were partly to blame, but it also seems to have been an off day for Uchida. The Sydney String Quartet from Australia, which had been formed six years earlier, was featured in the only Canadian concert of a three-week North American tour. Like the WMC season as a whole, the quartet promised rather more than it delivered.

The eighty-third season also featured two Canadian debuts, by the Chestnut Brass on 4 December 1980 and by the Sequoia String Quartet on 26 March 1981. The Chestnut Brass was a quintet from Philadelphia that performed mainly popular and light classical fare in a manner similar to the Canadian Brass, but without that group's panache. The WMC recital ranged from Renaissance dances played on cornetts and sackbuts to jazzy numbers written by the quintet's tubist. William Littler called it "a musical dog's breakfast" and wrote that "As admirable as it may be to be able to play anything, it can be even more admirable to refrain from doing so."[6] The Sequoia String Quartet from California was as understated and soft-toned as the Chestnut Brass was noisy and brash. Littler, commenting on the quartet's performance of Bartók's String Quartet No. 6, found it "perversely fascinating . . . to listen to the way music of such inner power could be rendered smoothly and genially harmless."[7]

The solo artists featured that season were the pianist Howard Shelley in a return appearance on 16 October 1980, the Israeli-born U.S. violinist Shmuel Ashkenasi on 29 January 1981, and the Toronto mezzo-soprano Catherine Robbin on 26 February 1981. Shelley and Ashkenasi both gave recitals of uneven quality, but Robbin provided the one outstanding musical event of the season with a "varied, agreeable and substantial song program"[8] of selections by English, German, and French composers.

At the annual meeting held in Heliconian Hall on 23 April 1981, Joan

Beryl Beynes Fox Wilch became the new president. She had been the social convenor of the WMC, and in November 1978, during Pauline McGibbon's term of office, she became the first official tea hostess to the office of the lieutenant governor of Ontario. In the second year of Joan Wilch's presidency, Lieutenant Governor John Black Aird officially opened the 1982–83 WMC season with "cheerful comments . . . paying tribute to the Club and its musical accomplishments,"[9] and in March 1983 he held the third reception for the club in the lieutenant governor's suite (the first two had been hosted by Pauline McGibbon in 1974 and 1978). Joan Wilch died on 16 March 1984, just ten months after stepping down as WMC president, and in her memory the club created the Joan B. Wilch Award in Voice.

The eighty-fourth season opened on 1 October 1981 with the Toronto debut of the Vega Wind Quintet from England, which was on tour with the Canadian pianist Tom Plaunt. Two days before the recital the quintet's French hornist had to return to England because of a death in the family, but the WMC recital was saved when Harcus Hennigar, the French hornist of Toronto's York Winds, agreed to step in. Next the Czech pianist Boris Krajny was featured in recital on 5 November 1981. He opened his program with the Liszt Sonata in B minor, but if he was hoping to startle the critics into submission with this act of reckless bravery, he was disappointed — instead they commented on how foolish it was to begin a recital with this work.[10] The Canadian debut of the Yugoslavian violinist Miha Pogacnik, a pupil of Joseph Gingold, Henryk Szeryng, and Max Rostal, followed on 3 December 1981. In a demanding program of works by Bach, Beethoven, Bartók, and Schubert he proved himself a worthy heir of the fine violin-playing traditions represented by his illustrious teachers. Jane Coop made her third WMC appearance on 4 February 1982, accompanying the Canadian soprano Rosemarie Landry, who had recently begun teaching voice at the University of Toronto. Both artists excelled in a recital of seldom heard songs ranging from Lully to Roger Quilter. The season came to a successful close on 11 March 1982 with the Canadian debut of the Audubon Quartet, an excellent young string quartet from Virginia.

Another U.S. string quartet opened the eighty-fifth season on 14 October 1982, the Muir String Quartet. The group was only two years old, yet was already the quartet-in-residence at Yale University and had toured Europe twice. For the WMC it performed works by Haydn and Ravel, as well as Bartók's String Quartet No. 6. Unlike the Sequoia String Quartet, the Muir Quartet did not take a gentle approach to the Bartók quartet; indeed its performance was so vigorous that the violist broke a string in the third movement. The second concert of the season, on 9 December 1982, featured the Lithuanian-born cellist David Geringas, whose brother Yaakov Geringas was a violinist in the Toronto Symphony at the time. Yaakov's wife, Marina Balter-Geringas, accompanied the cellist in his Toronto debut. Lynn Harrell, who had made his local debut with the WMC six years earlier, was performing in Toronto on the same evening as the Geringas recital, making it a banner day for cello fans. The Toronto-born tenor Mark DuBois was heard in recital accompanied by Stephen Ralls on 13 January 1983. Although only twenty-nine years old, DuBois was already at the height of his career, and the critics, though unimpressed by his rather hackneyed program, found much to admire in the quality of his voice and in Ralls's sensitive piano playing.

The chamber ensemble Musical Offering from California made its Canadian debut for the WMC on 3 February 1983. It was a sign of the times that this quintet, consisting of violin, oboe, cello, bassoon, and harpsichord, was already regarded as something of an anomaly because it performed Baroque music on modern instead of period instruments. Like the Sequoia String Quartet, Musical Offering was in residence at the California Institute of the Arts. The eighty-fifth season ended on 7 April 1983 with a recital by the oboist Louise Pellerin, a pupil of Heinz Holliger who was born in Sherbrooke but was resident in Switzerland. She was accompanied by the Montreal pianist Diane Mauger. At the end of his favourable review of Pellerin's recital, Kraglund noted that the WMC was in difficulty, stating that "the organization has experienced decreasing membership and attendance" and that "In desperation, the club is thinking of changing its name to get the few hundred new subscribers ... needed to prevent its demise."[11]

Indeed, the outlook was not good at the annual meeting, held at Heliconian Hall on 12 May 1983.[12] Nora Dawson, who had been a French teacher at Havergal College and in the public school system, was the incoming WMC president.[13] She reported optimistically that the brochures for the coming season had been printed in green, for growth. Helen Goudge pointed out that the WMC had survived a worse crisis in the past, though she had to look back to 1929 for that incident. Muriel Stafford noted, more realistically, that the club needed one hundred new members to meet its budget for the coming year. Although that target was not met, there was a modest increase in numbers to report at the next annual meeting. The increase did not help the WMC's financial situation much, but it was an important turning point, as it marked the first time in over a decade that there had been growth rather than decline in the number of members. A small improvement in the WMC's finances was also effected by the introduction of advertising into the club's concert programs. This had, in fact, been done in the past, but after a long absence the practice was resumed with the 1983–84 season.

The opening concert of the eighty-sixth season revealed another draw-back to Christ Church as a concert venue — the noise of the heating system. The Czapáry String Trio from Germany included the String Trio, Op. 20 by Anton Webern in its recital on 27 October 1983, but as John Kraglund reported, it was difficult to hear the work:

Webern's String Trio . . . did not last more than three minutes. . . . [T]he piece had an austere lyricism, which only failed to win enthu-siastic audience approval because it was so quiet it could barely be heard above the sound of the ceiling fans in the auditorium.

Once these air-circulators had made their presence felt, they could not be ignored. Even Schubert's String Trio in B flat, D 581, the highlight of the concert, did not manage to obliterate the distur-bance.[14]

The second concert of the season played to the church's strengths. A new organ had recently been installed in Christ Church, and it was heard in a joint recital on 1 December 1983 by Jeanne Baxtresser, the principal flutist of the Toronto Symphony at the time, and the Montreal organist Mireille Lagacé.

The third concert of the season, on 12 January 1984, featured the twenty-seven-year-old Canadian soprano Jane MacKenzie accompanied by the Toronto pianist Bruce Ubukata. In 1982, Ubukata and Stephen Ralls had founded the Aldeburgh Connection, an afternoon concert series that was similar in nature to the WMC series and had even success-fully revived the WMC's former practice of serving tea at intermission. (Perhaps taking its cue from the Aldeburgh Connection, the WMC switched from holding a private tea by invitation only after its concerts to having a general reception that was open to all the members beginning with the 1983–84 season.) The Aldeburgh Connection was sponsored in part by the Canadian Aldeburgh Foundation which, in an admirable spirit of cooperation, also gave the WMC a generous grant this season for the MacKenzie concert. (After retiring from the WMC executive, Françoise Sutton had established and was the first president of the Canadian Aldeburgh Foundation.) MacKenzie had studied at the Britten-Pears School for Advanced Musical Studies in Aldeburgh, England, and had worked with Ubukata there. Her teachers in Aldeburgh were Peter Pears, Hugues Cuénod, and Galina Vishnevskaya, and the influence of these singers was reflected in her choice of repertoire for the WMC recital, which included folk-song arrangements by Britten and songs by Fauré, Rachmaninov, and Tchaikovsky, in addition to lieder by Mozart and Brahms.

A highlight of the season was the concert by the Vermeer Quartet on 2 February 1984. The quartet was led by Shmuel Ashkenasi, who had not greatly impressed the critics on the occasion of his WMC solo recital three years earlier, but was evidently more in his element leading the quartet. The program consisted of works by Beethoven and Britten, followed after intermission by the Brahms Piano Quartet in G minor, Op. 25, in which the ensemble (minus the second violinist) was joined by Anton Kuerti. Ronald Hambleton wrote that "it was a concert of unusual beauty and clarity"[15] and that the musicians managed to work wonders with the acoustics of the church. The same could not be said of the final artist of the season, the twenty-two-year-old Bulgarian pianist Emile Naoumoff, who succeeded in "wearing out most of the audience and exposing some of the acoustical disadvantages of Christ Church, Deer Park, in the process," according to John Kraglund.[16] Naoumoff was heard in his Canadian debut on 22 March 1984 as a replacement for Mikhail Rudy. He had studied composition and counterpoint with Nadia Boulanger as a teenager, and his overly long WMC program included one of his own works, a virtuoso study titled *Impasse*, and also his transcription of excerpts from Stravinsky's ballet *The Firebird*.

The final season in Christ Church featured the Edinburgh Quartet on 11 October 1984, the French pianist Michèle Scharapan on 15 November 1984, Toronto's York Winds on 13 December 1984, the English baritone Brian Rayner Cook on 7 February 1985, and the Canadian cellist Shauna Rolston on 14 March 1985. The quartet and Scharapan were featured in their Toronto debuts, and Cook was making his Canadian debut for the WMC.

The York Winds gave the local premiere of the Woodwind Quintet (1981) by William Douglas, the Canadian musician whose *Collage* for clarinet and piano had not found much favour with the WMC audience in 1977. The quintet was no more appealing; it ranged from atonal bebop in the first movement to a rock-oriented rondo finale in which the players were instructed to tap their feet throughout. Cook also introduced the WMC members to a new, but more palatable work, the song cycle *The Threshold of the New* by the English composer Mary Chandler, which was heard in its Canadian premiere. Cook was accompanied by the Toronto pianist William Aide, who stepped in at short notice for an indisposed Stephen Ralls. The recital as a whole was judged to be "a concert of highs, with no single low point."[17]

But the highlight of the season was the recital of works by Beethoven, Bach, Schumann, and Franck performed by Rolston, accompanied by Valerie Tryon. Rolston had already matured from a child prodigy into a seasoned performer, with a New York debut at Town Hall and many other international appearances to her credit. At the end of her review, Gaynor Jones asked, "If Rolston is only 18 and plays this well, what will she be like at 20 or 25?"[18] The answer is — even better, for Rolston has continued to grow and develop as a performer. In 1994 she succeeded Vladimir Orloff as the cello instructor at the University of Toronto.

At the annual meeting in Heliconian Hall on 9 May 1985, Nora Dawson in her outgoing report as president noted that financial difficulties continued to plague the WMC. Because the club dealt with U.S. concert agencies, artists' fees had to be paid in U.S. funds, and with the decline in value of the Canadian dollar this represented a bigger investment each year. Another shortfall in the budget for the coming season was predicted, despite an increase in the membership fees from thirty dollars to thirty-five dollars.

There was, however, good news to report along with the bad. The executive committee had voted unanimously to move the concert series to Walter Hall in the Edward Johnson Building at the University of Toronto, beginning with the 1985–86 season. Nora Dawson explained some of the advantages of the new concert venue: "Walter Hall accommodates 492 people, has elevators, excellent washroom and backstage facilities and a spacious foyer for receptions. Transportation to this new facility is good. Shops and restaurants in the area are numerous and excellent."[19] Indeed, in the opinion of many, Walter Hall was "probably Toronto's best small concert hall,"[20] and it had been specifically constructed for the type of concerts sponsored by the WMC. It had excellent acoustics and unobstructed sight lines from every seat in the house, and it was equipped with both a concert grand piano and a two-manual Casavant organ. The bus and subway stopped a stone's throw from the Edward Johnson Building, and one of the finest music libraries in Canada was just an elevator ride away, should any of the artists turn up without their music, as had happened more than once in the past. With the WMC numbers stabilizing at 350 to 400 members, the hall was also just the right size. Hanna Gätgens Feuerriegel, the incoming WMC president, fully deserved the congratulations and thanks bestowed upon her by the members for having brought about the move to Walter Hall. After eight years in the wilderness, the WMC had at last found its promised land.

Hanna Feuerriegel was born in Hamburg and came to Canada in 1954, settling in Toronto in 1957. She joined the WMC in the early 1970s and had been involved in the executive committee for nine years, including a four-year term as concert convenor, before becoming president in 1985. After her two-year term as president she remained on the executive committee for another two years and has continued to be active behind the scenes in WMC affairs.

The first season in Walter Hall featured a return appearance by Musical Offering on 3 October 1985, the Canadian debut of the U.S. soprano Sylvia McNair on 7 November 1985, a recital by the Canadian pianist Angela Hewitt on 5 December 1985, the Toronto debut of the Korean violinist Dong-Suk Kang on 30 January 1986, and a concert by the Canadian Piano Trio on 6 March 1986.

Musical Offering's program was devoted to works by Bach and Handel to commemorate the three hundredth anniversary of the birth of those two composers. The ensemble now featured one performer on a period instrument: Owen Burdick played a harpsichord by the Toronto builder Matthew James Redsell that was a copy of an instrument from Bach's time. Sylvia McNair included in her recital Casa Guidi (1983), by the U.S. composer Dominick Argento; it was a cycle of five songs to texts by Elizabeth Barrett Browning which had been premiered in 1984 by Frederica von Stade. Both Argento's composition and McNair's singing were much enjoyed by the audience and critics alike. The concerts by Kang and the Canadian Piano Trio were also favourably received, but the highlight of the season was the Angela Hewitt recital. Further confirmation of the WMC's uncanny ability to spot rising young talent was given when the club contracted Hewitt several months before the twenty-six-year-old pianist from Ottawa won the 1985 International Bach Piano Competition. Hewitt outshone 165 contestants from thirty-eight countries to win the lucrative top prize in that competition, which was held in May 1985 in Toronto.[21] Hewitt's WMC recital attracted an unusual amount of interest, as it was her first local post-competition recital. Ronald Hambleton wrote that the concert "sparkled from beginning to end."[22]

At the annual meeting in Heliconian Hall on 8 May 1986, the most interest was generated by discussion of plans to celebrate the ninetieth anniversary of the WMC (see chapter 12).[23] But there were two other items of some importance. The first was the fact that the WMC had negotiated to have CBC Stereo tape four concerts from the coming season in a cost-sharing arrangement. This would not only help out with the financial situation, but would also raise the WMC's profile through the nationwide exposure that the broadcasts would bring. The second item of interest was the news that the WMC had received a grant from the Ontario Arts

Council for the 1985–86 season, a development that was not viewed favourably by all of the members. The WMC had long prided itself on the fact that it depended only on membership fees and donations for its funding. For the WMC to accept grants from government agencies, some members felt, meant that it was now just a concert-giving organization like any other, rather than a club. Others argued that since the WMC had become a registered charitable organization in 1969 and began to seek donations from foundations in 1978, the next logical step was to apply for any government assistance for which the club was eligible. The only loss in independence which this might involve would be that in future the WMC could be subject to guidelines set by the government funding agencies as a condition for receiving grants, but if these were found to be contrary to the wishes of the membership, the club could just decide not to apply for the grant.

The second season in Walter Hall was bracketed by two all-Canadian concerts; it opened with the violinist Chantal Juillet and the pianist William Tritt in a joint recital on 16 October 1986, and closed with the Toronto debut of the Hart Piano Quartet on 19 March 1987. In between came the Ridge String Quartet from California on 13 November 1986, the U.S. clarinettist David Shiffrin and his accompanist Irma Vallecillo, both making their Toronto debut on 11 December 1986, and the Bulgarian pianist Juliana Markova on 12 February 1987.

Juillet and Tritt attracted a near-capacity audience for their recital, which included the Sonata No. 2 (1983) for violin and piano by Oskar Morawetz, in addition to works by Beethoven, Strauss, and Ysaÿe. Unfortunately the musicians were inconvenienced backstage on this occasion, because the CBC equipment and personnel took over the greenroom. A further drawback in having the recitals taped for broadcast was demonstrated in the Ridge Quartet concert, when the first violinist broke a string near the end of the first movement of Beethoven's String Quartet in F major, Op. 59, No. 1. The players had to start the quartet over again from the beginning because of the CBC. Nevertheless the benefits of having the concerts taped for broadcast outweighed the minor disadvantages.

The Hart Piano Quartet took its name from the initials of its members, the violinist Betty-Jean Hagen, the violist Ralph Aldrich, the pianist Arthur Rowe, and the cellist Malcolm Tait, all of whom were then on the faculty of the University of Western Ontario. Hagen won the first WMC scholarship in 1950 and performed as a soloist in a WMC concert in 1953; the others were all making their first appearance before the club. Included on the program were two rarities, piano quartets by the Ottawa

composer Anne Eggleston (her earliest major work, dating from 1955)
and by Gustav Mahler (a student work written in 1876 but not published
until 1964). This was the last WMC concert to be reviewed by John
Kraglund,[24] who retired at the end of April 1987. Ten days before his
retirement, Kraglund wrote one final article about the WMC, in which he
gave a brief personal history of his involvement with the club and
outlined its forthcoming ninetieth anniversary season. He cited the
1956–57 and 1957–58 seasons as two of the most exciting he had witnessed, and praised the WMC for its "enviable ability to unearth young
performers," for providing "opportunities for Canadian performers,"
and for "its awarding of scholarships to talented young musicians." [25]
Kraglund's support had meant a great deal to the WMC over the past
thirty-five years, and the executive committee wrote to thank him on the
occasion of his retirement.

The WMC was also about to embark on a new phase of its life at this
time, not by retiring (it was well past retirement age) but by renewing
itself from within. The immediate past had seen the WMC's fortunes sink
to perhaps their lowest point ever, with financial difficulties, flagging
interest in the club, plummeting membership, and troublesome concert
venues. Throughout it all, the WMC had somehow managed, as always,
to continue sponsoring fine concerts — fifty of them in the previous ten
years — but the members could be forgiven for feeling a little shaken by
what they had collectively been through. Now, with the move to Walter
Hall successfully accomplished, a turnaround had begun, and to lift
everyone's spirits the WMC executive committee decided to celebrate by
throwing the biggest party in the club's entire history.

NOTES

[1] John Kraglund, "Orford's Beethoven Still Stylish," *Globe and Mail* 9 Dec.
1977: 18.
[2] John Kraglund, "Some Dazzling Virtuosity from Flute and Harp Duo,"
Globe and Mail 19 Jan. 1979: 14.
[3] Lauretta A. Forsythe, "Music Is Her Life," *Toronto Star* 20 Oct. 1979,
Starweek Magazine: 70.
[4] *Minutes of the Annual Meeting of the* WMC, 26 Apr. 1979.
[5] John Kraglund, "Chopin Doesn't Benefit from Muscular Approach," *Globe
and Mail* 22 Feb. 1980: 15; Ronald Hambleton, "Pianist Not Heard to Advantage," *Toronto Star* 22 Feb. 1980: D8.
[6] William Littler, "Five Chestnuts Roast Themselves with Hot Air," *Toronto
Star* 5 Dec. 1980: D9.

7 William Littler, "Californian Quartet Needs to Dig Deeper," *Toronto Star* 27 Mar. 1981: C8.

8 Arthur Kaptainis, "Robbin Triumphs in Several Styles," *Globe and Mail* 27 Feb. 1981: 18.

9 John Kraglund, "Quartet's Static Sound Thick, Heavy," *Globe and Mail* 15 Oct. 1982: E10.

10 John Kraglund, "Czechoslovak Pianist Has His Ups and Downs," *Globe and Mail* 6 Nov. 1981: 19; William Littler, "Czech Pianist Dives into the Maelstrom of Liszt," *Toronto Star* 6 Nov. 1981: D3.

11 John Kraglund, "Oboist Plays Superbly," *Globe and Mail* 8 Apr. 1983: E4.

12 Information in this paragraph is taken from *Minutes of the Annual Meeting of the* WMC, 12 May 1983 and 10 May 1984.

13 "Meet Nora Dawson," WMC *Newsletter* 7 (1993): 4.

14 John Kraglund, "Finale Only Flaw in Trio's Show," *Globe and Mail* 28 Oct. 1983: E6.

15 Ronald Hambleton, "Vermeer Quartet Works Wonders with Deer Park Acoustics," *Toronto Star* 5 Feb. 1984: H9.

16 John Kraglund, "Bulgarian Pianist Technically Brilliant but Unrestrained," *Globe and Mail* 23 Mar. 1984: E12.

17 Gaynor Jones, "Baritone's Voice Displays Passion," *Toronto Star* 10 Feb. 1985: E9.

18 Gaynor Jones, "Cellist a Knockout in Talent and Style," *Toronto Star* 15 Mar. 1985: D19. Rolston was actually only seventeen years old at the time of her WMC recital.

19 *Minutes of the Annual Meeting of the* WMC, 9 May 1985.

20 John Kraglund, "New Venue for WMC Concerts," *Globe and Mail* 10 May 1985: E8.

21 Patricia Wardrop, "The 1985 International Bach Piano Competition," *Encyclopedia of Music in Canada*, 2nd ed., 1992.

22 Ronald Hambleton, "Angela Hewitt Recital Sparkled All the Way," *Toronto Star* 6 Dec. 1985: D26.

23 Information in this paragraph is taken from *Minutes of the Annual Meeting of the* WMC, 8 May 1986.

24 John Kraglund, "Hart Quartet Shows Promise," *Globe and Mail* 20 Mar. 1987: D10.

25 John Kraglund, "Women's Musical Club Continues Its Tradition with Top-Notch Talents," *Globe and Mail* 20 Apr. 1987: C11.

12

Celebrations

The plans to celebrate the ninetieth anniversary of the WMC began during the 1985–86 season. A special committee was formed under the leadership of Isabel Jackson, and it was decided that the main event would be a gala concert, to be held in Massey Hall on 4 December 1987. The King's Singers were booked for that date, as was Toronto's CJRT Orchestra under Paul Robinson, which would accompany the King's Singers in the main work featured on the program, John Rutter's *The Reluctant Dragon* in its Canadian premiere.

It was quite a jump from the WMC's regular concert venue, Walter Hall, which seats 492 people, to Massey Hall, which seats 2,765 people. It had been forty-six years to the day since the previous WMC event in Massey Hall, a wartime benefit concert by the Ten-Piano Ensemble. None of the WMC members had any practical experience of the kind of public relations campaign that was necessary to fill a hall of that size. The fund-raising and ticket sales campaigns both began too late, and the concert proved to be a hard sell. *The Reluctant Dragon* is a charming English children's musical fable about St. George and the dragon, but it was not a work that was particularly well suited to the WMC's traditional audience. In trying to reach out to a different demographic group in order to fill the hall, the WMC faced stiff competition from other seasonal events, and ticket sales for the event remained disappointing. Just as had been the case in 1941, the Massey Hall concert seemed headed for ruin. In 1941, Mona Bates had come to the rescue and single-handedly sold enough tickets to make the event turn a profit. In 1987, it was

Esther Spence McNeil who saved the day with a massive fund-raising campaign, as we shall see later.

Aside from the large amount of money that was raised for the event, there were other benefits to the gala concert. John B. Withrow, the son of an early manager of Massey Hall, wrote a fine article about the WMC for *Bravo*, the house magazine of Massey Hall and Roy Thomson Hall,[1] and an article in *Music Magazine* by Jack Brickenden (whose wife, Ruth Brickenden, was the head of the WMC publicity committee at the time) included a brief history of the WMC and news of its ninetieth season.[2] For the concert itself, a twenty-eight-page commemorative program was produced, with congratulatory letters from the prime minister, Ontario's lieutenant governor, and other important public figures. A reception was held after the concert at the Eaton Tower, complete with a lavish supper. And after it was all over, Laura Muir wrote a useful evalutation of the gala concert to help the WMC learn from the experience, with a view to making the club's forthcoming centennial celebrations run as smoothly as possible.[3]

The actual concert was a mixed success. The hall's sound system was very poor indeed; Ronald Hambleton wrote that the microphones and amplification turned the King's Singers into ventriloquists: "The lips could be seen moving, but the sound could be heard coming loud and clear from a large black speaker 30 feet to their right."[4] The arrangements of seasonal music (by King's Singers member Robert Chilcott) were too heavily scored, and the orchestral selections did little to help create a sense of occasion. There were enjoyable moments in the program, to be sure, but the musical rewards were probably not commensurate with the extremely high financial cost of the event.

The ninetieth anniversary season itself was an unqualified success. The five concerts all featured previous WMC scholarship winners, which reinforced the club's commitment to Canadian performers and also provided an interesting sample of some of the fine talent that had benefitted from the awards over the years. As a further advantage, all of the artists' fees for the season could be paid in Canadian funds, thus avoiding the high exchange rate for U.S. dollars. To further improve the WMC's financial situation, the membership fee for the season was raised from $35 to $50, the largest single increase up to that time.

The featured performers (with the year of their WMC scholarship in brackets) were Robert Aitken (1959) with Erica Goodman on 1 October 1987; John Dodington (1968) and Catherine Robbin accompanied by John Greer on 12 November 1987; Edmond Agopian (1983 and 1984) accompanied by Janice Stephens on 14 January 1988; Bonnie Silver (1969

and 1971) with Norbert Kraft on 11 February 1988; and Jane Coop
(1970) on 17 March 1988. The concerts in November and March were
recorded for broadcast by CBC radio.

Of the nine pieces performed by Aitken and Goodman, eight dated
from the twentieth century and two were by Canadian composers
(Alexina Louie and Gilles Tremblay). Robert Everett-Green, who was
John Kraglund's successor as the *Globe and Mail* staff music critic, wrote
that the pieces were of a "contemporary slant . . . rarely glimpsed at the
Club's afternoon concerts,"[5] which was true on the whole, although
Aitken and Goodman had twice performed similar recitals for the club
in the past. Three of the other four recitals that season also featured
Canadian compositions. The violinist Edmond Agopian performed the
Suite for solo violin (1956) by Jean Papineau-Couture, Norbert Kraft
played R. Murray Schafer's *Le Cri de Merlin* (1987), and Jane Coop
included Barbara Pentland's *Vita Brevis* (1973) on her program. Agopian
came to Canada from Romania in 1977, graduated from the Unversity
of Toronto in 1985, and was on the faculty at Acadia University at the
time of his WMC recital (he later moved to the University of Calgary).
The other performers were all well-known figures on the Canadian music
scene, and all won favourable reviews for their concerts that season.

Mary Anderson Horwood was elected to succeed Hanna Feuerriegel
at the WMC annual meeting in Heliconian Hall on 14 May 1987, and thus
served as the president for the ninetieth anniversary season. Like Joan
Wilch, Mary Horwood enjoyed close ties to Queen's Park, for her
husband, Rudy Horwood, was aide-de-camp to four Ontario lieutenant
governors before his death in May 1989. Unfortunately, Mary Horwood
was in poor health and was unable to complete her term of office. On
29 September 1988 she resigned, and fifteen months later she died in
Toronto. The WMC concert on 7 February 1991 by the King's Consort
from England, which was attended by Ontario Lieutenant Governor
Lincoln Alexander, was dedicated to her memory, and the WMC's Mary
Horwood Memorial Fund, created with contributions from the Horwood estate and friends of the late president, helped to pay for the
concerts that season.

Mary Dennys, as the first vice-president, took over the duties of
president for the remainder of the 1988–89 season, and stayed on for a
two-year term thereafter. The daughter of a Presbyterian minister, Dennys
was born in Victoria, B.C., but moved to Toronto as a child and lived
there until her death in May 1996. She graduated from Havergal College
in 1940, and went on to study modern languages at Trinity College,
University of Toronto. After graduating from the Ontario College of

Education, she returned to Havergal College, first as a teacher, and from 1975 as the principal.[6] Upon retiring from Havergal College in 1985, she was given a WMC membership as a present, and quickly became involved in helping to run the club. Her administrative experience, business skills, and collegial approach were instrumental in helping the club forge ahead in a time of transition and make ambitious plans for the future. She remained associated with the WMC until the time of her final illness.

The ninety-first season was to have opened with the Toronto debut recital of the Quebec tenor Frederick Donaldson on 13 October 1988, but he became ill and the Toronto soprano Gaynor Jones substituted for him on less than a day's notice. She was accompanied by Stephen Ralls in a versatile program that ranged from Carissimi to Poulenc and from opera excerpts to folk-song arrangements, including Godfrey Ridout's *Folk Songs of Eastern Canada* (1967).

The second concert, on 24 November 1988, featured the Danish recorder virtuoso Michala Petri, accompanied by her mother Hanne Petri at the harpsichord. In one of the most thoughtful and probing reviews given a WMC concert, Tamara Bernstein wrote that it was "a dazzling, enjoyable performance," but one which raised problematic questions about the nature of virtuosity and the star system. Bernstein pointed out that while Petri "has openly dissociated herself from the period-instrument movement," her own approach to Baroque music was unconvincing because of a lack of musical freedom, the absence of a full continuo complement, and overly sparse ornamentation.[7]

The next event was a well-received performance by the New World String Quartet, the quartet-in-residence at Harvard University, on 15 December 1988. More intense excitement was generated, though, by a recital featuring the nineteen-year-old Canadian violinist Scott St. John, accompanied by Arthur Rowe, on 2 February 1989. In November 1988, St. John had been awarded the use of a Stradivarius violin from the Canada Council's Musical Instrument Bank, and the WMC recital marked the first time that he played the instrument in public.[8] The moment was captured both by CBC radio, which broadcast the entire recital, and by CTV, which featured excerpts from it on the network's evening news telecast. Robert Everett-Green wrote that St. John demonstrated "flair and individuality" in his program and that his new violin "sang out with enormous power and clarity."[9] In addition to showing off his new violin, St. John also demonstrated his versatility in the recital by performing violin sonatas by Mozart and Strauss, a viola sonata by Brahms, and *Steps...* (1978) for viola and piano by the Canadian composer Malcolm Forsyth.

The final concert of the season was a recital by the young German pianist Konstanze Eickhorst on 16 March 1989. Eickhorst, who had finished second to Angela Hewitt in the 1985 International Bach Piano Competition, played works by Mozart, Schubert, Beethoven, and Prokofiev. Unfortunately, she was up against even stiffer competition in her WMC recital, from the appallingly loud hammering noises of the adjacent building site. (The Rupert E. Edwards Wing of the Edward Johnson Building was under construction at the time.) It was hardly surprising that Eickhorst's playing, and the audience's enjoyment of the concert, suffered as a result of this disruption. As Tamara Bernstein wrote, "Eickhorst deserved an ovation simply for continuing to perform knowing that the hammering could resume at any time; few artists would have been able to do as much."[10]

The WMC Constitution was revised once again during the 1988–89 season by a committee under the leadership of Nora Dawson. Seventeen changes in all were proposed and subsequently ratified at the annual meeting, held in Heliconian Hall on 11 May 1989. In perhaps the most important innovation, Article III was changed to read, "General membership in the Club shall be open to women and men," thus doing away with the associate membership category, which had been on the books since 1958. Men were thus finally admitted to full and equal membership status in the WMC, with the right to vote for or even serve on the executive committee. In 1991 Frank Daley became the first man to join the WMC executive committee, and by 1993 there were about forty male members in the club, representing roughly ten percent of the total membership.

A major new initiative in 1989 was the launch of the WMC's Career Development Award. Its success was due in no small measure to Esther Spence McNeil, who chaired the first award committee and has been described by the Globe and Mail as a "powerhouse" fund-raiser.[11] She was born in Johnstown, Pennsylvania, and in 1956 moved to Canada with her English-born husband, John McNeil, an insurance executive who in 1988 became the chairman and CEO of the Sun Life Assurance Company of Canada. Esther McNeil first attended WMC concerts beginning in 1970, but then moved to Montreal, where she became a member of the Ladies' Morning Musical Club. After returning to Toronto she rejoined the WMC in 1986 and soon became involved in helping to run the club.

Esther McNeil's first task for the WMC was to spearhead the committee to raise money from government, corporate, and private sources for the ninetieth anniversary gala concert. Her efforts were so successful that after the considerable expenses for that concert had been paid, there was still more than $60,000 left over. It was decided to use this money to set up a competitive award that would be offered every two years. Unlike the other WMC scholarships and awards, which are given to local music students upon the recommendation of the Royal Conservatory of Music or the University of Toronto Faculty of Music, the Career Development Award is open to any music student across Canada who is under thirty years of age, and it is administered by the WMC itself. The award category has rotated between piano, strings, and voice. The first competition, for piano, attracted a total of forty-three applicants, whose taped submissions were evaluated by a jury at the Canadian Music Centre in Toronto from 14 to 16 November 1989. Francine Kay of Toronto won the award, which consisted of an eight-thousand-dollar cash prize and an appearance in the WMC's 1990–91 concert series. The runners-up were Michelle Mares and Kevin Fitz-Gerald.

An article in the *Globe and Mail* a month later stated that the jury had included the live-in paramour of one of the contestants.[12] The paper later printed a retraction of the item,[13] but even though the allegation was untrue, it brought home to the WMC the fact that conflict-of-interest guidelines had not been provided for the jury. This oversight was corrected in time for the next competition.

The second competition was organized slightly differently. It was for strings, and from the twenty-one applicants, four finalists, all violinists, were chosen to compete in front of a live audience at Walter Hall on 1 December 1991. James Ehnes, just fifteen years old and the youngest of the four contestants, won the top prize of eight thousand dollars and a WMC concert appearance. The other three finalists — Erika Raum, Catherine French, and Lara St. John (Scott St. John's younger sister) — were awarded smaller cash prizes. The third competition, for voice, offered two eight-thousand-dollar prizes, one from the WMC and the other from the Jean A. Chalmers Fund of the Canadian Opera Company Women's Committee. Six finalists competed before a live audience on 30 January 1994. The soprano Karina Gauvin of Montreal won the top prize of eight thousand dollars and a WMC recital, while Anita Krause won the Chalmers award. The other finalists were Brett Polegato, Lori Klassen, Randall Jakobsh, and Annie Larouche.

Meanwhile the regular WMC concert series continued as usual, though without any events of outstanding interest. The ninety-second season began with the Canadian pianist Alain Lefèvre in his Toronto recital debut on 19 October 1989. Next came the Trio d'Archi di Roma on 16 November 1989, followed by the English violist Sophie Renshaw, who had joined the Orford String Quartet in 1987, in her Toronto recital debut accompanied by Francine Kay on 14 December 1989, just one month after Kay had won the first WMC Career Development Award. The season ended with two WMC return appearances, the first by the baritone Brian Rayner Cook accompanied by Stephen Ralls on 8 February 1990, and the second by the Audubon Quartet on 22 March 1990. The Lefèvre recital was broadcast by CJRT, and the concerts by Renshaw and the Audubon Quartet were heard on CBC radio.

All of the artists in the ninety-third season were heard in their Toronto recital debuts, and two groups made their Canadian debuts: the Stockholm Arts Trio (a piano trio) on 18 October 1990 and the English soprano Gillian Fisher with a trio (oboe, cello, keyboard) from the period-instrument group The King's Consort on 7 February 1991. Local debuts were given by Francine Kay on 29 November 1990, by the Borealis Wind Quintet from the United States on 7 March 1991, and by the Hungarian cellist Csaba Onczay on 4 April 1991. The concerts by the trio, Kay, and the quintet were broadcast on CBC radio. Kay gave the Toronto premiere of *Four Contrasting Moods* (1986) by Oskar Morawetz in her recital, but otherwise the concerts this season, like those of the previous one, featured mainly standard repertoire in good but not great performances.

The annual meeting on 16 May 1991 took place not in Heliconian Hall as usual, but rather in the Women's Art Association on Prince Arthur Avenue. At that meeting Esther McNeil became the new WMC president. During her term of office, McNeil was often called away on business trips with her husband, and she relied on Mary Dennys, who was not only the past president but also a close personal friend, to keep the WMC sailing on an even keel during her absences from Toronto.[14] Despite her travels, McNeil had a very hands-on approach to running the WMC, and she effected many important changes during her two years as president. Some of her plans for reorganizing the WMC were drawn from Thomas Wolf's book *Managing a Nonprofit Organization*.

One of McNeil's first acts as president was to arrange a two-day retreat for the WMC executive committee in June 1991 in order to set up a five-year strategic plan with the help of a professional adviser. The idea for the two-day retreat was taken from the Wolf book,[15] and a strategic plan is recommended by the government arts councils which now supply a significant portion of the WMC budget. Next, a council of advisers was formed to facilitate input from people who were not WMC members but had useful arts management experience to share with the club. Then, at a meeting on 26 September 1991, it was moved that the WMC executive committee be renamed the board of directors, though as of 1995 the Constitution had not yet been changed to officially endorse the new term. The membership fee for the coming season was increased to $75, and finally, program advertising was done away with, but in its place corporate sponsorship of individual concerts was introduced.

In April 1992 the WMC moved into an office at 160 Bloor Street East, and soon thereafter Patricia Hiemstra was hired to be the WMC's part-time professional arts administrator. The cost of this move was minimized when Sun Life, which owned the building in which the office was located, returned the rent for the office space to the WMC as a charitable donation. The WMC committee meetings, which had been held for many years at the Royal Conservatory of Music, were now held at the new office, and historical materials from various locations were assembled there to form the WMC archives. The office and arts adminis-trator proved their usefulness so quickly that it was hard to imagine how the WMC had operated without them. In 1994 the WMC moved to a new office at 188 Eglinton Avenue East. At the end of the 1993–94 season Patricia Hiemstra resigned as the administrator, as she was moving to Ottawa. Alicia Sealey became the new administrator in 1994, and she was succeeded by Susan Corrigan in September 1995.

The annual meeting at the Women's Art Association on 14 May 1992 amounted to a sixth concert for the season, as it included an hour-long recital that featured Erika Raum and the Maple Trio, a local piano trio. The second season of Esther McNeil's presidency saw further important developments. An eight-minute-long promotional video outlining the history of the WMC was made in November 1992 with the cooperation of TSN and the veteran broadcaster Doug Maxwell; it is titled *For the Love of Music*. The centennial fund was created to finance the cele-brations of the club's hundredth anniversary, and the sustaining fund was reinvigorated. The annual operating budget for the WMC had by now grown to more than forty thousand dollars, and about twice that amount was invested in the club's scholarship accounts. The WMC's financial affairs were getting to be too complex for a person without extensive financial and investment experience to manage. Sylvia MacMillan, who had resigned as the secretary-treasurer in April 1989, was followed by Susan Crammond, who lasted only until December 1989 and was in turn succeeded by Marianne Weil. In 1992 the position of secretary-treasurer was changed to treasurer, and Dagmar Stafl, who had joined the WMC in 1990, took over the job. Stafl was highly qualified for the position, as she was the retired chief economist for the Ontario Ministry of Consumer and Commercial Relations.

Throughout all of this activity, the WMC concert series continued without missing a beat. The ninety-fourth season featured the Quink Vocal Ensemble from Holland in its Canadian debut on 10 October 1991, Trio Parnassus from Stuttgart (a piano trio with the Canadian pianist Chia Chou) on 7 November 1991, the U.S. clarinettist Charles Stier in his Canadian debut accompanied by William Bloomquist on 5 December 1991, the Fresk Quartet from Sweden in its Toronto debut on 30 January 1992, and the Canadian tenor Michael Schade in his Toronto recital debut accompanied by Mikael Eliasen and the violist Mark Podolsky on 5 March 1992. The last recital attracted much notice because Schade, like Hewitt and St. John, had recently won a major prize, the Canada Council's 1991 Virginia P. Moore Award. Stier gave the Toronto premiere of *Horovelé* (1979) for clarinet solo by the Montreal composer Petros Shoujounian. All of the concerts except the first one were broadcast on CBC radio.

The ninety-fifth season featured not one but three recent competition winners: James Ehnes, the holder of the WMC Career Development Award (19 November 1992); the U.S. pianist Mark Anderson, who won the Glory of Mozart International Piano Competition held in Joliette, Quebec, in June 1991 (25 February 1993); and the St. Lawrence String Quartet, awarded first prize in the fourth Banff International String Quartet Competition in April 1992 (15 April 1993). Also appearing that season were the Ames Piano Quartet from Iowa on 15 October 1992, and the Canadian baritone Russell Braun on 10 December 1992. Anderson, Braun, and Ehnes were all making their Toronto solo recital debuts. It was a season that lived up to the highest of WMC traditions, with memorable music making in every concert by exceptionally talented young performers.

Ehnes, accompanied by the Montreal pianist Louise-Andrée Baril, won a standing ovation from the capacity WMC audience for his recital, which was broadcast by CJRT. Included on the program was the Canadian composer Alfred Fisher's *Nameless Dances* (1988), a work dedicated to Ehnes. Braun, who had won a WMC scholarship in 1990 and graduated from the University of Toronto in 1991, was accompanied by the Toronto pianist Carolyn Maule. Urjo Kareda called him a "generously gifted young singer" and wrote that the recital demonstrated "wonderfully fresh and spontaneous singing from an artist who appears to have an instinctive compulsion for musicmaking."[16] Anderson also won rave reviews; Tamara Bernstein wrote that "his thoughtful interpretations encouraged listeners to hear familiar pieces in new ways." She complained, however, about the Faculty of Music's concert grand piano and wrote that it "sounds like a xylophone in its upper register."[17] Included in the St. Lawrence Quartet's sold-out concert was *Lament in the Trampled Garden* (1992) by the Canadian composer Marjan Mozetich. In addition to winning the top prize at Banff, the St. Lawrence Quartet also carried away the award for giving the best performance of Mozetich's work, which was the imposed test piece for the competition. Bernstein wrote that the Mozetich piece received "a passionate perfor-mance" and that the concert featured "the exciting kind of ensemble playing that not only reconciles, but thrives on the individualities of the players."[18]

At the annual meeting held at the Women's Art Association on 20 May 1993, Esther McNeil in her outgoing report as president announced that Maureen Forrester, Walter Homburger, and Ontario Lieutenant Governor Henry N.R. Jackman had agreed to become honorary patrons of the WMC.[19] She also reported that the Mary Osler Boyd and Joan B. Wilch awards had been combined to create one larger prize at the Faculty of Music. She congratulated the more than one hundred volunteers who had worked for the WMC during the past year, and announced that plans for celebrating the club's centennial were shaping up well. At the same meeting, Muriel Jones Roberts became the new president. A retired schoolteacher, she was born of Welsh parents in Windsor, Ontario, and had joined the WMC in 1983. In addition to serving as president for two years and in various other positions on the WMC executive, she assumed the responsibility of overall planning for the WMC's centennial celebrations.

The 1993–94 season saw another chamber music concert series com-petitor arrive on the scene in Metropolitan Toronto, with the opening of the $48 million North York Performing Arts Centre. The inaugural season of the centre's one-thousand-seat Recital Hall offered a breath-taking array of musical talent, including many artists who had earlier performed for the WMC, such as the Juilliard String Quartet, the Muir Quartet, Richard Goode, Anton Kuerti, and Norbert Kraft. It is a measure of the solid support for the WMC that a series of this magnitude could be launched just a twenty-minute subway ride away from Walter Hall without in any way diminishing the fortunes of the WMC's own concert series.

The WMC's ninety-sixth season opened with two Toronto debuts, the first by the London Winds (an octet) on 30 September 1993, and the second by the Armenian-born pianist Sergei Babayan on 18 November 1993. Next came the Alexander String Quartet from San Francisco on 9 December 1993, and then the venerable Haydn-Trio Vienna on 10

February 1994. The season ended with the third WMC appearance by Catherine Robbin on 31 March 1994, accompanied by Michael McMahon. As on her previous visits, Robbin was the highlight of the season. "Hers is a beautiful voice used with intelligence, polish and wisdom," wrote Urjo Kareda, who added that the two Canadian works featured were especially engaging — Robert Fleming's *The Confession Stone* (1966), a work of "heart-stopping power," and John Greer's *A Sarah Binks Songbook*, an "utterly funny" piece of "enlightened foolishness."[20] All of these concerts were broadcast on CBC radio. The WMC began admitting students from the Royal Conservatory of Music and the University of Toronto Faculty of Music to its concerts free of charge during this season, as a further sign of its support for young Canadian musicians.

The ninety-seventh season had the same mix of artists as the previous year, except that a flute and harp duo was substituted for the wind octet. The lineup included the Arden Trio (a U.S. piano trio) on 6 October 1994, the Moyzes Quartet (a Slovakian string quartet) in its Canadian debut on 3 November 1994, the U.S. team of Carol Wincenc (flute) and Nancy Allen (harp) on 15 December 1994, Career Development Award winner Karina Gauvin on 9 February 1995, and the Canadian pianist Michael Injae Kim on 16 March 1995. Gauvin, like Robbin, was accompanied by Michael McMahon and reviewed by Urjo Kareda, who once again felt that the singer was at her best in the Canadian work featured — Derek Holman's cycle *Ash Roses*, which was written for Gauvin and was heard in its premiere performance.[21] Kim also included a Canadian work on his program, the evocative four-movement work *Music for Piano* (1982) by Alexina Louie. Once again CBC radio broadcast all of the concerts.

At the annual meeting, held at the University Women's Club on 10 May 1995, Betty Taylor Gray became the new WMC president. She grew up in Collingwood, where she studied piano with Muriel Stephenson and completed her ARCT as a high school student. After completing teacher's college in Toronto, she taught school for five years but then retired to raise a family of five children. She attended her first WMC concert in 1989 at the invitation of Esther McNeil, and joined the executive committee two years later. Aside from installing Betty Gray and the new board of directors, the main business at the meeting was the discussion of plans for celebrating the WMC centennial. In addition to the regular concert series for the 1997–98 season, four projects were planned: the fourth Career Development Award competition, for piano, with the finals held on 9 February 1997; a commissioned work from the Canadian composer Jacques Hétu; a gala concert on 24 May 1998; and the present history of the WMC.

At the time of this writing, the WMC is in the midst of its ninety-eighth season, which has seen concerts by the Russian émigré Toronto pianist Alexander Tselyakov on 28 September 1995, and two Toronto debuts, the first by the Guild Trio with the French clarinettist Michel Lethiec on 26 October 1995, and the second by the Quatuor Parisii from Paris on 23 November 1995. The season concludes with the Canadian debut of the Welsh contralto Hilary Summers accompanied by Stephen Ralls on 15 February 1996, and a recital by Erika Raum and Francine Kay on 14 March 1996. For the third season in a row, CBC radio is taping all of the concerts for later broadcast. With a full slate of artists already booked for the ninety-ninth season and plans well underway for the centennial celebrations, the WMC can not only cast a backward glance on its distinguished past, but also look forward to an exciting future. The fact that the WMC has not just survived, but is in better shape than ever after an invigorating renewal process in the early 1990s, means that the celebrations will continue on and on into the future.

NOTES

1 John B. Withrow, "Celebrating 90 Years: The Women's Musical Club of Toronto Celebrates 90 Years of Achievement," *Bravo* Sept.–Oct. 1987: 70, 73, 74.

2 Jack Brickenden, "Women's Musical Clubs: A Canadian Tradition," *Music Magazine* 10.4 (1987): 14–17.

3 Laura Muir, "Ninetieth Anniversary Concert Evaluation," typescript, 1988, WMC archives. This report is based on a questionnaire filled out by members of the WMC executive committee and the ninetieth anniversary committee.

4 Ronald Hambleton, "Club Rings in 90th Year with Charming Concert," *Toronto Star* 6 Dec. 1987: C4.

5 Robert Everett-Green, "Alumni Return to WMC with Contemporary Slant," *Globe and Mail* 2 Oct. 1987: D5.

6 See "Dennys, Mary Grace Amelia," obituary, *Globe and Mail* 30 May 1996: A19, and "Lives Lived: Mary Dennys," *Globe and Mail* 5 June 1996: A22.

7 Tamara Bernstein, "Dazzling Recorder Recital Raises Unsettling Questions," *Globe and Mail* 26 Nov. 1988: C4.

8 Robert Everett-Green, "Musician Wins Five-Year Loan of Canada Council Stradivarius," *Globe and Mail* 25 Nov. 1988: D11.

9 Robert Everett-Green, "Recital Demonstrates St. John's Mature and Flexible Talent," *Globe and Mail* 4 Feb. 1989: C12.

10 Tamara Bernstein, "Pianist Forced into Untimely Competition," *Globe and Mail* 18 Mar. 1989: C5.

[11] Rosemary Sexton, "MPs, Friends Celebrate Robbie Burns' Birthday," *Globe and Mail* 28 Jan. 1988: A19. The second half of this column is about the WMC.

[12] "Notes on 1989," *Globe and Mail* 30 Dec. 1989: C11. The article is anonymously authored but appears as a sidebar to an article by the music critic Robert Everett-Green.

[13] "Our Mistake," *Globe and Mail* 4 Jan. 1990: A2.

[14] Esther McNeil and Mary Dennys, personal interview, 2 Aug. 1995.

[15] Thomas Wolf, *Managing a Nonprofit Organization* (New York: Simon, 1990) 246.

[16] Urjo Kareda, "Braun Shows Abundant Promise," *Globe and Mail* 11 Dec. 1992: C9.

[17] Tamara Bernstein, "Anderson Gives Brahms His Full Due," *Globe and Mail* 27 Feb. 1993: C13.

[18] Tamara Bernstein, "New Level of Ease," *Globe and Mail* 17 Apr. 1993: C13.

[19] Esther McNeil, "The President's Report," WMC *Annual Report for 1992–93*.

[20] Urjo Kareda, "Artist Proves Worthy of Her Supporters," *Globe and Mail* 2 Apr. 1994: C12.

[21] Urjo Kareda, "Gauvin's Voice an Unformed Bloom," *Globe and Mail* 11 Feb. 1995: C5.

13

Reflections:
An Afterword

The WMC has been restructured from the ground up several times in the course of its one hundred years of activity, and there is no doubt that it will continue to evolve as it heads into its second century. Like any other living, vital organism, the WMC changes over time; it grows, develops, matures, and learns from its past mistakes as it heads into the future. But as it travels through time, the WMC also influences its environment. The impact that the club has had and continues to have on the musical life of Toronto is extraordinarily rich. Many thousands of people have been associated with the WMC over the years, among them the featured performing artists, those who have helped to run the organization, the regular members of the club and their guests, and the music students who have attended concerts or received scholarships. The WMC will always hold a special place in the hearts of these people and bring back a flood of memories of the many benefits gained through contact with the club — memories of the fine music heard and enjoyed at the concerts, of the financial help received at a crucial point in a career, of the satisfaction of working with others and seeing the tangible results of those labours, or perhaps most importantly, of the friendships made over the years.

The emphasis in this book has been on the things that have made the WMC unique — the people, the concerts (some 875 to date), and the close association with Toronto, the great city in which the club has woven its counterpoint of music and good deeds. However, the WMC is but one member of a huge network of women's musical clubs in the United States and Canada, and it is worth reflecting on what the WMC shares in common with those other groups.

The study of the women's musical club movement is still in its infancy, despite the fact that thousands of such organizations have flourished in centres large and small throughout North America during the past 125 years. Information on these clubs is scattered in a myriad of places — in libraries and archives the length and breadth of the continent, in countless magazine and newspaper articles, in a host of ephemeral pamphlets outlining the histories of the various clubs, and in the personal papers, memoirs, and memories of club women.

Linda Whitesitt is one of the few people to have studied the important role that women's musical clubs have played in American concert life over the years. She has examined the histories of numerous such clubs in the United States, and has summarized her findings on the history and evolution of the club movement. The experience of the very first women's musical club, the Rossini Club of Portland, Maine, is representative, as Whitesitt has explained:

> From an initial emphasis on self-education, the Rossini Club soon set a course that other clubs would later follow: it turned its energy to serving the community — presenting public concerts, raising money for civic welfare organizations, providing educational opportunities for youth, and offering scholarships to local musicians.[1]

The WMC followed these very steps. In its initial stage, self-education played an important role; many of the earliest concerts included a talk on some aspect of music appreciation to inform as well as entertain the members. Public concerts followed: in 1899, at the end of the first season, the WMC held its first open recital, and beginning in 1902 these concerts reached a more ambitious level when the Kneisel Quartet became the first professional group to be engaged. The goal of community service was uppermost at the time of the First World War, when the WMC formed a Philanthropic Committee that was engaged in various charitable deeds. Such activity continued during the early years of the Second World War, when the club raised thousands of dollars for the Canadian Red Cross Society. Scholarship awards to young local musicians, first planned in 1930, became a reality in 1950, and in the ensuing forty-five years nearly one hundred such awards have been given (see appendix 3 for details).

Whitesitt describes other general features of women's musical clubs in the United States that are applicable to the WMC: a division in the early years of the century into active and associate membership categories (a feature of the WMC from 1899 to 1914), a fondness for "theme" recitals devoted to a specific composer or country (numerous such events were held in the early seasons of the WMC), the sponsoring of a separate student music club (the WMC's Rehearsal Club, which flourished from 1930 to 1947), and the promotion of music by indigenous composers (e.g., the WMC's concerts of music by Toronto composers in 1908 and 1909, and an all-Willan concert in 1927). Whitesitt also found that many clubs disappeared during the Depression (the WMC came close to disbanding in 1929, and then ceased operating for four seasons because of the Second World War), and that those clubs which managed to survive the 1930s had switched from giving concerts by amateur members to sponsoring professional performances (the WMC effected this change in 1914).

The achievements of some individual clubs in the United States are impressive. The Women's Music Club of Columbus, Ohio, is said to have been the largest in the world, with 3,500 members by 1907. Three major orchestras were formed either directly by or with major financial assistance from the local women's musical club — the Cincinnati Symphony Orchestra, the Cleveland Orchestra, and the National Symphony Orchestra of Washington, D.C. Other clubs, such as those in Grand Rapids and Tucson, were able to raise enough money to build their own meeting place or concert hall. Collectively, women's musical clubs in the U.S.A. were responsible for three-quarters of all concert engagements outside of the major urban centres in 1927.

Turning from Whitesitt's analysis of women's musical clubs in the U.S.A. to an examination of the history of the movement in Canada, we see that the above generalities dissolve into a sea of individual stories. Although they were all cut from the same cloth, no two clubs followed exactly the same pattern. As in any other area of human activity, the influence of one strong-willed, energetic leader can shape and mould the actions and destiny of an entire organization. The distinguishing features of each club are the result of the creative ideas of the many individuals who have guided and shaped that club over the years.

Of the sixteen women's musical clubs that have entries in the second edition of the *Encyclopedia of Music in Canada*, only six are now inactive.[2] Twelve of the sixteen were founded in the twenty-year period following 1889; in chronological order these were the clubs in Hamilton (founded in 1889), Quebec City (1891), Montreal (1892), Ottawa (1892–1974), Winnipeg (1894), Toronto (1899), Calgary (1904–64), Halifax (1905), Vancouver (1905), Victoria (1906–89), Regina (1907), and Edmonton (1908–73). The other clubs with entries are those in Saskatoon (1912–78) and Lethbridge (1932–74), and two clubs founded by Eva

Clare in Regina (1915) and Winnipeg (1933). Eva Clare (1884–1961) was a Canadian pianist and teacher who recruited the members of these two music clubs from among her pupils and friends.[3] She also wrote a valuable book describing how to organize and run a music club, with short essays on seven composers and suggestions for music club concert programs.[4]

Cautionary tales for the future can be read from the history of those clubs that are now defunct. The Morning Music Club of Ottawa did not survive two name changes, the city's curious lack of interest in chamber music and solo recitals, and the increased cost of presenting artists in the inflationary 1970s. Declining interest led the clubs in Calgary and Victoria to disband and use their assets to set up awards for local young musicians. The Victoria club seems to have been the first to open its membership up to men when it reconstituted itself as the Victoria Musical Art Society in 1930, but this did not prevent an eventual decline in the club's fortunes. The Ladies' Morning Musical Club of Montreal, on the other hand, was one of the last to invite males to attend when it opened its doors to them in 1969, but both before and since that time it has been one of the most successful of all Canadian women's musical clubs. Indeed, a recurring theme in WMC executive committee minutes over the years has been the desire to emulate the success of the Montreal club.

Not a few clubs have been the victims of their own success. In many cities across Canada it was the local women's musical club that first organized concert-giving activity in the community in an attempt to foster an appreciation for fine music and encourage its growth and development.[5] As a result of these pioneering efforts, concert activity took hold and then increased by leaps and bounds in many cities. If a women's musical club did not adjust to the changing musical life of the community, its role could easily be usurped by other organizations, resulting in declining membership and the loss of a sense of purpose. The Halifax Ladies' Musical Club has been one of the most successful at adapting over the years. It was one of the only Canadian women's musical clubs to join the National Federation of Music Clubs, but left the U.S. organization in 1913 to set off on its own path. Over the years it has sponsored concerts, offered scholarships and prizes, promoted music in the local school system, and given performance opportunities to young musicians, continually inventing new ways of proving its usefulness and value to the cultural life of Halifax.

If the history of these other clubs teaches anything, it is that each organization must find its own way. What works for one club can and often has spelled disaster for another. Each club must reflect the needs and qualities of the community in which it is located. Perhaps it is not by coincidence that so many of the women involved in the WMC have also been expert gardeners. A healthy plant needs strong roots and proper nourishment, and a good gardener must know not only the plant but also the ground that she cultivates. What grows in Victoria may well wither and die in Toronto, and this applies not just to flowers but also to women's musical clubs. In the end, success depends not on any easily applied formula or panacea, but on the sound judgement and inspired decisions of the individuals in whose hands the fate of the club lies — the members themselves.

If Mary Irene Gurney Evans and the others who founded the Women's Musical Club of Toronto in 1899 could witness the present-day structure and activities of their organization, they would likely be surprised at how different an entity it is from the one that they knew, but they would surely be pleased by the healthy condition of their offspring. And no doubt they would still enjoy themselves thoroughly at WMC events, for the philosophy of the club may have evolved and changed over the years, but the goal has remained the same: to present fine concert music for the benefit of club members and the general public, and to support young Canadian musicians. As long as people are alive to the satisfaction and joy that this activity brings, there will be a need for the Women's Musical Club of Toronto.

NOTES

1 Whitesitt 664.

2 "Women's Musical Clubs," *Encyclopedia of Music in Canada*, 2nd ed., 1992.

3 Ronald Gibson, "Clare, Eva," *Encyclopedia of Music in Canada*, 2nd ed., 1992.

4 Eva Clare, *Music Appreciation and the Studio Club*, 2nd ed. (New York: Longmans, 1930).

5 See Maria Tippett, *Making Culture: English-Canadian Institutions and the Arts before the Massey Commission* (Toronto: U of Toronto P, 1990) 103.

Women's Musical Club of Toronto Presidents

1. 1899–1904 Mary Henderson Flett Dickson [Mrs. George Dickson]
2. 1904–05 Constance Bodington Hamilton [Mrs. L.A. Hamilton]
3. 1905–07 Sarah Trumbull Van Lennep Warren [Mrs. H.D. Warren]
4. 1907–08 Anna Mueller Farini [Mrs. Guillermo Antonio Farini]
5. 1908–10 Mary Henderson Flett Dickson [Mrs. George Dickson]
6. 1910–13 Mary Richmond Kerr Austin [Mrs. A.W. Austin]
7. 1913–14 Helen Daly Pepler [Mrs. Arthur Pepler]
8. 1914–18 Mary Henderson Flett Dickson [Mrs. George Dickson]
9. 1918–19 May Thompson Lash [Mrs. Miller Lash]
10. 1919–21 Carrie Reid Lambe [Mrs. William G.A. Lambe]
11. 1921–24 Mary Wylie Meikle [Mrs. W.B. Meikle]
12. 1924–29 Elsie Johnston Bongard [Mrs. R.R. Bongard]
13. 1929 Georgina Dennistoun Russel [Mrs. A.M. Russel]
14. 1929–31 Judith Grant Howse Finch [Mrs. Gordon T. Finch]
15. 1931–39 Mary Osler Boyd [Mrs. Edmund Boyd]
16. 1939–42 Bertha Mason Woods [Mrs. W.B. Woods]
   1942–46 WMC ceases activities because of wartime conditions
16. 1946–48 Bertha Mason Woods [Mrs. W.B. Woods]
17. 1948–52 Pearl Steinhoff Whitehead [Mrs. Roy B. Whitehead]
18. 1952–55 Doris Godson Gilmour [Mrs. Harrison Gilmour]
19. 1955–57 Kathleen (Kay) Irwin Wells [Mrs. Dalton C. Wells]

20. 1957–59   Jessie Macpherson [Miss/Dr. Jessie Macpherson]
21. 1959–61   Eustella Burke Langdon [Mrs. John E. Langdon]
22. 1961–63   Margaret (Peggy) Young Snell [Mrs. F. Van V. Snell]
23. 1963–65   Amy Fleming Timmins [Mrs. Harold W. Timmins]
24. 1965–67   Muriel Gidley Stafford [Mrs. Merrill C. Stafford]
25. 1967–69   Helen Christilaw Goudge [Mrs. T.A. Goudge]
26. 1969–71   Elizabeth Lodi Mittler [Mrs. Nicholas Mittler]
27. 1971–73   Juliette Abreu del Junco [Mrs. Emilio del Junco]
28. 1973–75   Françoise Dreyfus Sutton [Mrs. Marshall B. Sutton]
29. 1975–77   Elizabeth McCowan Thomas [Mrs. William B. Thomas]
30. 1977–79   Mildred Levagood Toogood [Mrs. Arthur F. Toogood]
31. 1979–81   Isabel Laidler Jackson [Mrs. Alan T. Jackson]
32. 1981–83   Joan Beryl Beynes Fox Wilch [Mrs. Peter J. Wilch]
33. 1983–85   Nora C.E. Dawson [Miss/Dr. Nora Dawson]
34. 1985–87   Hanna Gätgens Feuerriegel [Mrs. F.W. Feuerriegel]
35. 1987–88   Mary Anderson Horwood [Mrs. G.W. Horwood]
36. 1988–91   Mary Dennys [Miss Mary Dennys]
37. 1991–93   Esther Spence McNeil [Mrs. John McNeil]
38. 1993–95   Muriel Jones Roberts [Mrs. Michael F. Roberts]
39. 1995–97   Elizabeth (Betty) Taylor Gray [Mrs. Joe Gray]

APPENDIX 2

Women's Musical Club of Toronto Concert Convenors

The early concerts of the WMC were performed largely by the members themselves, and for each concert a member of the program committee was responsible for arranging the event. When the WMC switched to sponsoring concerts by visiting professional artists, the role of concert convenor was created.

1. 1921–23 Elsie Keefer
2. 1923–27 Georgina Dennistoun Russel [Mrs. A.M. Russel]
3. 1927–31 Mary Osler Boyd [Mrs. Edmund Boyd]
4. 1931–34 F.M. Warren [Mrs. Douglas Warren]
5. 1934–42 Marjorie Counsell [Mrs. John L. Counsell]
   1942–46 WMC ceases activities because of wartime conditions
5. 1946 Marjorie Counsell [Mrs. John L. Counsell]
6. 1946–54 Mary Osler Boyd [Mrs. Edmund Boyd]
7. 1954–64 Eustella Burke Langdon [Mrs. John E. Langdon]
8. 1964–66 Trudy Graf [Mrs. H.G. Graf]
9. 1966–69 Elizabeth Lodi Mittler [Mrs. Nicholas Mittler]
10. 1969–71 Juliette Abreu del Junco [Mrs. Emilio del Junco]
11. 1971–73 Françoise Dreyfus Sutton [Mrs. Marshall B. Sutton]
12. 1973–77 Božena Brajsa Naughton [Mrs. Michael H. Naughton]
13. 1977–81 Laura Kenton Muir [Mrs. J.S. Muir]
14. 1981–85 Hanna Gätgens Feuerriegel [Mrs. F.W. Feuerriegel]

15. 1985–87   Consuela Corbett [Mrs. Gary Corbett]
16. 1987–89   Doreen Allison Ryan [Mrs. Noel Ryan]
17. 1989–92   Isabel Laidler Jackson [Mrs. Alan T. Jackson]
18. 1992–   Pamela Richards MacKenzie [Mrs. William MacKenzie]

APPENDIX 3

Women's Musical Club of Toronto Award Winners

Abbreviations

BSG	Banff study grant (1964)
CDA	Career Development Award (est. 1989)
ISH	Irene Simons Hume Award (1966–71)
JGF	Scholarship in memory of Mrs. J.G. Fitzgerald (1957)
MOBA	Mary Osler Boyd Award (WMCS as renamed in 1955)
WMCB	WMC Bursary (est. 1966)
WMC-JBW	Joan B. Wilch Award in Voice (est. 1985)
WMC-MOB	MOBA as renamed in 1973 and increased
WMC-OMG	Ottilie M. Gunning Piano Scholarship (est. 1992)
WMC-RCM	WMC Royal Conservatory Scholarship (est. 1975)
WMCS	WMC Scholarship (1930–73) / WMC Scholarship in memory of MOB, JBW (est. 1993)

1950–51	Betty-Jean Hagen, violin	WMCS	($250)
1951–52	Ray Dudley, piano	WMCS	($250)
1952–53	Bernard Turgeon, baritone	WMCS	($100)
1953–54	Bernard Turgeon, baritone	WMCS	($100)
1954–55	Paul Helmer, piano	WMCS	($100)
1955–56	Pierrette Lepage, piano	MOBA	($125)
1956–57	Bruce Mather, piano and composer	MOBA	($150)

1957–58	Teresa Stratas, soprano	MOBA	($150)
	Walter Buczynski, piano and composer	JGF	($100)
1958–59	Orval Ries, oboe	MOBA	($150)
1959–60	Robert Aitken, flute	MOBA	($200)
1960–61	No award given		
1961–62	Janet Thom, piano	MOBA	($200)
1962–63	Ruth Shakarian, soprano	MOBA	($200)
1963–64	Ruth Shakarian, soprano	MOBA	($200)
1964–65	Ruth Shakarian, soprano	MOBA	($200)
	Maria Pellegrini, soprano	BSG	($200)
1965–66	Nancy Greenwood, contralto	MOBA	($200)
1966–67	Isabel Vila, violin	MOBA	($300)
	Paul Brown, baritone	ISH	($100)
	Burnetta Day, soprano	WMCB	($100)
1967–68	Renee Rosen, soprano	MOBA	($300)
	Judith Kenedi, piano	WMCB	($200)
	Sonya Rohozynsky, contralto	ISH	($100)
1968–69	Judith Kenedi, piano	MOBA	($300)
	Adele Armin, violin	WMCB	($200)
	John Dodington, bass-baritone	ISH	($100)
1969–70	Mary Lou Fallis, soprano	MOBA	($300)
	Bonnie Silver, piano	WMCB	($200)
	Madeleine Courtney, contralto	ISH	($100)
1970–71	Jane Coop, piano	MOBA	($300)
	Allan Stellings, cello	WMCB	($200)
	Roderick Campbell, baritone	ISH	($100)
1971–72	Bonnie Silver, piano	MOBA	($300)
	Fujiko Imajishi, violin	WMCB	($200)
	Caralyn Tomlin, soprano	WMCS	($150)
1972–73	Jill Pert, contralto	MOBA	($300)
	Connie Stewart, piano	WMCS	($200)
1973–74	Helena Bowkun, piano	WMC-MOB	($500)
1974–75	Caralyn Tomlin, soprano	WMC-MOB	($500)
1975–76	Galia Shaked, piano	WMC-MOB	($500)
1976–77	Colleen Farrier, piano	WMC-MOB	($500)
1977–78	Giselle Dalbec, violin	WMC-MOB	($500)
1978–79	Lise Vaugeois, French horn	WMC-MOB	($500)
1979–80	Raymond Bisha, French horn	WMC-MOB	($500)
	Chia-Lin Chou, piano	WMC-RCM	($200)
1980–81	Joseph Orlowski, clarinet	WMC-MOB	($600)

	Elina Doverman, piano	WMC-RCM	($250)
1981–82	Hamish Gordon, oboe	WMC-MOB	($700)
	Melana Karpinsky, piano	WMC-RCM	($250)
1982–83	Jean Ducharme, saxophone	WMC-MOB	($700)
	Laura Ippolito, piano	WMC-RCM	($250)
1983–84	Edmond Agopian, violin	WMC-MOB	($700)
	Elina Doverman, piano	WMC-RCM	($300)
1984–85	Edmond Agopian, violin	WMC-MOB	($700)
	Mami Kuroda, piano	WMC-RCM	($300)
1985–86	Mark David Cavlovic, piano	WMC-MOB	($700)
	David Chokroun, piano	WMC-RCM	($300)
	Mary Hahn, soprano	WMC-JBW	($200)
1986–87	Jack Bakker, classical guitar	WMC-MOB	($700)
	Mariko Anraku, harp	WMC-RCM	($300)
	Laura Schatz, soprano	WMC-JBW	($200)
1987–88	Meredith Hall, soprano	WMC-MOB	($700)
	Elise Desjardins, piano	WMC-RCM	($300)
	Shelagh Tyreman, mezzo-soprano	WMC-JBW	($200)
1988–89	Nicholas Papadakis, violin	WMC-MOB	($700)
	Julianne Schoen, piano	WMC-RCM	($300)
	Lori Klassen, mezzo-soprano	WMC-JBW	($200)
1989–90	Mary Catherine Duff,		
	mezzo-soprano	WMC-MOB	($900)
	Francine Plouffe, piano	WMC-RCM	($500)
	Russell Braun, baritone	WMC-JBW	($500)
	Francine Kay, piano	CDA	($8,000)
1990–91	Xia Liao, violin	WMC-MOB	($900)
	Susan Archibald, piano	WMC-RCM	($500)
	Hope Nightingale, soprano	WMC-JBW	($400)
1991–92	Dianne Wells, mezzo-soprano	WMC-MOB	($900)
	Susan Archibald, piano	WMC-RCM	($500)
	Cheryl Hickman, soprano	WMC-JBW	($400)
	James Ehnes, violin	CDA-1st	($8,000)
	Erika Raum, violin	CDA-2nd	($2,000)
	Catherine French, violin	CDA-3rd	($1,000)
	Lara St. John, violin	CDA-4th	($500)
1992–93	Erika Tanner, soprano	WMC-MOB	($900)
	Micah Yui, piano	WMC-RCM	($500)
	Teri Dunn, soprano	WMC-JBW	($400)
1993–94	Elissa Lee, violin	WMCS	($1,400)
	Stephen Ham, piano	WMC-OMG	($700)

	Karina Gauvin, soprano	CDA-1st	($8,000)
	Brett Polegato, baritone	CDA-2nd	($2,000)
	Lori Klassen, mezzo-soprano	CDA-3rd	($1,000)
	Randall Jakobsh, bass-baritone	CDA-4th	($500)
	Annie Larouche, mezzo-soprano	CDA-5th	($500)
1994–95	David Braid, piano	WMCS	($1,400)
	Yeo-Jung Kim, piano	WMC-OMG	($700)
1995–96	Measha Gosman, voice	WMCS	($1,400)
	Gillian Frost, piano	WMC-OMG	($700)
1996–97	Joni Henson, soprano	WMCS	($1,400)
	Kirsten Olafson, piano	WMC-OMG	($700)
	Jeanie Chung, piano	CDA-1st	($8,000)
	Nara Matsuura, piano	CDA-2nd	($3,000)
	Lana Henschel, piano	CDA-3rd	($2,000)
	Joel Ross Hastings, piano	CDA-4th	($1,000)

Nara Matsuura: best performance of
the commissioned composition

APPENDIX 4

Women's Musical Club of Toronto Concert Venues

January 1899   Yonge Street Arcade, 131–9 Yonge Street, Unit 71, Studio U (Mary Hewitt Smart's private music studio); WMC is founded and holds its first season of concerts here

May 1899   St. George's Hall, 14 Elm Street (now the Arts and Letters Club); the first open concert of the WMC

November 1899   Temple Building, northwest corner of Bay and Richmond; the regular meeting place until 1903

May 1899   Normal School, corner of Church and Gould streets; special concert at the end of the second season

May 1902   YMCA Association Hall, corner of Yonge and McGill streets; Kneisel Quartet concert and many subsequent open concerts

November 1903   Toronto Conservatory of Music concert hall, corner of College Street and Queen's Avenue (now University Avenue); the regular meeting place until circa 1914 and again from November 1925 to November 1929

October 1908   St. Margaret's College hall, 144 Bloor Street East; special WMC event held here this month and on occasion in later years

March 1909   Margaret Eaton School hall, North Street (now Bay Street), south of Bloor (moved to Yonge Street in 1925);

WMC invited to give a special concert. The hall was used on occasion in later years (e.g., for a concert by Wanda Landowska on 21 January 1926).

1914–18 Various concert venues used, including Massey Hall (used on occasion thereafter for major events, including most recently the ninetieth anniversary concert in December 1987) and Oddfellows' Hall (2 College Street), in addition to some of the above venues

January 1918 Masonic Hall, corner of Yonge Street and Davenport Road; the regular meeting place to November 1921 and again from January 1924 to March 1925

November 1921 Jenkins' Art Galleries, 23 Grenville Street (the former Lucius R. O'Brien residence)

January 1922 Assembly Hall of the King Edward Hotel, 37 King Street East, at the corner of Toronto Street

October 1923 Uptown Theatre, 764 Yonge Street

January 1924 Masonic Hall

November 1925 Toronto Conservatory of Music concert hall

November 1929 Hart House Theatre, University of Toronto

October 1931 Eaton Auditorium, on the seventh floor of Eaton's College Street, 444 Yonge Street, at the corner of College Street, used for the first time; Hart House Theatre remains the regular meeting place

1941–42 Eaton Auditorium used for two of three events this season

1942–46 WMC ceases activities owing to wartime conditions

October 1946 Eaton Auditorium becomes the regular venue

November 1977 St. Andrew's Presbyterian Church, 189 King Street, at the corner of Simcoe Street

October 1979 Christ Church, Deer Park, 1570 Yonge Street

October 1985 Walter Hall, Edward Johnson Building, University of Toronto

Works Consulted

Alexander, Andrea, et al. *The Toronto Symphony Women's Committee 1923–1983*. Toronto: Toronto Symphony Women's Committee, 1984.

Ammer, Christine. *Unsung: A History of Women in American Music*. Westport, CT: Greenwood, 1980.

Anderson, Marian. *My Lord, What a Morning*. New York: Viking, 1956.

Baillie, Joan Parkhill. *Look at the Record: An Album of Toronto's Lyric Theatres 1825–1984*. Oakville: Mosaic, 1985.

Beckwith, John. *Music at Toronto: A Personal Account*. Toronto: U of Toronto P, 1995.

Blair, Karen J. *The Clubwoman as Feminist: True Womanhood Redefined, 1868–1914*. New York: Holmes & Meier, 1980.

Block, Adrienne F., and Carol Neuls-Bates, eds. *Women in American Music: A Bibliography of Music and Literature*. Westport, CT: Greenwood, 1979.

Bowers, Jane, and Judith Tick, eds. *Women Making Music: The Western Art Tradition, 1150–1950*. Urbana: U of Illinois P, 1986.

Breton, Raymond, et al. *Ethnic Identity and Equality: Varieties of Experience in a Canadian City*. Toronto: U of Toronto P, 1990.

Brickenden, Jack. "Women's Musical Clubs: A Canadian Tradition." *Music Magazine* 10.4 (1987): 14–17.

Bridle, Augustus. "Chamber Music in Toronto." *The Yearbook of Canadian Art 1913*. Toronto: Dent, n.d. [ca. 1914]. 143–48.

Butkovich, Sister Mary Virginia. "Hans Kindler, 1892–1949." Diss. Catholic U of America, 1965.

"Canadian Women in the Public Eye: Mrs. George Dickson." *Saturday Night* 8 Jan. 1921: 25.

Citron, Marcia J. *Gender and the Musical Canon*. Cambridge: Cambridge UP, 1993.

Clare, Eva. *Music Appreciation and the Studio Club.* 2nd ed. New York: Long-
mans, 1930.
Clark, C[hristopher]. S[t. George]. *Of Toronto the Good.* 1898. Toronto: Coles,
1970.
Cook, Ramsay, and Wendy Mitchinson, eds. *The Proper Sphere: Woman's Place
in Canadian Society.* Toronto: Oxford UP, 1976.
Copland, Aaron, and Vivian Perlis. *Copland 1900 through 1942.* New York: St.
Martin's Marek, 1984.
Duet Club of Hamilton: Anniversary Book. Hamilton: Duet Club of Hamilton,
1989.
Dutton, Phyl. *Music Clubs, Festivals and Concerts and How to Organize Them.*
Old Woking, Surrey: Gresham, 1981.
Elson, Arthur. *Music Club Programs from All Nations.* Rev. ed. Boston: Ditson,
1928.
———. *Woman's Work in Music.* Boston: Page, 1904.
Fischer-Dieskau, Dietrich. *Reverberations: The Memoirs of Dietrich Fischer-
Dieskau.* Trans. Ruth Hein. New York: Fromm, 1989.
Forrester, Maureen, with Marci McDonald. *Out of Character: A Memoir.*
Toronto: McClelland, 1986.
Friedrich, Otto. *Glenn Gould: A Life and Variations.* Toronto: Lester, 1989.
Godden, Reginald, and Austin Clarkson. *Reginald Godden Plays.* Etobicoke,
ON: Soundway, 1990.
[Godfrey, H.H.] *A Souvenir of Musical Toronto.* Toronto: n.p., 1897. 2nd ed.
Toronto: n.p., 1898.
Goudge, Helen. *Look Back in Pride: A History of the Women's Musical Club of
Toronto 1897–98 to 1972–73.* Toronto: Women's Musical Club of Toronto, 1972.
Graham, Jean. "Among Those Present, XLII: Mrs. H.D. Warren." *Saturday Night*
5 Nov. 1932: 10.
———. "Representative Women: Mrs. W. Sanford Evans." *The Globe* 30 Dec.
1911, Globe Magazine: 3.
Green, J. Paul, and Nancy F. Vogan. *Music Education in Canada: A Historical
Account.* Toronto: U of Toronto P, 1991.
Griffiths, N.E.S. *The Splendid Vision: Centennial History of the National Coun-
cil of Women, 1893–1993.* Ottawa: Carleton UP, 1993.
Hall, Alfreda. *Per Ardua: The Story of Moulton College, Toronto 1888–1954.*
Toronto: Moulton College Alumnae Association, 1987.
Hall, Roger. *A Century to Celebrate, 1893–1993: The Ontario Legislative Build-
ing.* Toronto: Dundurn, 1993.
Harney, Robert F. *Gathering Place: Peoples and Neighbourhoods of Toronto,
1834–1945.* Toronto: Multicultural History Society of Ontario, 1985.
Howard, Richard B. *Upper Canada College 1829–1979: Colborne's Legacy.*
Toronto: Macmillan, 1979.
"An Important Event in Toronto's Musical History: The Silver Anniversary of
the Women's Musical Club." *Saturday Night* 4 Nov. 1922: 26, 34.

Jones, Gaynor G. "The Fisher Years: The Toronto Conservatory of Music, 1886–1913." *Three Studies.* CanMus Documents 4. Toronto: Institute for Canadian Music, 1989.

Kallmann, Helmut. *A History of Music in Canada 1534–1914.* 1960. Toronto: U of Toronto P, 1987.

——, and Gilles Potvin, eds. *Encyclopedia of Music in Canada.* 2nd ed. Toronto: U of Toronto P, 1992.

Kazdin, Andrew. *Glenn Gould at Work: Creative Lying.* New York: Dutton, 1989.

Kilbourn, William. *Intimate Grandeur: One Hundred Years at Massey Hall.* Toronto: Stoddart, 1993.

Kluckner, Michael. *Toronto the Way It Was.* Toronto: Whitecap, 1988.

Kresz, Mária, and Péter Király. *The Violinist and Pianist Géza de Kresz and Norah Drewett: Their Life and Music on Two Continents.* Toronto: Canadian Stage and Arts, 1989.

Lazarevich, Gordana. *The Musical World of Frances James and Murray Adaskin.* Toronto: U of Toronto P, 1988.

Lefebvre, Marie-Thérèse. *La création musicale des femmes au Québec.* Montreal: Les éditions du remue-ménage, 1991.

Léger, Cécile. *Fifty Years of Musical Recollections 1892–1942.* Montreal: Victoria, 1942.

MacMurchy, Marjory. *The Woman — Bless Her.* Toronto: Gundy, 1916.

Macpherson, Jessie. "Women's Musical Clubs." *Canadian Music Journal* 5.4 (1961): 45–47.

Magner, Brian. "Impresarios with a Mission." *Globe and Mail* 17 Oct. 1959, Globe Magazine: 14, 25.

Malcolm, Noel. *George Enescu: His Life and Music.* London: Toccata, 1990.

Marsh, James H., ed. *The Canadian Encyclopedia.* Edmonton: Hurtig, 1985.

Martin, Theodora Penny. *The Sound of Our Own Voices: Women's Study Clubs 1860–1910.* Boston: Beacon, 1987.

McDowall, Duncan. *The Light: Brazilian Traction, Light and Power Company Limited 1899–1945.* Toronto: U of Toronto P, 1988.

McInnes, Graham. *Finding a Father.* London: Hamish Hamilton, 1967.

Middleton, Jesse Edgar. *The Municipality of Toronto: A History.* Toronto: Dominion, 1923.

Moore, Gerald. *Am I Too Loud? Memoirs of an Accompanist.* London: Hamish Hamilton, 1962.

Morey, Carl. "Orchestras and Orchestral Repertoire in Toronto before 1914." *Musical Canada: Words and Music Honouring Helmut Kallmann.* Ed. John Beckwith and Frederick A. Hall. Toronto: U of Toronto P, 1988. 100–14.

——. "Toronto Women's Musical Club." *Performing Arts in Canada* 9.1 (1972): 19.

Morgan, Henry James, ed. *The Canadian Men and Women of the Time: A Hand-Book of Canadian Biography of Living Characters.* Toronto: Briggs, 1898. 2nd ed. Toronto: Briggs, 1912.

National Council of Women of Canada. *Women of Canada: Their Life and Work.* 1900. Ottawa: National Council of Women of Canada, 1975.

Neel, Boyd. *My Orchestras and Other Adventures: The Memoirs of Boyd Neel.* Ed. J. David Finch. Toronto: U of Toronto P, 1985.

Neuls-Bates, Carol, ed. *Women in Music: An Anthology of Source Readings from the Middle Ages to the Present.* New York: Harper, 1982.

Nothing New under the Sun: A History of the Toronto Council of Women. Toronto: Local Council of Women of Toronto, 1978.

Parker, C.W., ed. *Who's Who in Western Canada.* Vancouver: Canadian Press, 1911.

Peacock, Shane. *The Great Farini: The High-Wire Life of William Hunt.* Harmondsworth, Middlesex: Penguin, 1995.

Peglar, Kenneth W. *Opera and the University of Toronto 1946–1971.* Toronto: n.p., 1971.

Reich, Nancy B. "Women as Musicians: A Question of Class." *Musicology and Difference: Gender and Sexuality in Music Scholarship.* Ed. Ruth A. Solie. Berkeley: U of California P, 1993.

Rieger, Jennifer, and Mary F. Williamson. *Toronto Dancing Then and Now.* Exhibition catalogue. Toronto: Metropolitan Toronto Reference Library, 1995.

Schabas, Ezra. *Sir Ernest MacMillan: The Importance of Being Canadian.* Toronto: U of Toronto P, 1994.

Schafer, R. Murray. *On Canadian Music.* Bancroft, ON: Arcana, 1984.

Seranus [Susie Frances Harrison]. "Canada." *The Imperial History and Encyclopedia of Music.* Ed. W.L. Hubbard. Toronto: Ford, n.d. [ca. 1910].

Solway, Maurice. *Recollections of a Violinist.* Oakville: Mosaic, 1984.

Story, Rosalyn M. *And So I Sing: African-American Divas of Opera and Concert.* 1990. New York: Amistad, 1993.

Thompson, Austin Seton. *Spadina: A Story of Old Toronto.* Toronto: Pagurian, 1975.

Tick, Judith. "Passed Away Is the Piano Girl: Changes in American Musical Life, 1870–1900." Bowers and Tick 325–48.

——. "Women in Music." *The New Grove Dictionary of American Music.* Ed. H. Wiley Hitchcock and Stanley Sadie. London: Macmillan, 1986.

Tippett, Maria. *Making Culture: English-Canadian Institutions and the Arts before the Massey Commission.* Toronto: U of Toronto P, 1990.

Vehanen, Kosti. *Marian Anderson: A Portrait.* 1941. Westport, CT: Greenwood, 1970.

Wells, Kathleen Irwin. "The Women's Musical Club of Toronto." *BSS Bulletin* Apr. 1956: n.p.

Whitesitt, Linda. " 'The Most Potent Force' in American Music: The Role of Women's Music Clubs in American Concert Life." *The Musical Woman: An International Perspective.* Ed. Judith Lang Zaimont. Vol. 3. Westport, CT: Greenwood, 1991. 663–81.

Withrow, John B. "Celebrating 90 Years: The Women's Musical Club of Toronto Celebrates 90 Years of Achievement." *Bravo* Sept.–Oct. 1987: 70, 73, 74.

Wolf, Thomas. *Managing a Nonprofit Organization.* New York: Simon, 1990.

NEWSPAPERS, PERIODICALS, AND ANNUAL REFERENCE BOOKS CONSULTED

Bravo [Toronto]
Canadian Jewish News [Toronto]
Canadian Journal of Music [Toronto]
Canadian Who's Who
Conservatory Bi-monthly [Toronto]
Conservatory Monthly [Toronto]
Conservatory Quarterly Review [Toronto]
Conservatory Review [Toronto]
Etude [Philadelphia]
Globe [Toronto]
Globe and Mail [Toronto]
Mail and Empire [Toronto]
Might's Toronto City Directory
Musical Canada [Toronto]
Musical Courier [New York]
New York Times
Saturday Night [Toronto]
Society Blue Book of Toronto, Hamilton and London
Telegram [Toronto]
Toronto Daily Star/Toronto Star
Toronto World
Torontonian Society Blue Book and Club List
Who's Who in Canada
Women's Musical Club of Toronto Annual Reports
Women's Musical Club of Toronto Executive Committee Minutes
Women's Musical Club of Toronto Newsletter

ARCHIVAL SOURCES

Metropolitan Toronto Reference Library: Special Collections,
    Baldwin Room
National Library of Canada, Music Division
Thomas Fisher Rare Book Room, University of Toronto
University of Toronto Archives
Women's Musical Club of Toronto Archives

Index